AQA
GCSE
Drama

Illuminate Publishing

Published in 2017 by Illuminate Publishing Ltd, PO Box 1160,
Cheltenham, Gloucestershire GL50 9RW

Orders: Please visit www.illuminatepublishing.com
or email sales@illuminatepublishing.com

British Library Cataloguing-in-Publication Data

A catalogue record for this book is available from the British Library.

ISBN 978-1-911208-21-1

Printed by Cambrian Printers Ltd, Aberystwyth

1st impression: 07 17

The publishers' policy is to use papers that are natural, renewable and recyclable products made
from wood grown in sustainable forests. The logging and manufacturing processes are expected
to conform to the environmental regulations of the country of origin.

Every effort has been made to contact copyright holders of material produced in this book.
Great care has been taken by the author and publishers to ensure that either formal permission has
been granted for the use of copyright material reproduced, or that copyright material has been used
under the provision of fair-dealing guidelines in the UK – specifically that it has been used sparingly,
solely for the purpose of criticism and review, and has been properly acknowledged. If notified,
the publisher will be pleased to rectify any errors or omissions at the earliest opportunity.

This material has been endorsed by AQA and offers high-quality support for the
delivery of AQA qualifications. While this material has been through an AQA
quality assurance process, all responsibility for content remains with the publisher.

Editor: Dawn Booth
Design and layout: emc design ltd
Cover design: Nigel Harriss
Cover photograph: Paul Fox

Extracts in this book are taken from:
A Midsummer Night's Dream, William Shakespeare, Penguin Classics, 978-0-14-1396-66-8
A Raisin in the Sun, Lorraine Hansbserry, Plume, 0-45-226485-6
A View from the Bridge, Arthur Miller, Penguin, 0-14-048-029-3
Blood Brothers, Willy Russell, Methuen Modern Classics, 978-0-41-3767-70-7
Citizenship, Mark Ravenhill, Metheun, 978-0-7136-8398-1
Collected Grimm Tales, adapted by Carol Ann Duffy, dramatised by Tim Supple, Faber and Faber, 0-571-22142-4
Hansel and Gretel, Carl Grose (Kneehigh Theatre), Oberon Books, 978-1-84-9430-57-9
Kindertransport, Diane Samuels, Nick Hearn Books, 978-1-85459-527-0
Macbeth, William Shakespeare, Oxford School Shakespeare, 9778-0-19-8324-00-3
Noughts and Crosses, Malorie Blackman and Dominic Cooke, Nick Hearn Modern Plays, 978-1-85-4599-39-1
The 39 Steps, John Buchan and Patrick Barlow, Samuel French, 978-0-57-3114-40-3
The Crucible, Arthur Miller, Methuen Student Editions, 978-1-4081-0839-0
The Importance of Being Earnest, Oscar Wilde, Penguin Plays, 0-14-048-019-1
The Play of George Orwell's Animal Farm, adapted by Peter Hall, Heinemann, 978-0-435-23291-7
The Trial, Steven Berkoff, Amber Lane Press, 0-906399-84-X

CONTENTS

Acknowledgements

The author would like to thank the following theatre makers for their generous help in the preparation of this book: Jonathan Brody, Jordan Castle, Peter Forbes, Kerry Frampton, Nikki Gunson, Alex Harland, Mark Hutchinson, Gavin Maze, Baker Mukasa, Max Perryment, Tim Shortall, Alice Smith and Zöe Wilson. Thanks also to Rachel Izen for her introductions to two of our theatre makers.

Photo acknowledgements

p1 © Paul Fox; p5 Pavel L Photo and Video; p6 Pavel L. Photo and Video; p10 Public domain; p11 Public domain; p14 (top) © Joan Marcus; (bottom) Wordpress; p15 Meilun; p16 (top) Meilun; (middle) Khakimullin Aleksandr; (bottom) aerogondo2; p17 NY Studio; p18 (top) © Simon Mayew; p18 (bottom) Zoë Wilson; p28 Everett Collection; p29 (top) Everett Historical; (bottom) Courtesy Pearson Scott Foresman; p30 (top left) Chris Peterson; (top right); littleny; (middle) INTERFOTO / Alamy Stock Photo; (bottom left) Everett Historical; (bottom right) patrimonio designs ltd; p32 (top) Morphart Creation; (middle) Stephen Dorey / Alamy Stock Photo; Alamy Classic Image / Alamy Stock photo; p33 (top) Everett Historical; (bottom) Creative commons; p48 (top to bottom) Monkey Business Images; Monkey Business Images; Monkey Business Images; Joana Lopes; stockyimages; Dragon Images; Ashwin; Kdonmuang; p51 Trinity Mirror / Mirrorpix / Alamy Stock Photo; p52 Shaun Jeffers; p53 (top) chrisdorney; (top middle) chrisdorney; (top bottom) Jason Wells; (bottom) kenny1; p55 (top) kenny1; (bottom) seehooteatrepeat / Shutterstock.com; p56 V.Kuntsman; p57 Heritage Image Partnership Ltd / Alamy Stock Photo; p58 (top) © Van Dyke; (bottom) Trinity Mirror / Mirrorpix / Alamy Stock Photo; p61 Aratemida-psy; (bottom) Marbury; p71 Fer Gregory; p74 Gaumont British; p76 (right) wales_heritage_photos / Alamy Stock Photo; (top left) Everett Collection; (bottom left) Sandy Stevenson; p77 (top) Public domain; (bottom) Public domain; p79 Katarina Tauber; p80 Public domain; p85 © Diana P. Rowe; p95 (top) Steven Barber; (bottom) Pinterest; p100 (all) © Steve Tanner / Kneehigh; p101 Allan Warren Creative Commons Attribution-Share Alike 3.0 Unported; p102 (top) Dano Sabljak; (bottom left and right) Lokichen; p103 Gorbash Varvara; p104 keith morris / Alamy Stock Photo; p105 Polka Theatre, The Other Richard; p108 aberCPC / Alamy Stock Photo; p120 (left) © Brinkhoff Mögenburg; p120 (right) Little Angel Theatre; p126 Brinkhoff Mögenburg; p130 Geraint Lewis / Alamy Stock Photo; p138 (top) Oleksandr Berezko; (bottom) © Alice Philipson; p144 (top) Chronicle / Alamy Stock Photo; (2nd top) Chronicle / Alamy Stock Photo; (3rd top) mart; (bottom left) rusty426; (bottom middle) North Wind Picture Archives / Alamy Stock Photo; (bottom right) smoxx; p145 (top) pavila; (bottom) Pinterest; p.150 © Photostage; p153 © Globe Theatre; p157 (top) Tumblr; (bottom) © Keith Pattison; p163 seeshooteatrepeat / Shutterstock.com; p166 aerogondo2; p168 © Greg Veit; p170 (top) © Alastair Muir; p170 (bottom) © Brinkhoff Mögenburg; p171 (top right) © Paul Fox; (2nd top right) © Paul Fox; (top left) © Paul Fox; (middle left) ostill; (middle right) Darrin Henry; (bottom left) pathdoc; (bottom right) Ozgur Coskun; p175 (top) © Paul Fox; (bottom) © Paul Fox; p179 (top) © Paul Fox; (middle) © Paul Fox; (bottom) © Paul Fox; p185 Vibrant Pictures / Alamy Stock Photo; p188 Splendid Productions; p192 (all) Splendid Productions; p193 Chris Bull / Alamy Stock Photo; p194 Kerry Frampton; p195 (top) dpa picture alliance / Alamy Stock Photo; (bottom) Inga Nielsen; p196 (bottom) © Yinka Shonibare/Victoria and Albert Museum; (top) *Slumdog Millionaire*, dir. Danny Boyle [DVD], 2008, Celador Films, Channel 4 & Twentieth Century Fox; p197 Everett Historical; p198 (top) Chronicle / Alamy Stock Photo; (bottom) Jeffrey Blackler / Alamy Stock Photo; p200 © Paul Fox; p201 (top) © Paul Fox; (bottom) Splendid Productions; p205 Splendid Productions; p206 Splendid Productions; p207 (top) © Brian Roberts; (middle) © Brian Roberts; (bottom) © Greg Veit; p208 (top) Norman Chan; (2nd) fotogestoeber; (3rd) Guzel Studio; (4th) Dmitry Kolmankov; (5th) passion artist; (bottom) pavila; p209 Rawpixel.com; p211 (top) Splendid Productions; (bottom) Splendid Productions; p215 © Paul Fox; p216 (top) Splendid Productions; (bottom) Splendid Productions; p218 Splendid Productions; p222 Nir Alon / Alamy Stock Photo; p225 Splendid Productions; p228 Cedarville University; p231 (top) © Clare Park; (bottom) © Paul Fox; p232 © Clare Park; p233 © Clare Park; p234 © Clare Park; p235 (top) ID1974; (bottom) Elnur; p236 Gavin Maze; p237 (top left) FrameAngel; (top right) StudioADFX; (middle) Epitavi; (bottom) Creative commons; p238 (top right) Andrii Zhezhera; (top left) Andrii Zhezhera; (middle) Gavin Maze; (bottom) © Paul Fox; p239 Gavin Maze; p240 © Dan Court; p241 © Paul Fox; p242 © Dan Court; p243 © Dan Court; p246 (left) © Tim Shortall; (right) © Tim Shortall; p247 © Paul Fox; p250 Rawpixel.com; p251 Pinterest; p253 (top) © Paul Fox; p253 (bottom) © Sharronwallace.com; p254 Nikki Gunson; p255 Nikki Gunson; p256 Nikki Gunson; p257 ESB Professional

Text acknowledgements

p10 Copyright © A VIEW FROM THE BRIDGE, Arthur Miller, 1983, 1985, 1988 used by permission of The Wylie Agency (UK) Limited; pp35, 36, 39, 41, 43, 44, 49, 50 Copyright © THE CRUCIBLE, Arthur Miller, 1952, 1953 used by permission of The Wylie Agency (UK) Limited; p100 Copyright Guardian News and Media Ltd 2017; p173 © Paul Taylor, The Independent; p173 © Telegraph Media Group Limited 2007; p173 © The Guardian; p193 'What If?' reprinted by kind permission of Canongate Books Ltd © Lemn Sissay (2016); pp223–224 © Mark Ravenhill, 2015, 'Citizenship', Bloomsbury Methuen Drama, an imprint of Bloomsbury Publishing plc; p225 Copyright © Steven Berkoff 1981, originally published by Amber Lane Press.

INTRODUCTION TO GCSE DRAMA

How to get the most out of Drama

Drama is an exciting subject that uses your knowledge, talent and imagination. Throughout the course there will be opportunities to act, devise, design, review and analyse. It is a creative subject that will give you the chance to employ a wide variety of skills and test your abilities. You may explore an idea or interpretation, try it out practically and then evaluate how well it worked. You will learn not only from your teacher, but also from your fellow students, as you work together to achieve a devised or scripted production. It is an active course where you will not only be up and doing, but also one where you must be able to reflect on your work and the work of others.

At the beginning of the course, you will probably not feel equally confident in all of these areas – very few people do. However, you will have the chance to learn and grow in these skills. At times, you may make choices in order to play to your strengths. For example, you may choose to perform or design for Component 2 Devising Drama and Component 3 Texts in Practice. However, do be open to trying new skills – you may discover talents you didn't know you had.

Understanding

By reading and through practical tasks, you will become familiar with several plays. You will study a set play for Component 1, Section B and will work practically on a contrasting play for Component 3. You will also view and analyse a production of a third play for Component 1, Section C. This will expose you to different periods or types of dramatic literature and you will learn how theatre is created.

Creativity

One of the pleasures of Drama is that you have the opportunity to express your own ideas, thoughts and interpretations. In Drama there can be many different 'right' answers.

Responsibility

Drama requires self-discipline. You need to be an active, trustworthy group member. You will need to be on time, meet deadlines and fulfil your responsibilities.

Making connections

Although the course is divided into three components, there is a great deal of crossover between the skills in each one. When you review a professional actor's performance, this can aid your understanding and development of your own acting. When you notice a technique used in a set text, you may want to recreate that in your devising. Build on the skills you are learning to enrich your work in each component.

▲ *The choice of colour and fabric is an important element of costume design.*

COMPONENT 1 UNDERSTANDING DRAMA (WRITTEN EXAMINATION)	COMPONENT 2 DEVISING DRAMA (PRACTICAL AND DEVISING LOG)	COMPONENT 3 TEXTS IN PRACTICE (PRACTICAL)
What is assessed	**What is assessed**	**What is assessed**
Knowledge and understanding of drama and theatre Study of one set play from a choice of six Analysis and evaluation of the work of live theatre makers	Process of creating devised drama Performance of devised drama (students may contribute as performer or designer) Analysis and evaluation of own work	Performance of two extracts from one play (students may contribute as performer or designer). Free choice of play but it must contrast with the set play chosen for Component 1
How it's assessed	**How it's assessed**	**How it's assessed**
Written exam: 1 hour and 45 minutes Open book (clean book, no annotations in it) 80 marks 40% of GCSE	Devising log (60 marks) Devised performance (20 marks) 80 marks in total 40% of GCSE	Performance of Extract 1 (20 marks) Performance of Extract 2 (20 marks) 40 marks in total 20% of GCSE
This component is marked by AQA examiners Section A: Theatre roles and terminology: multiple choice (4 marks) Section B: Study of a set play: four questions on a given extract from the set play chosen (44 marks) Section C: Live theatre production: one question (from a choice) on the work of theatre makers in a single live theatre production (32 marks)	This component is marked by teachers and moderated by AQA	This component is marked by a visiting AQA examiner

TIP

It is very possible that you will not study these components in this order. However, keep looking for opportunities to apply the learning gained in one component to another.

Actors rehearsing in a proscenium theatre. ▶

How to get the best out of this book

The book is arranged to cover each of the assessed components of the course:

▶ Component 1 Understanding Drama (divided into three sections)

▶ Component 2 Devising Drama

▶ Component 3 Texts in Practice

This book isn't designed to be read from cover to cover, but for you to use the sections which apply to the texts you are studying or the skills you are developing. In order to help you get the most from it, we have created some special features:

ASSESSMENT FOCUS:

these panels will remind you of the assessment objectives that underpin the specification itself and how they are covered in each section.

COMPONENT 1

UNDERSTANDING DRAMA

SECTION A

THEATRE ROLES AND TERMINOLOGY

THE SPECIFICATION SAYS...

Students must develop knowledge and understanding of:

▶ Drama and theatre terminology and how to use it appropriately.

▶ The roles and responsibilities of theatre practitioners in contemporary theatre practice.

▶ Stage positioning.

▶ Staging configuration.

ASSESSMENT FOCUS

Assessment objective AO3: Demonstrate knowledge and understanding of how drama and theatre is developed and performed.

In Section A, you will be asked multiple choice questions in which you must demonstrate your understanding of how theatre works, such as what various theatre makers do, the different areas of a stage or possible staging configurations.

Roles and responsibilities

Drama is a team effort in which many people contribute to create the final production. When you go to see a play you are, of course, aware of the performers, but you might not think about the efforts of all the other theatre makers who do not appear onstage. For Component 1, Section A, you need to be able to identify theatre roles for a multiple choice question.

Below is a chart that summarises some of the key personnel.

THEATRE MAKER: PLAYWRIGHT

PRACTICE QUESTIONS:

there are examples of practice questions so that you can become familiar with the type of questions you will be asked and can practise answering.

SAMPLE RESPONSES:

these are samples of a typical student's work Some of them have comments to indicate how the responses demonstrate various skills.

You are performing the role of _____

Describe how you would use your vocal and physical skills to perform the lines below and explain the effects you want to create.

Sample:

> HANSEL: page 10: 'It says here the universe is infinite, that is has no end ... Imagine that!'

This is the audience's introduction to Hansel and I would like to create through my vocal and physical choices what a bright but dreamy character he is. ❶ As they live in the countryside, I will use a rural accent, perhaps Scottish with a soft burr to it, making my 'r's very distinctive. ❷ I will pronounce the words precisely, fascinated by the idea of the universe. There will be a hint of wonder on the words 'no end'. I will exclaim loudly 'Imagine that' hoping to get a reaction from Gretel ❸ and, for the first time, making direct eye contact with her. Physically, I will walk, around the stage, taking large confident steps, with my nose stuck in a comically large book. ❹ I will handle the book with care, showing how important it is to me. ❺ my facial expression will be serious and engrossed until I look up at Gretel, smiling and wide-eyed at my discovery. To add to the comedy, I will nearly bump into things onstage, but Gretel, who is following me around, will guide me away from them, without my apparently noticing. This establishes our relationship as team players – while I may think about big ideas, she is the one who gets things done practically. ❻

Vocal skills and effect

Physical skills

Understanding of character

Vocal skills and explanation

Physical skills and effect

Physical skills and effect. Understanding of play and characters

THEATRE MAKER ADVICE:

these are excerpts from interviews with professional theatre makers, such as designers and performers. They provide up-to-date insights into the practical aspects of theatre and offer ways of improving your own work.

During rehearsals

Jordan Castle, understudy and musical theatre performer

I am currently the understudy for two roles in the musical 'Cats'. As an understudy you get a lot less rehearsal time than if you were actually playing the part, which can be difficult because you don't get the same one-to-one time with the director to explore the character. In rehearsals, I pay attention to everything the actors I am covering do, and make notes. I know I will need to add some of my own interpretation because we are very different people. But it is important to learn all the blocking and not to change that. Luckily I was well-prepared, because I did end up going on and performing each role with very little actual rehearsal.

KEY TERMS:
Covering: learning the words and movements for a part that you do not usually perform.

During performance

During a performance of 'Richard III' I was stage managing...

Zoë Wilson,

REFLECTION:

at the end of some tasks, there will be guidance for thinking about what you have learned and how that learning can be applied to your assessment tasks.

REFLECTION

Perform the dialogue in front of your group, choosing the vocal interpretation that you thought worked best. Discuss the way these different ways of delivering the lines affected how the audience might perceive the characters.
- Do they seem angrier?
- Frightened?
- Comic?
- Tense?
- Which character seems more dominant and in control?

EDDIE: What do you mean?

MARCO: From here

EDDIE: Sure, why not? Gee, that's hard, I never knew that. It's on an angle, that's why, heh?

MARCO: Here.

a Speak the lines making clear that Marco is challenging Eddie by emphasising certain words (for example, saying them more loudly or slowly or with a particular tone of voice).

b Speak the lines experimenting with how loudly or softly the characters speak in order to show the relationship between them (for example, who is in control).

c Speak the lines attempting the accents of the characters: Marco has an Italian accent and Eddie an American one.

d Speak the lines showing that the characters are being polite to each other, but that the subtext is that Marco is threatening Eddie.

e Speak the lines using at least one pause in the dialogue to increase the sense of tension.

12

▸ To read about tragedies see page 199.

LOOK HERE:

these notices point out other pages of the book where you may find further information on a topic. For example, when revising sound design for Component 1, you may be directed to look at the sound design advice and technical terms in Component 3.

Lyons – middle class, private home

reet sign outside the night the street name

main colours used?
ls are the walls made one? Wood? Concrete?)
n are the walls in?
special features that e seem prosperous?
eps?, Balcony? Window

size, shape and colour and windows?
external features such
athway or plants?
do you think the home built?

 CHALLENGE

Research online the furniture from the time. Based on your research, draw sketches of key furniture items, such as the Lyons' dining table or Mrs Johnstone's kitchen table, which you believe would be appropriate for your design. Explain how they could be used in a scene.

CHALLENGES:

exercises to really stretch and extend your drama skills.

TIP

Consider how you will accomplish the quick scene changes. For example, how will you move on Mrs Johnstone's kitchen set (page 75) and then remove it (page 79)? Will you use trucks? Casters on the furniture? Fly the set pieces in? Have actors carry or push the set pieces on/off?

TIPS:

guidance to help you with your assessments and to avoid common errors.

KEY TERMS:
Truck: a platform on wheels upon which scenery can be mounted and moved.
Fly: raising and lowering scenery or other items onto the stage using a system of ropes and pulleys.

KEY TERMS:

definitions of terms to help you understand how drama works and express your ideas fluently. There is also a glossary at the back of the book to remind you of the definitions.

55

Learning how to work with performance texts and dramatic works

The GCSE Drama specification is set out as follows:

▶ There are SIX set plays – you will read ONE of them.

▶ Component 1 Section C: you will watch a performance of another play.

▶ Component 1 Section C: you will study another play.

You may read all or some of the play that you see for Component 1, Section C. Your knowledge of plays may influence your devising in Component 2 when you will be creating your own dramatic work. So it is important that you are aware of how to read a performance text and learn the correct terminology for discussing it.

THE SPECIFICATION SAYS...

You must develop knowledge and understanding of characteristics of performance texts and dramatic works.

Genre: a category of drama, such as historical drama or musical.

Dialogue: what the characters say.

Monologue: a long speech spoken by one character.

Performance style: the way in which something is performed. A realistic performance has a believable or life-like performance style, or a comedy might feature multi-role or physical comedy as its performance style.

COMMON FEATURES OF A PLAY

Character: a person or other being (such as a talking animal) in a play, novel or film.

Plot: the main events of the play presented in a particular sequence by the playwright.

P L O T

Character list: a list of the characters that appear in the play. Some lists include a short description of the characters, such as their age or occupation.

Resolution: the end of the plot when the problems of the play are resolved.

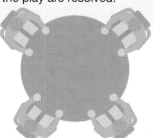

Dramatic climax: the moment of greatest dramatic **tension** in a play.

Stage directions: descriptions of aspects of the play not conveyed by the actors' speeches. These may include a description of what the set or characters look like, and the actions of the characters and how certain lines of dialogue are spoken. It may also note pauses, silences or beats to indicate when characters are not speaking.

EXIT STAGE LEFT

KEY TERM:

Tension: a sense of anticipation or anxiety.

Moving from 'page to stage'

Throughout the course you will have chances to study scripts and then to think about how a script could be moved from the page to the stage. One way is by considering how your interpretation of it could be realised by performance and design choices. Over the next few pages there are examples of exploring a sample script, '**A View from the Bridge**', which will introduce you to some of the skills and terminology that will be useful throughout the course.

Sample exploration of a play

Beyond identifying the different features of a script, you must also learn to analyse its meaning, genre, **characterisation** and **style**. Read the excerpt below from the end of Act 1 of the modern **tragedy** '**A View from the Bridge**' (1955) by the American **playwright** Arthur Miller. This scene is considered the climax of the play's first act.

Earlier in the play, Eddie, a middle-aged American dockworker, and his wife, Beatrice, have agreed to allow two of Beatrice's cousins, the young Rodolpho and Marco, to live with them. The cousins have arrived from Italy without work papers. Rodolpho has begun to date Eddie's niece, Catherine, much to Eddie's annoyance. Right before this scene, Eddie has tried to show that he is the most powerful person in his home by hitting Rodolpho while pretending to give him a boxing lesson. Shortly afterwards, Rodolpho and Eddie's niece, Catherine, begin to dance. Marco approaches Eddie (pages 57–58).

[RODOLPHO *takes her in his arms. They dance.* EDDIE *in thought sits in his chair, and* MARCO *takes a chair, places it in front of* EDDIE, *and looks down at it.* BEATRICE *and* EDDIE *watch him.*] ❶

MARCO: Can you lift this chair? ❷

EDDIE: What do you mean?

MARCO: From here. [*He gets on one knee with one hand behind his back, and grasps the bottom of one of the chair legs but does not raise it.*] ❸

EDDIE: Sure, why not? [*He comes to the chair, kneels, grasps the leg, raises the chair one inch, but it leans over to the floor.*] Gee, that's hard, I never knew that. [*He tries again, and again fails.*] It's on an angle, that's why, heh? ❹

MARCO: Here.

[*He kneels, grasps, and with strain slowly raises the chair higher and higher, getting to his feet now.* RODOLPHO *and* CATHERINE *have stopped dancing as* MARCO *raises the chair over his head.*

MARCO *is face to face with* EDDIE, *a strained tension gripping his eyes and jaw, his neck stiff, the chair raised like a weapon over* EDDIE's *head – and he transforms what might appear like a glare of warning into a smile of triumph, and* EDDIE's *grin vanishes as he absorbs his look.*] ❺

▲ Playwright Arthur Miller (1915–2005)

KEY TERMS:

Characterisation: how the qualities of a character are conveyed, typically through description, dialogue and actions.

Style: the way in which something is written or performed, such as the use of realistic dialogue or choreographed movement.

Tragedy: a play involving the downfall of its lead character leading to an unhappy ending.

Playwright: responsible for the writing of the script of the play. This includes the dialogue and stage directions.

TASK 1

After reading the excerpt from the play, refer to the numbered passages and answer the related question in your notebook.

1. What **motivations** might be revealed by this stage direction? For example, is Marco just pleasantly passing the time or is he confronting Eddie?

2. What might be the **subtext** of Marco's line? What is he thinking and feeling? How might his voice, body language or facial expression show his thoughts and feelings?

3. How do these stage directions create tension? If the stage directions are performed slowly or quickly do you think they would create more or less tension?

4. What do we learn about the **character** of Eddie from this dialogue? How might Eddie's facial expression, tone of voice or use of eye contact show how he feels?

5. How does this stage direction suggest **conflict** between Eddie and Marco?

▲ *Although written and first performed in the 1950s, 'A View from the Bridge' is frequently produced in revival productions.*

KEY TERMS:

Motivations: what a character wants or needs in a scene. For example, 'I need to escape' or 'I want you to admire me'. These are sometimes called 'objectives'.

Subtext: the unspoken meaning, feelings and thoughts 'beneath' the lines, which may be shown in the characters' body language, tone of voice and facial expressions, for example, although not explicitly stated in the text.

Character: a person or other being (such as a talking animal) in a play, novel or film.

Conflict: when two or more characters' desires are in opposition (external conflict) or when a character experiences opposing emotions (internal conflict).

TIP

As you study plays, look for the characters' motivations and how the characters' subtexts might be revealed through their actions. When thinking as a performer, consider how you can explore these elements of the character and play.

THE SPECIFICATION SAYS...

Performers' vocal interpretation of character such as accent, volume, pitch, timing, pace, intonation, phrasing, emotional range and delivery of lines.

Performers' physical interpretation of character such as build, age, height, facial features, movement, postures, gesture and facial expression.

Introduction to performance skills

Throughout the course, you will be exploring how you might perform certain characters or evaluating how others have performed them. When performing or writing about performance you will often focus on:

- vocal skills
- physical skills.

In addition, you will learn about:

- characterisation
- interaction between characters (how they react to each other)
- use of the performance space (how they are positioned in or move around the space).

You will need to think about the effects that are being created:

- Do you want the audience to feel tense and anxious about the situation your character is in?
- Do you want them to sympathise with your character?
- Do you want them to laugh at your character?

To begin working on characterisation, you might consider the character's background, their motivations and their relationship to the other characters in the play.

Vocal skills

Using only the dialogue from the scene from '**A View from the Bridge**', explore different vocal choices a performer might make.

TASK 2

Working in pairs, speak the dialogue from the scene from '**A View from the Bridge**' in the different ways suggested below:

> **MARCO:** Can you lift this chair?
>
> **EDDIE:** What do you mean?
>
> **MARCO:** From here.
>
> **EDDIE:** Sure, why not? Gee, that's hard, I never knew that. It's on an angle, that's why, heh?
>
> **MARCO:** Here.

a Speak the lines making clear that Marco is challenging Eddie by emphasising certain words (for example, saying them more loudly or slowly or with a particular tone of voice).

b Speak the lines experimenting with how loudly or softly the characters speak in order to show the relationship between them (for example, who is in control).

c Speak the lines attempting the accents of the characters: Marco has an Italian accent and Eddie an American one.

d Speak the lines showing that the characters are being polite to each other, but that the subtext is that Marco is threatening Eddie.

e Speak the lines using at least one pause in the dialogue to increase the sense of tension.

 REFLECTION

Perform the dialogue in front of your group, choosing the vocal interpretation that you thought worked best. Discuss the way these different ways of delivering the lines affected how the audience might perceive the characters.

- Do they seem angrier?
- Frightened?
- Comic?
- Tense?
- Which character seems more dominant and in control?

▶ To read about tragedies see page 199.

Physical skills

One of the main ways actors create their characters is through their use of posture, gesture and facial expression.

▶ Both Eddie and Marco are used to physical labour – how might that affect the way they move?

▶ Eddie is older than Marco – how might that be shown in his posture?

▶ Marco is a guest in Eddie's apartment – will that change how he behaves in Eddie's living room?

Working with a partner and using the same scene as above, try Task 3.

TASK 3

a   Many people interpret this scene as showing a transfer of power from Eddie to Marco. Create two **still images**, one showing their relationship at the beginning of the scene and the second showing their relationship at the end. Either take a photograph of these images or quickly sketch them and label them, showing how you used physical skills to show what is happening in the scene.

b   Perform the scene trying the following:

   i   Create one clear gesture for each character that they use at a significant moment.

   ii   Choose when the characters maintain eye contact and when they look away.

   iii   Choose when the characters should move during the scene and how close or far away they are from each other at key points.

   iv   Choose one moment for each character when their facial expression changes.

Introduction to design skills

Throughout the components there are opportunities to explore design specialisms that include:

▶ lighting design

▶ sound design

▶ set design

▶ costume design

▶ puppet design.

Designers use their skills to create an element of the production that helps to contribute to the meaning of the play. One aspect they may consider when creating their designs is the **context** of the play, such as where and when it takes place.

The context of the setting of '**A View from the Bridge**' is that it takes place in New York in the 1950s. However, a designer may choose to **interpret** that context in different ways.

KEY TERM:

Still image: a frozen image showing the facial expressions and physical positions, including posture and gesture, of one or more characters.

 REFLECTION

Discuss if any of the choices you made for Task 3 revealed physical choices that you could use in an actual performance. Are there any sections of the dialogue where changing levels or moving towards or away from each other seem to help convey the action of the scene?

KEY TERMS:

Designer: person responsible for an aspect of the production, such as lighting, costumes, set, sound or puppets.

Context: the circumstances of the setting of a play, such as the location, period of time or conventions.

Interpret: to make choices about a play. There may be many possible interpretations.

 TIP

Throughout all the components of the course, you will have opportunities to explore how plays and their designs may be interpreted. Whatever your interpretation, it is important to explain why you have made your design choices.

TIP

Be aware if a question is asking you to refer to the context or not. In Section B, there will be one design question that asks you to refer specifically to the context. However, other design questions allow you to update, change or reinterpret the context.

KEY TERMS:

Naturalistic: life-like, realistic, believable.

Abstract: not realistic or life-like, but instead using colours, shapes, textures, sounds and other means to achieve an effect.

Stylised: non-realistic, done in a particular manner, perhaps emphasising one element.

Minimalistic: simple; using few elements; stripped back.

Symbolic: using something that represents something else. Examples of symbolic design might be characters dressed in white to symbolise their purity or a set resembling a boxing ring to symbolise the conflict between the characters.

TIP

Although these two designs are very different, both of these productions were successful. This shows that there is no single correct way of interpreting a play. If you were designing the set or costumes for this play, you might make very different choices.

KEY TERMS:

Costumes: what the characters wear on stage.

Sets: items put on stage such as furniture or backdrops to create the world of the play; sometimes called scenery. There may also be **props**, which are objects used on stage.

Props: small items that actors can carry on stage.

For example, they may choose to research that period of time and location to recreate the furniture, fabrics and music associated with them. Many **naturalistic** productions do this in order to create a believable world for the characters to inhabit. On the other hand, a designer may make more **abstract** or **stylised** choices where they do not attempt to create a realistic version of the world, but instead make choices which might be **minimalistic** or **symbolic**. Some productions may ignore the original context and choose another context, for example by updating the production to a different time or changing the location.

Below are production photographs showing the set and costumes of two different productions of '**A View from the Bridge**'.

Naturalistic production

◀ *From a Broadway production, 2010, starring Liev Schrieber, sets by John Lee Beatty, costumes by Jane Greenwood.*

Minimalistic and abstract production

◀ *Young Vic production, starring Mark Strong, design and lighting by Jan Versweyveld, and costumes by An D'Huys, 2014.*

TASK 4

a   What differences do you see between the **costumes** in the two productions? Note the choice of fabrics, colours, the fit or shape of the clothes, the footwear, and the hair and make-up.

b   What differences do you see between the **sets** in the two productions? Note the furniture, walls, colours and flooring.

c   Read the script on page 10 again and then explain which of the costume and set designs most closely matches your ideas about the design of the play, and explain why?

The above tasks are just an introduction to some of the skills, terminology and ideas that you will be developing over the different components of the course. Throughout the course consider the different ways that plays can be interpreted.

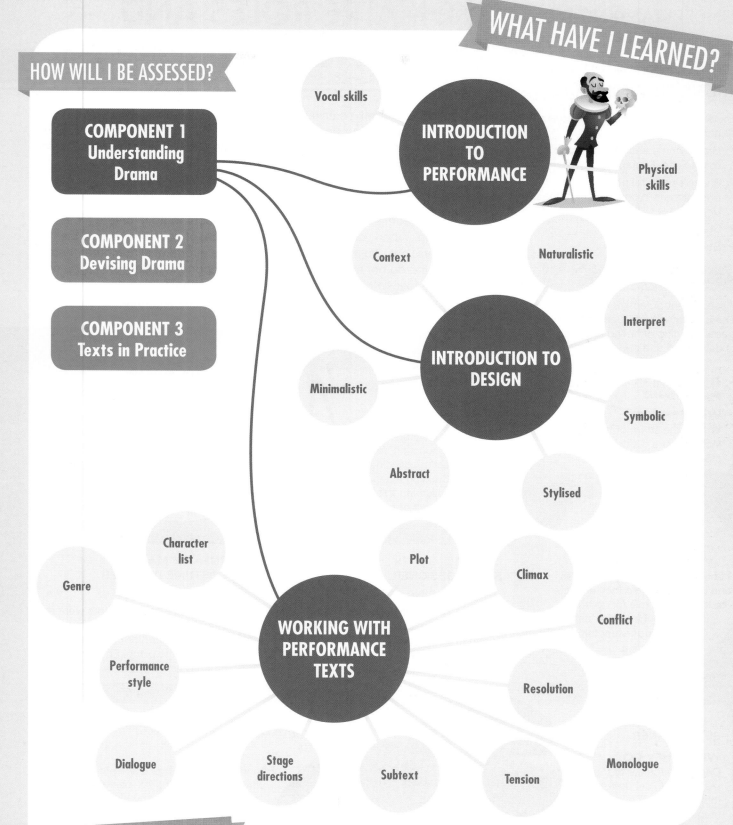

WHAT HAVE I LEARNED?

HOW WILL I BE ASSESSED?

COMPONENT 1
Understanding Drama

COMPONENT 2
Devising Drama

COMPONENT 3
Texts in Practice

Vocal skills

INTRODUCTION TO PERFORMANCE

Physical skills

Context

Naturalistic

Interpret

INTRODUCTION TO DESIGN

Symbolic

Minimalistic

Abstract

Stylised

Character list

Plot

Climax

Genre

Conflict

WORKING WITH PERFORMANCE TEXTS

Resolution

Performance style

Dialogue

Stage directions

Subtext

Tension

Monologue

CHECK YOUR LEARNING If you are uncertain of the meaning of any of the terms above, go back and revise.

Why not use the downloadable version of this summary as a basis for your own checklist of what you have learned from Samples & Downloads at www.illuminatepublishing.com?

SECTION A

THEATRE ROLES AND TERMINOLOGY

THE SPECIFICATION SAYS...

Students must develop knowledge and understanding of:

▶ Drama and theatre terminology and how to use it appropriately.

▶ The roles and responsibilities of theatre practitioners in contemporary theatre practice.

▶ Stage positioning.

▶ Staging configuration.

ASSESSMENT FOCUS

Assessment objective AO3: Demonstrate knowledge and understanding of how drama and theatre is developed and performed.

In Section A, you will be asked multiple choice questions in which you must demonstrate your understanding of how theatre works, such as what various theatre makers do, the different areas of a stage or possible staging configurations.

Roles and responsibilities

Drama is a team effort in which many people contribute to create the final production. When you go to see a play you are, of course, aware of the performers, but you might not think about the efforts of all the other theatre makers who do not appear onstage. For Component 1, Section A, you need to be able to identify theatre roles for a multiple choice question.

Below is a chart that summarises some of the key personnel.

THEATRE MAKER: PLAYWRIGHT

WHAT THEY DO:
Writing the script of the play, including the dialogue and stage directions.

THEATRE MAKER: PERFORMER

WHAT THEY DO:
Appearing in a production, for example by acting, dancing or singing. Creating a performance or assuming a role on stage in front of an audience.

THEATRE MAKER: LIGHTING DESIGNER

WHAT THEY DO:
Designing the lighting states and effects that will be used in a performance. Understanding the technical capabilities of the theatre and creating a lighting plot.

THEATRE MAKER: UNDERSTUDY

WHAT THEY DO:
Learning a part, including lines and movements, so they are able to take over a role for someone if needed when there is a planned or unexpected absence.

THEATRE MAKER: SOUND DESIGNER

WHAT THEY DO:
Designing the sound required for the performance, which may include music and sound effects. Considering if amplification, such as the use of microphones, is needed, and creating a sound plot.

THEATRE MAKER: COSTUME DESIGNER

WHAT THEY DO:
Designing what the actors wear on stage. Making sure that costumes are appropriate for the style and period of the piece. Ensuring the costumes fit the actors.

THEATRE MAKER: SET DESIGNER

WHAT THEY DO:
Designing the set of the play and the set dressing (objects placed on the stage). Providing sketches and other design materials before overseeing the creation of the set.

THEATRE MAKER: STAGE MANAGER

WHAT THEY DO:
Running the backstage elements of the play and supervising the backstage crew. Organising the rehearsal schedule and keeping lists of props and other technical needs. Creating a prompt book and calling the cues for the performance.

When theatre makers undertake their responsibilities

It is useful to see in context when professional theatre makers undertake their responsibilities and to read what some professional theatre makers do before rehearsals, during rehearsals and during performances.

THE SPECIFICATION SAYS...

Knowledge and understanding should cover:

▶ The activities each may undertake on a day-to-day basis.

▶ The aspects of the rehearsal/performance process each is accountable for (their contribution to the whole production being a success).

BEFORE REHEARSALS

1 Playwright prepares script

2 Director reads and studies play, decides concept

3 Designers (set/costume/lighting/sound/puppet) research play/context, develops design ideas

4 Director casts performers

DURING REHEARSALS

1 Director rehearses performers

2 Performers learn lines and blocking

3 Stage manager creates rehearsal schedules and prop lists; notes blocking; creates prompt book

4 Costume designer organises costume fittings for performers

5 Understudy learns the roles they are covering

6 Set designer ensures that set is built and operates correctly

7 Sound and lighting designers create plot sheets and cues for sound and lighting

8 Puppet designer makes and provides puppets for rehearsals

9 Technicians run technical elements during technical rehearsals and dress rehearsals

IN PERFORMANCE

1 Stage management ensures smooth running of show; 'calls' the show by announcing cues to cast and technicians

2 Technicians operate sound and lighting equipment.

3 Theatre manager oversees operation of Front of House and box office

4 Performers appear before audience and perform their roles

5 Understudy is prepared to go on in case of absence of a performer

TIP

Some productions do not begin with a finished script but are created collaboratively during rehearsals. This is called devising, which you will learn more about in Component 2.

THEATRE MAKER:
PUPPET DESIGNER

WHAT THEY DO:
Designing the puppets for a production, taking into account the style of puppets and how they will be operated.

THEATRE MAKER:
DIRECTOR

WHAT THEY DO:
Overseeing the creative aspects of the production. Developing a 'concept' or central unifying idea for the production. Liaising with designers, rehearsing the actors and ensuring that all technical elements of the play are ready. Giving 'notes' to the actors to help improve their performances and agreeing the blocking (or movements) of the actors.

THEATRE MAKER:
TECHNICIAN

WHAT THEY DO:
Operating the technical equipment, such as the lighting and sound boards, during the performance.

THEATRE MAKER:
THEATRE MANAGER

WHAT THEY DO:
Running the theatre building, including overseeing the Front of House staff (ushers) and the box office staff who sell tickets.

THEATRE MAKER ADVICE

Before rehearsals

Tim Shortall, West End costume and set designer

What I ideally aim for upon very first reading the script is purely an overall direct personal response to it, much as you would have when reading a book.

Then I'll read it again, but this time looking specifically at the likely physical/design requirements of each scene. These may be literally stated in the script or be in some way evident from the scenes. This is most probably at such an early stage in the proceedings that I have not yet discussed anything with the director, or heard their views and intended approach.

That discussion can then of course often change my whole view of the script.

During rehearsals

Jordan Castle, understudy and musical theatre performer

I am currently the understudy for two roles in the musical '**Cats**'. As an understudy you get a lot less rehearsal time than if you were actually playing the part, which can be difficult because you don't get the same one-to-one time with the director to explore the character. In rehearsals, I pay attention to everything the actors I am covering do, and make notes. I know I will need to add some of my own interpretation because we are very different people. But it is important to learn all the blocking and not to change that. Luckily I was well-prepared, because I did end up going on and performing each role with very little actual rehearsal.

KEY TERMS:

Covering: learning the words and movements for a part that you do not usually perform.

Blocking: the movements of the actor. These are often written down by the stage manager to ensure that they can be repeated. For example, *'Jo enters and moves DSL (downstage left)'*.

Interval: a break in a performance for both the performers and the audience. This often occurs between the first and second acts of plays. Some plays have more than one interval and some run without an interval.

During performance

During a performance of '**Richard III**' I was stage managing, there was a table with wheels on one end which gets taken on and off the stage during scene changes. At one point, two actors sit in chairs on top of this table. During one performance, in the first half, one of the wheel's rubber surfacing fell off which made the table slightly wobbly. Although it was only a slight wobble this could cause a risk

Zoë Wilson, stage manager

to the actors in the second half. So in the interval I had to make the decision to take the table offstage with my ASM [assistant stage manager] and call for our construction member and crew backstage to take both wheels off to make the table more stable. I then had to inform the actors of what had happened so they were updated and aware. We ended up getting the table on in good time to end the interval on time.

Stage positioning

In order to discuss theatre, you need to be able to explain quickly and simply where you want something to occur. To do this, imagine that the stage (an end on stage in this instance) has been turned into a grid as below:

TIP

To understand if it is 'right' or 'left', imagine you are an actor standing on the centre of the stage facing the audience. Stage right is to your right and stage left is to your left.

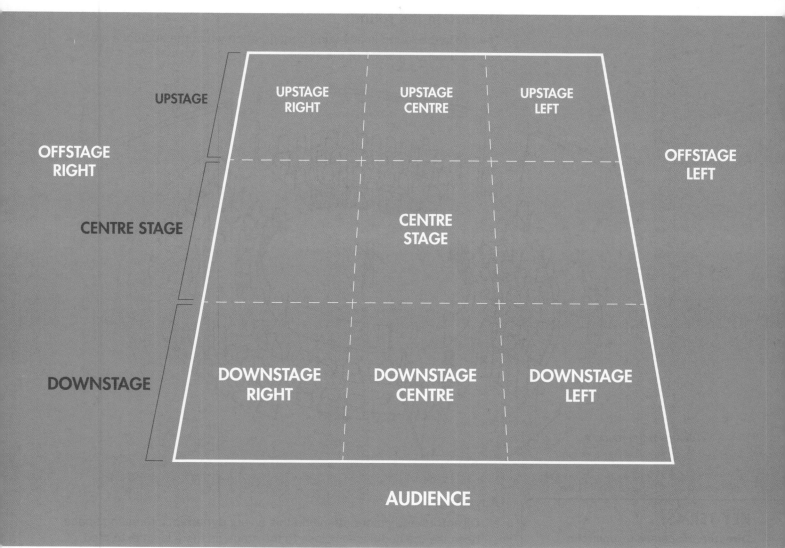

TASK 1

Copy the above end on stage positioning guidance. Then use it to complete the follow directions:

a   Mark an X to show where a doorway could be positioned for an entrance upstage left.

b   Draw a sofa centre stage.

c   Draw a ramp coming from downstage right into the audience.

d   Draw a large projection screen that will hang upstage centre.

Staging configurations

Although the stage positions shown on the previous page are designed for theatres where the audience sits looking straight on at a rectangular stage, as is typical of 'end on' or proscenium stages, there are many other **staging configurations** that influence how the actors perform and what the audience experiences. Below are examples of different types of stages.

Theatre in the round

Theatre in the round is a staging configuration when the audience are seated around all sides of the stage.

KEY TERM:

Staging configuration: the type of stage and audience arrangement.

Theatre in the round ▶

KEY TERMS:

Director: the person responsible for the overall production of a play, including the performances and overseeing the designers.

Dynamic: energetic, forceful.

Fourth wall: an imaginary wall between the audience and the actors giving the impression that the actors are unaware they are being observed.

Backdrop: a large painted cloth hung as part of the scenery.

Sightline: the view of the audience.

Advantages:

▶ **Directors** and actors often find this a very **dynamic**, interesting space because the audience is close to the stage as there is an extended first row.

▶ The actors enter and exit through the audience, which can make the audience feel more engaged.

▶ Unlike spaces such as proscenium theatres, there is no easily achieved 'artificial **fourth wall**' separating the audience from the acting area.

Disadvantages:

▶ Designers cannot use **backdrops** or flats that would obscure the view of the audience.

▶ Stage furniture has to be chosen carefully so that **sightlines** are not blocked.

▶ Actors have to be carefully blocked so that no section of the audience misses important pieces of action or facial expressions for too long.

Proscenium arch

Proscenium arch is a common form of theatre, popular for larger theatres or opera houses. The proscenium refers to the frame around the stage, which emphasises that the whole audience is seeing the same stage picture. The area in front of the arch is called an **apron**.

▲ A proscenium arch

Advantages:

▶ Stage pictures are easy to create as the audience look at the stage from roughly the same angle.

▶ Backdrops and large scenery can be used without blocking sightlines.

▶ There may be **fly space** and **wing spaces** for storing scenery.

▶ The frame around the stage adds to the effect of a fourth wall, giving the effect of a self-contained world.

Disadvantages:

▶ Some audience members may feel distant from the stage.

▶ The auditorium could seem very formal and rigid.

▶ **Audience interaction** may be more difficult.

> ### KEY TERMS:
>
> **Apron:** the area of the stage nearest the audience, which projects in front of the curtain.
>
> **Fly space:** area above the stage where scenery may be stored and lowered to the stage.
>
> **Wing spaces:** areas to the side of the stage. This is the area where actors, unseen by the audience, wait to enter and where props and set pieces may be stored.
>
> **Audience interaction:** involving the audience in the play, for example by bringing them onstage, going into the audience to speak with them or passing them props to hold.
>
> **Box set:** a set with three complete walls, often used in naturalistic set designs, for example to create a believable room.

Thrust stage

A thrust stage protrudes into the auditorium with the audience on three sides. This is one of the oldest theatre types of stage.

Advantages:

▶ Combine some of the advantages of proscenium and theatre in the round stages.

▶ As there is no audience on one side of the stage, backdrops, flats and large scenery can be used.

▶ The audience may feel closer to the stage as there are three first rows – one on each of the stage's three sides

◀ A thrust stage

Disadvantages:

▶ Sightlines for those on the extreme sides may be limited or obstructed.

▶ The audience on the right and left sides of the auditorium have each other in their view.

▶ **Box sets** (where three sides of a room are constructed) cannot be used as this would block views for much of the audience.

📊 CHALLENGE

Greek amphitheatres, with their audience seated around almost half the curved stage, are a type of thrust theatre. Elizabethan theatres are thrust stages and the audience in the lowest level, 'the pit', would stand around three sides of the stage.

Why do you think this has remained such a popular type of theatre configuration?

Traverse

On a traverse stage the acting area is a long, central space with the audience seated on either side facing each other.

Advantages:

▶ The audience feel very close to the stage as there are two long, front rows.

▶ They can see the reactions of the other side of the audience who are facing them, which can work well for audience interaction.

▶ Sometimes, extreme ends of the stage can be used to create extra acting areas.

Disadvantages:

▶ Big pieces of scenery, backdrops or set can block sightlines.

▶ The acting area is long and thin, which can make some blocking challenging.

▶ Actors must be aware of making themselves visible to both sides of the audience.

▶ Lighting for traverse stages needs to be arranged carefully to avoid shining lights into the audience's eyes or light spilling onto them unnecessarily.

A traverse stage ▲

End on staging

End on staging is similar to a proscenium stage, as the audience is seated along one end of the stage, directly facing it. However, it doesn't have the large proscenium frame.

Advantages:

▶ The audience all have a similar view.

▶ Stage pictures are easy to create.

▶ Large backdrops or projections may be used.

Disadvantages:

▶ Audience members in the back rows may feel distant from the stage.

▶ It doesn't have the 'frame' of the proscenium arch theatre, which can enhance some types of staging.

▶ It may not have the wing and fly areas typical of proscenium arch theatres.

End on staging ▲

Promenade theatre

To promenade means 'to walk' and promenade theatre is when the audience stand or follow the actors through the performance. This may occur in a conventional theatre space or it may be designed for a **site specific** show when an unconventional space is used for the production.

> **KEY TERM:**
>
> **Site specific:** a performance in a location, such as a warehouse or park, which is not a conventional theatre. The space has often been adapted to suit the production.

Promenade theatre ▲

Advantages:

▶ This is an interactive and exciting type of theatre where the audience may feel very involved.

Disadvantages:

▶ The audience may find moving around the space difficult or get tired of standing.

▶ Actors or crew need to be skilled at moving the audience around and controlling their focus.

▶ There can be health and safety risks.

TASK 2

a Using the excerpt from '**A View from the Bridge**' on page 10 or another play that you know well, experiment with staging it for all the different configurations: theatre in the round, end on, thrust, traverse, proscenium and promenade. It is important to agree where entrances/exits will be and where you will place any pieces of set furniture.

b Discuss what adjustments you had to make for the different spaces, and decide which you think worked best for the style and content of that particular scene.

 TIP

Understanding staging configurations will help you not only with Component 1, Section A, but will also be useful in Component 1, Sections B and C and Components 2 and 3 when analysing or creating set designs.

PRACTICE QUESTIONS FOR SECTION A

You will answer a number of multiple choice questions.

1 In professional theatre, who is responsible for operating the technical equipment such as lighting during a performance?

   A The theatre manager

   B The stage manger

   C The technician   [1 mark]

2 When performing on a thrust stage which of the following is true?

   A You can only perform centre stage.

   B The audience is positioned along three sides of the stage.

   C The audience is encouraged to walk around during the performance.   [1 mark]

3 What type of stage is shown in Figure 1 on the right?

   A Proscenium arch

   B Traverse stage

   C Thrust stage   [1 mark]

4 With reference to Figure 1 on the right, in what position is the gate?

   A Upstage left

   B Upstage centre

   C Downstage centre   [1 mark]

▲ Figure 1

Additional practice for Section A

1 In the professional theatre, if a performer is unable to perform, who should go on in their place to play the role instead?

   A The stage manager

   B The theatre manager

   C The understudy   [1 mark]

2 Which of the following staging configurations is best suited for using large, high **pieces of set and backdrops**?

   A Proscenium

   B Theatre in the round

   C Traverse   [1 mark]

3 What type of stage is shown in Figure 2 on the right?

   A Thrust stage

   B Theatre in the round

   C End on stage   [1 mark]

4 With reference to Figure 2 on the right, what stage position is the table in?

   A Centre stage

   B Upstage left

   C Downstage right   [1 mark]

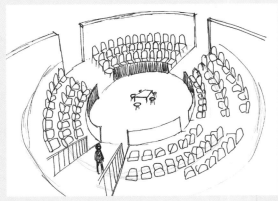

▲ Figure 2

 TIP

Check your work for careless errors. One of the most common is to confuse stage left with stage right.

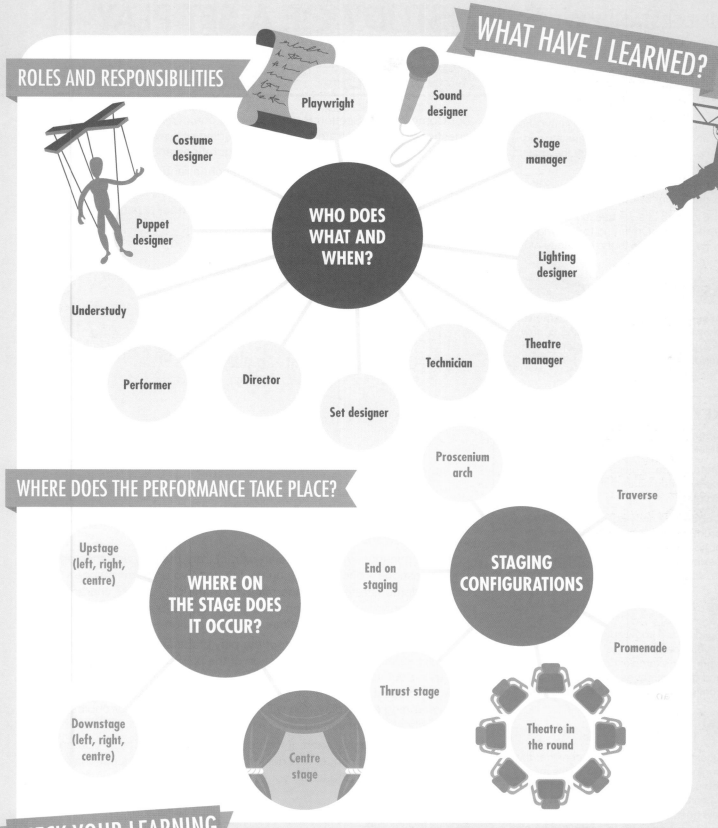

ROLES AND RESPONSIBILITIES

WHAT HAVE I LEARNED?

- Playwright
- Sound designer
- Costume designer
- Stage manager
- Puppet designer

WHO DOES WHAT AND WHEN?

- Lighting designer
- Understudy
- Theatre manager
- Technician
- Performer
- Director
- Set designer
- Proscenium arch

WHERE DOES THE PERFORMANCE TAKE PLACE?

- Upstage (left, right, centre)

WHERE ON THE STAGE DOES IT OCCUR?

- End on staging

STAGING CONFIGURATIONS

- Traverse
- Promenade
- Thrust stage
- Downstage (left, right, centre)
- Centre stage
- Theatre in the round

CHECK YOUR LEARNING

If you are uncertain of the meaning of any of the terms above, go back and revise.

Why not use the downloadable version of this summary as a basis for your own checklist of what you have learned from Samples & Downloads at www.illuminatepublishing.com?

SECTION B
STUDY OF A SET PLAY

THE SPECIFICATION SAYS...

▶ Students are expected to know and understand the characteristics and context of the whole play they have studied.

▶ One extract from each set play is printed in the question paper.

▶ Students answer questions relating to that extract, referring to the whole play as appropriate to the demands of the question.

ASSESSMENT FOCUS

Assessment objective AO3: Demonstrate knowledge and understanding of how drama and theatre are developed and performed.

KEY TERMS:

Genre: a category or type of music, art or literature.

Melodrama: a piece of drama with exaggerated characters and exciting events.

Concept: a unifying idea about the production, such as when it is set or how it will be interpreted and performed.

TIP

Build on the knowledge you have gained in your 'page to stage' and Section A work. For example, consider the benefits and disadvantages of the different staging configurations covered in Section A.

TIP

Question 1 will ask you to consider the original context of the play. This means the play's setting or style, not necessarily when it was written. Your design ideas for this question should show how you have used your research in context to inspire your design.

For Component 1 Section B you will study one of six set plays and be asked questions to demonstrate your understanding of how those plays may be interpreted through acting, staging configurations and design decisions.

The set plays have been chosen to represent a range of theatrical **genres**:

The Crucible – a historical drama

Blood Brothers – a musical

The 39 Steps – a **melodrama**

Hansel and Gretel – a play based on a fairy or folk tale

Noughts and Crosses – a teen drama

A Midsummer Night's Dream – a comedy

Whichever play you study, you will have the chance to explore how the plays could be performed, staged and designed, and each will offer you the opportunity to show your creativity.

In the examination, you will read an extract from the play and then answer three questions – one focusing on design and two on performance – in order to demonstrate your understanding of the play and its characters, style and context. You will then have a choice of a fourth question where you may choose to focus on either acting or design.

It is important that you think about the play practically. It's not expected that you will mount a complete production of the play, but you should be on your feet trying out your performance ideas or sketching your design **concepts** in order to see if these ideas will work. The best ideas come from a deep understanding of the play. You will need to explain how your choices work in a practical theatre setting.

In the following pages, each of the set texts is analysed for its content, context and performance, and design elements. Sample questions and responses are provided to aid your study.

TIP

There is a strong element of interpretation based on your own insight into the play, so there may be many 'right' answers.

▶ There are additional detailed notes on the practical aspects of the different specialisms in Component 3.

SET PLAY 1: 'The Crucible' by Arthur Miller

Synopsis

The play opens in a bedroom in the house of **Reverend Parris** in the town of **Salem** in **America**, during **1692**. His daughter, **Betty**, is ill in bed. Various Salem residents, including servant girls and neighbours, as well as **Tituba**, a slave from Barbados, come to enquire how she is. When the servant girls, led by **Abigail**, are left alone with Betty, they discuss how they were discovered, with Tituba, dancing in the woods. **Mary Warren** is afraid they will be called witches.

John Proctor, a neighbour, enters and sends Mary Warren, his servant, home. When he and Abigail are left alone, she asks him for a 'soft word' and he tells her that he is 'done with' that. There is conflict between Parris and Proctor over matters of money, community and religion. **Reverend Hale**, an educated minister from another parish, arrives to treat Betty. Parris describes finding the girls, including Betty and Abigail, dancing in the woods. Abigail is asked if they were calling the Devil. Abigail blames Tituba who, she says, made them drink blood. Tituba claims that the Devil has visited her, accompanied by women of Salem. Abigail cries out that she wants the light of God and begins naming people she saw with the Devil. Betty rises from her bed and joins in the accusations.

Act 2, in the Proctor home, Proctor and his wife, **Elizabeth**, discuss Mary Warren and the upcoming court case. Many people have been put in jail, based on the girls' accusations. Elizabeth wants Proctor to declare Abigail a fraud. They argue over Elizabeth's suspicions. Mary Warren returns and presents Elizabeth with a doll she has made. Mary tells Elizabeth that she was accused in court. Elizabeth asks Proctor to intervene with Abigail, who she believes wants to kill her in order to be with him.

Hale arrives and questions the Proctors' commitment to the Church. Proctor admits a dislike of Reverend Parris. Proctor tells Hale that Abigail said they made up the witchcraft story to avoid punishment for dancing in the woods. **Giles Corey** and **Francis Nurse** arrive to say their wives have been taken by the court. Elizabeth is arrested. The doll Mary Warren gave Elizabeth is to be used as evidence against her. Proctor orders Mary to tell the truth in court.

TIP

'**The Crucible**' is a complex play with many characters. One way to keep them clear in your mind is to divide them into groups such as: the judges; servants; neighbours. Then put a few notes, either in pencil in your script or on the notes you make accompanying your script, next to each name, such as: Giles Corey: older, troublesome, a bit foolish but brave.

Act 3 takes place in the Salem meeting house where the court is held. Proctor brings Mary before the judges. She tells them the stories were false. The Deputy Governor, **Danforth**, reveals that Elizabeth has told the court that she is pregnant, which could spare her life for at least another year. Proctor presents a statement by neighbours in support of the accused women.

Giles Corey, who states that **Thomas Putnam** is making false accusations of witchcraft for monetary gain, is arrested. Proctor hands the court Mary's deposition. The accusing girls are brought into court which hears Mary's faltering account of their dishonesty. The girls, led by Abigail, claim that Mary is sending an evil spirit or a 'bird' to control them. Proctor calls Abigail a 'whore'. He confesses that he has 'known' Abigail and that is the motivation for her actions. Elizabeth is brought into court and asked if her husband is a 'lecher'. To protect her husband's good name, she says, 'No, sir.' Elizabeth is taken away and the girls begin screaming. Mary turns and accuses Proctor of being the Devil. Proctor is taken to jail.

Act 4 takes place in a cell in the Salem jail. Reverend Parris tells Danforth that his niece, Abigail, stole money from him and has vanished. Parris expresses doubts about executing members of high standing in their community such as Rebecca Nurse and John Proctor. Hale meets with the accused hoping to get them to confess to witchcraft in order to spare their lives. Hale asks Elizabeth to plead with Proctor to confess so he won't be killed.

Proctor is brought in. He asks for Elizabeth's forgiveness. He declares that he wants to live. He is asked to sign a confession. Danforth wants him to name others who he has seen with the Devil. Proctor refuses and declares he cannot sign his name to the false confession, 'Because it is my name!' He kisses a weeping Elizabeth. Rebecca Nurse and Proctor are taken out to be executed, while Hale weeps in prayer.

TASK 1

a   After reading the synopsis above, with your group choose ten key plot points and create a still image for each one. Discuss what you think are the most important moments in the play.

b   With your group, make a bullet point list of some of the challenges in performing and designing a production of the play. You could try to find at least two points for each of the following design areas: sound; costume; lighting; and setting. You might begin by:

▶ creating the period setting

▶ differentiating between the different characters.

Context

The play is set in Salem, Massachusetts, in 1692 and is based on historic events. The 'witch trials' of this time were among the most famous events of Colonial America.

New England, on the east coast of America, had been settled by people, called Puritans, seeking freedom from the Church of England, in order to practise their particular branch of Christianity. The Puritans were fiercely religious and had strong ideas about appropriate Christian behaviour, which they hoped to practise without interference.

In the community of Salem there were many disputes about legal and religious issues. The Church and local minister were central to the community and the appointment of Reverend Parris, their first ordained minister, was a controversial one, adding to the discontent.

At this time, the roles of women and men were clearly divided. Women were in charge of the home and, in many cases, would have servant girls to help them with their chores.

Child-bearing was an important role for women and it is a source of conflict in the play that Rebecca Nurse has so many surviving children while Mrs Putnam had buried 'all but one' of hers. Women who were pregnant would not be executed, so it is significant when Elizabeth reveals that she is pregnant.

Abigail, who is the orphaned niece of Reverend Parris, was a servant to the Proctors until she was replaced by Mary Warren when Elizabeth learned of Abigail's relationship with her husband. Tituba, Reverend Parris' slave from Barbados, is treated with suspicion by other characters due to her different background and beliefs. The men in the play are shown in a variety of roles, including farmers, ministers and judges. Money is discussed in some detail, such as Reverend Parris' salary or Giles Corey's various lawsuits. Reverend Hale is an outsider to the community. Miller's description of him as an 'intellectual' or a man of learning, is backed up by his entrance carrying 'a dozen heavy books'. His education is respected by others.

▲ *The Salem witch trials*

▲ *Architecture of the period: a) interior; b) exterior of Judge Corwin's house, known as Witch House, in Salem.*

KEY TERM:

Clapboards: wooden boards used to cover the outside of buildings.

▲ *Costumes of the period* ▶

Buildings in Salem at this time would usually be simple wooden structures. In Act 2, John Proctor tells how the community 'built the church', which was a '**clapboard** meeting house'. There would be limited decorative adornments inside, with many objects being obviously hand-made by the residents.

Women would dress modestly in long dresses, often with an apron, a shawl and cap. Petticoats or underskirts were worn under skirts for warmth and modesty. When outside, they might wear a hooded cape.

Men would dress differently depending on their occupations. A minister or wealthy man might wear a wide-brimmed hat, a doublet or long waistcoat, breeches (knee-length trousers) and buckled shoes. Outdoor work would require simpler, sturdy clothing, such as woollen breeches, a collarless shirt, a neckcloth (a strip of fabric tied around the neck), hard-wearing boots and a leather or coarsely woven waistcoat. Puritans dressed in plain colours, often earth tones, such as tan or brown, or grey, with white or off-white cuffs and collars. Black was a more expensive dye, so that was used for formal clothes or for wealthier people, such as the judges. Linen and wool were the most popular fabrics.

Men's hair was usually shoulder-length and some wore expensive wigs. Although very young girls might wear their hair down, women would put their hair in a bun, usually tucked under a cap for modesty.

TASK 2

Look at the images of Puritan clothing on this page and decide which characters in the play might wear costumes that look like them. Make notes in your notebook describing their outfits and why they are suitable for those characters.

Costume, hair and make-up design inspired by context

TASK 3

Use your understanding of the play's context and the prompts below to design a costume for **Reverend Hale** for Act 1.

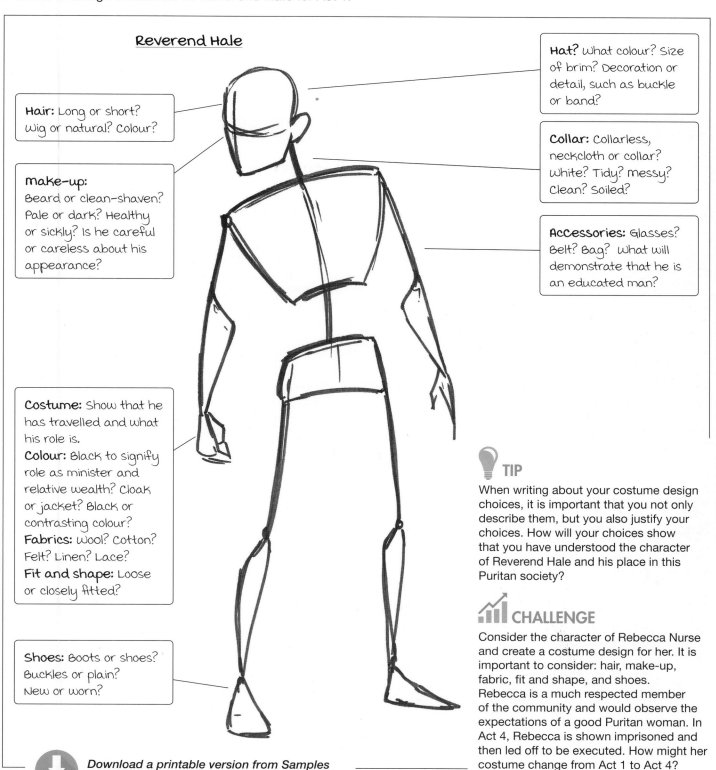

Reverend Hale

Hair: Long or short? Wig or natural? Colour?

make-up: Beard or clean-shaven? Pale or dark? Healthy or sickly? Is he careful or careless about his appearance?

Hat? What colour? Size of brim? Decoration or detail, such as buckle or band?

Collar: Collarless, neckcloth or collar? White? Tidy? messy? Clean? Soiled?

Accessories: Glasses? Belt? Bag? What will demonstrate that he is an educated man?

Costume: Show that he has travelled and what his role is.
Colour: Black to signify role as minister and relative wealth? Cloak or jacket? Black or contrasting colour?
Fabrics: Wool? Cotton? Felt? Linen? Lace?
Fit and shape: Loose or closely fitted?

Shoes: Boots or shoes? Buckles or plain? New or worn?

TIP

When writing about your costume design choices, it is important that you not only describe them, but you also justify your choices. How will your choices show that you have understood the character of Reverend Hale and his place in this Puritan society?

CHALLENGE

Consider the character of Rebecca Nurse and create a costume design for her. It is important to consider: hair, make-up, fabric, fit and shape, and shoes. Rebecca is a much respected member of the community and would observe the expectations of a good Puritan woman. In Act 4, Rebecca is shown imprisoned and then led off to be executed. How might her costume change from Act 1 to Act 4?

Download a printable version from Samples & Downloads at www.illuminatepublishing.com.

Set design inspired by context

Each act of **'The Crucible'** has a different setting in the context of a Puritan community in the 17th century. Although it can be interpreted in different ways, typically the play is performed and designed in a naturalistic style when the aim is to make the interpretation as realistic as possible. The first question will ask you to refer specifically to the context. As a designer, you will need to consider how your design will:

▶ serve the practical needs of the play

▶ show the period setting

▶ suggest the appropriate atmosphere.

After choosing your stage configuration, use the following to begin formulating ideas for your set design (the requirements have been started for you, but you may discover additional aspects of the set or props that you wish to include):

ACT 1 — Small upper bedroom in the home of Reverend Samuel Parris. Spring 1692.

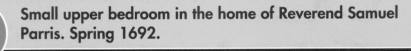

REQUIREMENTS OF LOCATION

Window. Candle. Chest. Chair. Table. Door. Bed.

DESIGN CHOICES

1 How will you show that this is a 17th-century building? What specific period features, such as wooden beams or leaded windows, could you use?

2 What choices of materials would you make for the walls and flooring? Wood? Stone? Plaster?

3 What are the main colours in the room?

4 Where would you arrange the furniture? For example, how central should the bed be? Where will others sit or stand?

5 What, if anything, can be seen outside the window?

ACT 2 — The common room (living room) of Proctor's house. Eight days later.

REQUIREMENTS OF LOCATION

Outside door. Fireplace with pot. Opening leading to stairway. Basin. Table. Chairs. Plates, drinking utensils, cutlery.

DESIGN CHOICES

1 What is the atmosphere in the room? What can we learn about the Proctors from this room?

2 How can the room indicate the period (for example, how cooking and washing were done)?

3 What are the main colours in the room?

4 Where will you place the outside door for maximum effect when characters make their entrances?

5 What is the size of the table and where will you place it on stage?

The Salem meeting house, now serving as the courthouse.

REQUIREMENTS OF LOCATION

High windows. Heavy beams. Two doors leading into the meeting house. Another door leads outside. Two benches. A long meeting table. Stools. One armchair.

DESIGN CHOICES

1 How will the set show the difference in the atmosphere in contrast with the previous two sets?

2 Where will you position the judges' table and the benches to give the impression of a court and the importance of the judges?

3 Where will you position the doors to create dramatic effects, for example when Giles is carried in or the girls enter?

4 Where on the set will the girls claim to see 'the bird'?

5 What are the main colours in the room and what materials will you use for the set?

ACT 4

A cell in the Salem jail. Autumn, 1692.

REQUIREMENTS OF LOCATION

High, barred window. Heavy door. Two benches.

DESIGN CHOICES

1 How will this set demonstrate the different atmosphere in this act in contrast with the previous acts?

2 How can you create a design that makes clear this is a prison, how harsh the conditions are in the 17th century and how difficult it would be to escape? (Think about the door and window, for example.)

3 How can you make it clear that when this act begins it is night-time? How can you use light and shadow to create atmosphere?

4 What materials can you use to emphasise how uncomfortable the jail is?

5 Where will you position the door where Proctor finally exits to emphasise the importance of that moment?

MARTHA CORY AND HER PERSECUTORS.

▲ *Rebecca Nurse's homestead*

TASK 4

You are designing a setting for a performance of Act 2 of '**The Crucible**'. The setting must reflect the context of '**The Crucible**', set in a Puritan community in the 17th century. Describe your design ideas for the setting.

You may wish to include:

▶ How the Proctors' living room reflects the simple beliefs of the Puritan community.

▶ How the materials used in the set reflect those available in the 17th century and the needs of those living in the house.

▶ What the set shows about the lives of Elizabeth and John Proctor.

 TIP

When considering how you will design your set, it is important to know that you will often not use the actual materials of the time, but create the set out of materials that can be made to look like them. For example, you would probably paint plywood or other lightweight material to create the effect of stones in the jail, or stain a lighter wood to create dark wooden beams in the meeting house.

Writing about your design ideas

Question 1 will always ask you to consider an aspect of design for the play in relation to its context. Below is a student's plan for the following question:

You are designing a costume for Reverend Hale to wear in a performance of this extract from the first act. The costume must reflect the context of 'The Crucible', set in a Puritan community in the 17th century. Describe your design ideas for the costume.

1 Understanding of character in play:

Reverend Hale is an educated, religious man. ① —————————————— *Demonstrates understanding of character*

His costume must reflect this.

2 Period:

Colours and fabrics: black breeches, white collar, black, *Understand typical clothing of this period* —— long waistcoat. ② Emphasise his role as a Puritan minister in Colonial America in the 17th century. ③ White linen shirt. —— *Refers to his role in this context*

Black wool for other items.

3 His relationship to the community:

Understanding of play and what has happened before this scene —— Enters wearing cloak, shows he has travelled and comes from another community. ④ Wears glasses and carries a leather satchel of books to indicate his studious nature. ⑤ —— *Shows understanding of how accessories can help establish character*

4 Character:

His clothing is neat, well-pressed, suggesting a slight vanity. He is clean-shaven, with shoulder-length clean, fair hair. His buckled shoes are well polished showing that he does not do heavy manual or dirty work. ⑥ —— *Considers hair and other period details and what they reveal about character*

 TIP

It is important to know that there are other interpretations of how Reverend Hale might be costumed.

 TIP

It is important that you justify your ideas. Explain why you are making these specific choices, don't just describe what she will look like. What do we learn about Mary as a young servant and her role in Puritan Salem from these costume choices?

1 Understanding of character in play:

2 Period:

3 Her relationship to the community:

4 Character:

TASK 5

Using the above plan as a guide, create your own plan for the character of Mary Warren in answer to the following question:

You are designing a costume for Mary Warren to wear in a performance of this extract from the second act. The costume must reflect the context of 'The Crucible', set in a Puritan community in the 17th century. Describe your own design ideas for the costume.

Practical exploration of play's style and themes

When writing about performing roles in the play, you must demonstrate that you understand the characters and how they interact. You need to use the performance space to show your understanding of the play. Below are two themes from the play that you can explore practically to develop your understanding of the play and its characters.

Reputation

Reputation is an important theme in the play, with consequences for many characters. Proctor loses his reputation as a good Christian man in his community when he confesses to his 'lechery' with Abigail; Mary Warren risks her reputation with the girls by speaking up against them; Abigail lies to protect her own reputation by accusing Tituba and others; in the final act, Proctor chooses his reputation over his life.

TASK 6

a Focus on the character of Proctor. Read the scene with Proctor, Danforth and Hale in Act 4, starting with Danforth's line: 'Mr. Proctor. When the Devil came to you did you see Rebecca Nurse in his company?' and ending with Danforth's 'Why? Do you mean to deny this confession when you are free?'

b With your group create a 'Conscience Alley' to help Proctor make up his mind. One of you will be Proctor and the rest will form two facing lines. One side of the line must think of reasons why Proctor should sign the confession and the other side should think of reasons why he should not. As 'Proctor' walks down the alley between the two lines, each person shouts out a reason for or against signing the confession. At the end of the alley, 'Proctor' must refuse to sign and say the line 'Because it is my name.'

c Discuss how it felt to hear all the conflicting reasons and how the performer playing Proctor made their decision.

d Everyone in the group should have a turn saying 'Because it is my name'. Write your observations on the following in your notebook:

▶ projection/volume

▶ emotion

▶ pace, pause and timing

▶ inflection (words said with particular emphasis).

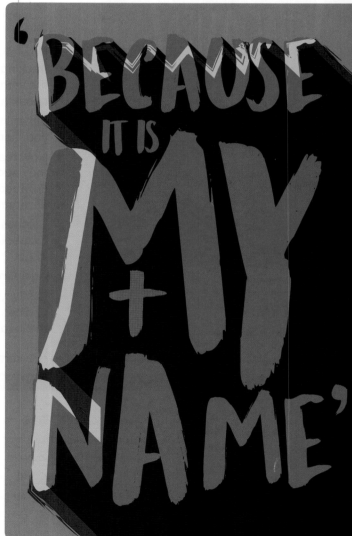

Love

There are several examples of love in the play, most particularly the love between Elizabeth and Proctor. In Act 2, their relationship is strained and there is a great deal of unspoken tension between them. Beneath their lines, there is a subtext, which is influenced by Proctor's former relationship with Abigail.

KEY TERM:

Thought-track: speaking aloud the thoughts of the character.

KEY TERM:

Repressing: holding back or restraining.

TASK 7

a   With a partner, read a section of Act 2 from Proctor's line: 'It's well seasoned' to Elizabeth's line 'I couldn't stop her.'

b   Now read the scene again, but **thought-track** what the characters are really thinking after each line.

Here is an example:

> **Proctor:** It's well seasoned.
>
> `Thought-track:` Only because I put more salt in.
>
> **Elizabeth:** I took great care. She's tender.
>
> `Thought-track:` I'm so happy – I am really trying to please him. Does he mean it though? Is everything all right? Or is he just saying it?

c   Now read through the scene a third time, without saying the thought-tracking lines, but keeping them in mind with the way you speak. Do these thoughts create more pauses or awkwardness in the way they speak to each other?

d   Either in pencil in your script or on the notes you make accompanying your script, jot down any discoveries you have made.

e   Now read the scene between Proctor and Elizabeth in Act 4, when they speak frankly of their feelings for each other, starting with Elizabeth's line 'It is not for me to give, John I am' and ending with Elizabeth's line 'It were a cold house I kept!'

f   Discuss with your partner the contrasts between how Proctor and Elizabeth speak to each other in this scene compared with the scene in Act 2.

g   Again, note in your script in pencil any discoveries you have made.

h   Lastly, write a few sentences describing the physical and vocal choices that could be made when performing these scenes and how the love between the characters could be shown.

Here is a sample response:

Explains why choices are made

Describes vocal and physical choices

Detail of use of eye contact

> In Act 4, Elizabeth finally speaks frankly to John about her feelings. Instead of judging him and repressing her feelings, she is emotional and open. ❶ Playing her, I would speak harshly when I say 'cold wife' and I would gesture angrily at myself. ❷ When I say 'so plain', I would look down, unable to meet John's eyes. ❸ However, I would look up at him and take a step closer when I say 'I should say my love.' ❹ I think this is the first time Elizabeth has actually said the word 'love' to him and it would be said in a 'trembling way'. ❺

Detail of use of eye contact and stage space

Explains why choices are made

Interpretation of character

You will need to show how you can interpret a character. This means that you understand the character's motivations and goals and the obstacles they face. Then you must be able to use your vocal and physical skills to portray the character and create particular effects for the audience, such as tension, comedy, surprise, pity or sorrow.

Look below at one interpretation of the character of **Giles Corey** (your interpretation may differ).

SET PLAY 1:
'The Crucible'
by Arthur Miller

1

FACTS:

Age: he is an old man, eighty-three

Job: farmer, still active

Interpretation:

PHYSICAL APPEARANCE:

I imagine Corey to be short and, for his age, muscular.

HAIR:

Long, grey, somewhat tangled and not recently washed.

VOICE:

Speaks in a stronger dialect than other characters – 'readin'. He is simple and straightforward with a tendency to repeat himself 'deep, deep'. Low-pitch, gruff, often shouts.

MAKE-UP:

Emphasise his age, with deep grooves on his forehead. Skin is rough from outdoor work.

BODY LANGUAGE:

Solid, rooted to the ground, ready for a fight, often raises his fists. At his age, he may have a slight limp from decades of hard work, but that doesn't slow him down. Possibly hard of hearing, so leans forward to make sure he catches everything.

COSTUME:

Rough, practical clothes. Brown breeches, sturdy plain leather shoes, no buckle. Poorly repaired stockings – he would think it a waste to get new ones. Coarse woollen, brown waistcoat, off-white linen shirt, with some stains.

EFFECT ON AUDIENCE:

Giles Corey is the most comic character in the play and his stubbornness and, early in the play, his willingness to fight should cause some amusement. However, he is also very brave and when the audience hear about his death in Act 4 they should be sad.

TASK 7

Using your own understanding of the characters in the play and how they could be interpreted, create an interpretation on paper, with the following as a guide, of Mary Warren, Rebecca Nurse or Ann Putnam. In this instance, think about total characterisation, which includes facts about the characters and their appearance as well as how they could be interpreted through acting, costume and make-up choices. This will help you to think about all aspects of interpreting the character, even when writing about acting or design.

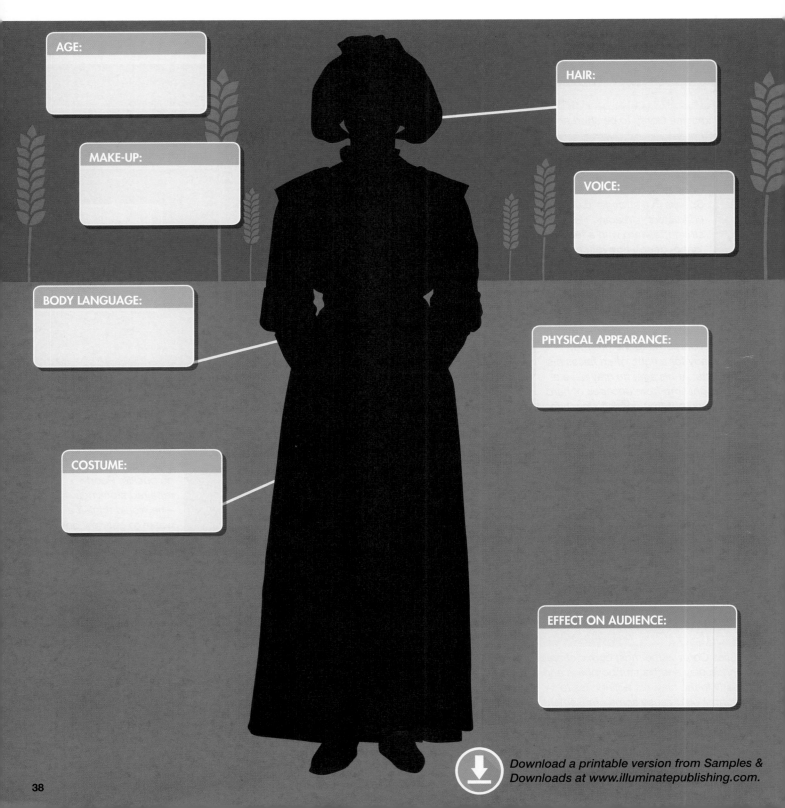

AGE:

MAKE-UP:

BODY LANGUAGE:

COSTUME:

HAIR:

VOICE:

PHYSICAL APPEARANCE:

EFFECT ON AUDIENCE:

Download a printable version from Samples & Downloads at www.illuminatepublishing.com.

Performing choices

In question 2, you will be asked to discuss in detail how you would perform a particular line as a given character.

For example:

SET PLAY 1:
'The Crucible'
by Arthur Miller

1

You are performing the role of _____ .
Describe how you would use your vocal and physical skills to perform the lines below and explain the effects you want to create.
Sample:

> **ABIGAIL. Act 1:** And you must. You are no wintry man.
> I *know*, John. I *know* you.

Effect —
Physical skills —
Physical skills —
Effect —
Vocal skills —

In this scene, Abigail wants to win Proctor's affections again. ① As Abigail, I would move closer to Proctor on 'And you must.' ② I would put my hand on his chest on the word 'wintry' and maintain eye contact, ③ making clear that I can see that he is attracted to me. ④ On the word 'wintry' my tone will be sarcastic ⑤ because I know he is warm-hearted and passionate. On 'I know John' I will move even closer and put my arms around him. ⑥ I will speak those words slowly and softly as if to mesmerise him, ⑦ but also making sure that we cannot be overheard by others. ⑧ I will emphasise the word 'know' ⑨ because, in those days, know, in the biblical sense, meant having sexual relations, so my tone will suggest our past. ⑩ I will speak those words with a breathy, seductive voice, with my face close enough to him that we could kiss. ⑪ The effect of these choices for these lines will show the power that Abigail wants to have over Proctor. ⑫

Physical skills
Vocal skills
Effect
Vocal skills

Effect

Vocal and physical skills

Effect

TIP

It is important that you write in the first person ('I') so you can fully imagine your own performance of the role. Don't only describe the vocal and physical skills you will use, but also think about how your choices will add to the audience's understanding of the play's meaning, the character and the character's relationship with others.

TASK 8

Experiment with different ways of using your vocal and physical skills for each of the following lines:

TITUBA: Act 1: Oh, how many times he bid me kill you, Mr Parris!

PROCTOR: Act 2: Oh, Elizabeth, your justice would freeze beer!

HALE: Act 2: Aye. But the Devil is a wily one, you cannot deny it.

MARY: Act 3: Let me go, Mr Proctor, I cannot, I cannot –

ELIZABETH: Act 3: She – dissatisfied me. [*Pause.*] And my husband.

PARRIS: Act 4: Thirty-one pound is gone. I am penniless.

DANFORTH: Act 4: Why, for the good instruction of the village, Mister; this we shall post upon the church door.

TASK 9

a Make notes in your notebook on the following:
  - Vocal skills:
  - Physical skills:
  - Effects achieved:

b Then, using the example answer above as a guide, write an answer to the same question referring to each of the characters and lines.

c Check your work by writing 'V' next to each vocal skill, 'P' next to each physical skill and 'E' next to an effect. Make sure that you have answered this queston fully.

Character revision sheet

Below is an example of a character revision sheet based on the character of **Abigail Williams**, which has been partially completed. Copy the grid and complete it.

Character and importance to the play	Abigail Williams Leader of the girls and the cause of conflict between Elizabeth and John.
What do they want?	Wants to be with John. Wants adventure.
What obstacles do they face?	John rejects her. The Puritan society confines and restricts her.
What are their key scenes?	Act 1: Scene with Parris about being found in the woods. Act 1: Scene with Proctor about their previous relationship. Act 1: Scene with Hale and others accusing Tituba of leading them in witchcraft. Act 3: Scene in court responding to Mary Warren's accusations.

How might they be costumed?	How might their hair and make-up be done?
Draw a simple sketch or write a description of it. Consider: • colours • fabrics • shape and fit • character's personality and status	Draw a simple sketch or write a description of it. Consider: • style and colour of hair • type of make-up (realistic or fantasy; colours; how it is appropriate for character, setting and period)

How might they use body language?	
• posture • gait (the way they walk) • facial expression	

How might they use their voice?	
Emotional range (angry, sad, happy, irritated, desperate, dominating, etc.) Pitch and volume (how low or high; how loud or soft) Accent or other distinctive vocal features	

Choose one important line and analyse how they might say it.	Act 1: 'A wild thing may say wild things.'

TASK 10

Using the above grid for guidance, create similar revision sheets for all major characters including: Elizabeth, Proctor, Hale, Mary Warren, Danforth, Tituba and Parris.

Download a printable version from Samples & Downloads at www.illuminatepublishing.com.

Using the performance space and interaction with others

There are opportunities to explore the space and interaction with others in a number of different ways in the four settings of the play. There are intimate two-person scenes, such as the scenes between Proctor and Elizabeth or Proctor and Abigail, and busy, crowded scenes, like the trial; there are scenes set during the day and others at night; scenes in domestic settings and others in public places. When you are writing about how you will use the performance space and interaction with others, make sure that you focus on the effects you wish to achieve, such as tension, surprise, humour, pity or sorrow, and how you will use your skills to achieve them.

TASK 11

Look closely at the entrance of John Proctor in Act 1, starting from '*Enter* JOHN PROCTOR. *On seeing him,* MARY WARREN *leaps in fright*' and ending with Abigail's 'Give me a word, John.'

a Read the scene, taking particular notice of any stage directions.

b Agree what stage configuration you are going to use: end on, theatre in the round, thrust, promenade, proscenium or traverse. Mark where the entrances will be and any pieces of furniture.

c Decide what effects you wish to achieve in this scene. To help you do this, answer the following questions on the following issues:

   ▶ Proctor's character: Miller describes him as having 'a quiet confidence' and 'an unexpressed, hidden force'. How might this influence how the performer playing him stands and moves?

   ▶ Mary's reaction to him: she is his servant and is frightened of him. Yet when she leaves she tries to 'retain a shred of dignity' and exits slowly. Explain how the performer could make clear what she wants to show the others?

   ▶ Abigail's reaction to him: how obvious is her attraction to him? Does she do anything to try to catch his attention?

   ▶ How Mercy (one of the girls in Abigail's group) reacts to him: what does the stage direction for Mercy ('*both afraid of him and strangely* **titillated**') mean and how could the performer show this?

> **KEY TERM:**
> **Titillated:** excited, thrilled.

   ▶ Do John and Abigail behave differently when Mercy and Mary leave the room? How does it add to the tension of the scene that they may be overheard or interrupted at any time?

d How will you use stage space? Try the following:

   Proctor's entrance:

   ▶ Have Proctor enter and stand in the doorway, slowly observing the other characters.

   ▶ Have Proctor enter quickly and stand centre stage, ignoring Abigail.

   ▶ Have Proctor enter at a steady pace, stop and see Abigail, briefly make eye contact with her, and then continue walking across the room.

   Mary's reaction:

   ▶ Have Mary jump up, let out a small shriek, and then hide her face in her hands.

   ▶ Have Mary hide behind Abigail, while nervously twisting the end of her apron.

   ▶ Have Mary run past John towards the door, avoiding eye contact.

e Continue working through the scene, experimenting with different staging configuration ideas. When you have finished, answer the following question:

> You are performing the role of **John Proctor**.
>
> Focusing on the lines 'Be you foolish, Mary?' to '… my wife is waitin' with your work', explain how you and the actor playing Mary might use the performance space and interact with each other to create tension for the audience.

TIP

It is important to know that you will have your own interpretation of this character, this is just one example.

Answering a question about character interpretation

If you choose to answer question 4, you will need to write about how you would use your acting skills to interpret a character both in the extract provided and **in the play as a whole**.

An example of this sort of question might be:

> You are performing the role of **Parris**.
>
> Describe how you would use your **acting skills** to interpret Parris' character in this extract (Act 1, lines 'And what shall I say to them' to 'There is a faction that is sworn to drive me from my pulpit. Do you understand that?') and explain why your ideas are appropriate both for **this extract** and the **play as a whole**.

Below is a sample student plan for this question.

This extract:

1 Character of Parris and reasons for making acting choices:

minister, self-important, but also distressed because of daughter and what he has seen of the girls' actions. Wants high status. Suspicious of others.

2 Acting skills: vocal:

well-spoken. Orders others: 'Sit you down.' Tries to dominate, uses volume and speaks directly and with authority. Speaks more quickly on 'And what shall I say to them?' and more softly so as not to be overheard on 'my daughter and my niece' – he's embarrassed. More emotion on 'This child is desperate' and 'There is a faction ...' – is fearful both for his daughter and his position.

3 Acting skills: physical:

upright posture. Eye contact with Abigail, willing her to tell the truth. Remains standing when he makes Abigail sit. Towers over her, trying to dominate. Towards end of extract, gestures become more pleading – points towards Betty, wrings his hands anxiously. Moves towards Abigail trying to convince her. Looks over his shoulder, suspicious, anxious, when talking about a 'faction'. Shows his fear.

Rest of play:

1 Character of Parris and reasons for making acting choices:

by end of the play, a broken man who has lost almost everything. His certainty and status are gone. Important that status is established in earlier scenes, so loss of it at the end is felt.

2 Acting skills: vocal:

Act 3: speaks bitterly of Giles Corey and Proctor. Suspicious, complaining. Shocked when Proctor brings in Mary Warren, shouts out. More confident tone when discussing the Bible, takes a condescending, knowing tone. Totally different in Act 4. He is troubled. Speaks quickly, with high emotion, breaks into sobs. Voice ragged, shouts final line.

3 Acting skills: physical:

in Act 4: anxious, nervous energy, quick gestures. Afraid of Proctor. Tries to be kind to Proctor but has to accept his rejection. Bows his head before Proctor. Clear loss of status in his movements at ending.

TIP

It is important to include both vocal and physical skills. Highlight key moments when these skills can be discussed.

1 Character of Parris and reasons for making acting choices:

2 Acting skills: vocal:

3 Acting skills: physical:

TASK 12

Using the above plan as a guide, create your own plan in answer to the following question using the headings on the left:

> You are performing the role of **Elizabeth**.
>
> Describe how you would use your **acting skills** to interpret Elizabeth's character in Act 2, from Elizabeth's 'Oh, the noose, the noose is up!' to Elizabeth's 'John – grant me this,' and explain why your ideas are appropriate both for **this extract** and the **play as a whole**.

Design choices

If you choose to answer question 5, you will be thinking as a designer and commenting on one aspect of design.

For example, see the question in the margin.

You may choose to focus on set design, costume design, lighting design, sound design or puppet design. Whichever you choose, you must explain why your ideas are appropriate to the play as a whole. You might refer to:

▶ how your design helps to show the action and the nature of the characters

▶ how your design for the extract is consistent with the design requirements of the rest of the play (for example, don't suddenly change mid-scene from a period to a modern setting)

▶ how you have used design methods that fit in with the mood of the play

▶ props, anything that the actors may carry on stage.

'**The Crucible**' is usually performed and designed in a naturalistic way, with an emphasis on its period setting. However, some productions use symbolism to emphasise certain themes or choose more minimalistic sets to focus on the acting. A production may introduce a colour, such as red, at certain points to indicate danger. Others show the woods where the girls were dancing in every act to indicate their importance to the plot.

You may choose to use modern techniques such as projections to suggest the New England countryside or to highlight religious imagery. You could use music or sound effects to create the sense of doom in the final act or to underscore the girls' visions of the Devil. You could choose lighting effects to pick out key moments or to emphasise the passing of time.

> You are a designer working on one aspect of design for this extract.
>
> Describe how you would use your design skills to create effects that support the action of this extract and explain why your ideas are appropriate for **this extract** and the **play as a whole**.

 TIP

Whatever design choices you make, you must make sure that they show your understanding of the play and its needs.

**Robert Innes Hopkins,
designer**

Can you explain your design for 'The Crucible'?

As a Puritan community in Massachusetts in the 1600s, the characters in '**The Crucible**' would have built their own homes and would not have had many possessions. Therefore, everything on-stage is very simple, with a handmade feel that uses natural materials such as wood. For the first half, I have the challenge of housing all the actors on-stage, even when they are not in the scene. To achieve this, I have made a playing space on a circular disc in the middle of the stage, with benches alongside where the actors will sit and enter and exit the performance space without the use of doorways – eliminating that level of naturalism. It is not designed to be a naturalistic actual space, but we represent the three main settings with unique pieces of set, for example a window or a door to demonstrate a change in environment. (Bristol Old Vic, Education Pack)

THEATRE MAKER ADVICE

Costume design

For the costume design, you might consider:

- ▶ style, cut and fit of costume
- ▶ colour, fabric, decorative features
- ▶ condition (worn or new; neat or wrinkled; clean or stained, etc.)
- ▶ footwear/headgear
- ▶ accessories
- ▶ status or social role of character
- ▶ make-up and hairstyle.

Below is an extract from a sample response for a question based on Abigail in Act 1, in her scene with John Proctor.

In this scene, I would have Abigail dressed in clothing typical of the other servant girls: a long, plain, brown woollen dress, white apron, cap and white shawl-like collar. ① However, I want to show her character through her costume, by emphasising her awareness of her own beauty. ② Although she is wearing a cap, there will be tendrils of hair escaping from it, creating a softer, more seductive look. ③ Her clothes will be neater and in better condition than the other girls. ④ Her brown leather shoes will be unmarked and shiny. She will wear the modest collar of the others, but it will be more open at the neck, exposing a little more of her chest than the others. ⑤ Her dress will be closely fitted at the waist, showing her attractive shape. ⑥ Abigail is a rebel and, although ornamentation would be frowned upon by Puritans, I would have her wear a little decorative object, like a feather, pinned under her collar, to show her willingness to break the rules. ⑦ In this extract, her costume should demonstrate how she stands out from the other girls and her sensual appeal to John Proctor. ⑧

In Act 3, I would remove any of the features from the first act that made her stand out, with her hair tucked neatly into a cap, looking proper, so her testimony would be believed. ⑨

Annotations (right):
- Fabric, colours and style consistent with setting and period of the play
- Understanding of character and action of the scene
- Discusses hairstyle and effect on portrayal of character
- Shape and fit of costume
- Ornamental detail
- How costume helps to convey action of play
- How costume would be altered for her role in the rest of the play

Annotations (left):
- Condition of clothing
- Costume detail to portray character

TASK 13

Draw a sketch showing Elizabeth's costume, make-up and hair for Act 2. Then create a contrasting sketch of her for Act 4. Label the drawings, showing the differences between the costumes.

 TIP

You might want to consider the following about Deputy Governor Danforth when answering Task 14: his status and authority; his relative wealth; what we learn about his character.

TASK 14

Write an answer, as a costume designer, to the following question:

> Focus on Act 3, from '*Enter* DEPUTY GOVERNOR DANFORTH' to 'GILES [*through helpless sob*]: It is my third wife, sir.'
>
> You are a designer working on one aspect of this extract. Describe how you would use your design skills to create effects which support the action of this extract and explain why your ideas are appropriate both for **this extract** and the **play as a whole**.

After you have completed your work, check to make sure you have:

✓ Referred to fabric, colours, shape/fit, condition.
✓ Included headwear/footwear, if appropriate.
✓ Considered make-up and hairstyle.
✓ Explained how the use of costume helps the action of the extract.
✓ Related your answer to the play as a whole.

Set design

For the set design, you might consider:

▶ stage configuration
▶ if you will use one main set to represent all locations or will have four separate sets
▶ the scale (how large) your set will be
▶ if there will be any levels, ramps or stairs
▶ the entrances/exits
▶ if there will be backdrops, flats or projections
▶ the colour palette you will use
▶ how the materials, textures and shapes will help to create a suitable setting
▶ which props are needed.

TASK 15

You have been asked to design the set for Act 4 for the stage configuration of your choice.
You need to emphasise the dark, frightening nature of the jail and how entrapped the characters are.
Create a sketch showing your ideas. The sketch below shows you one of many ways of beginning a sketch.

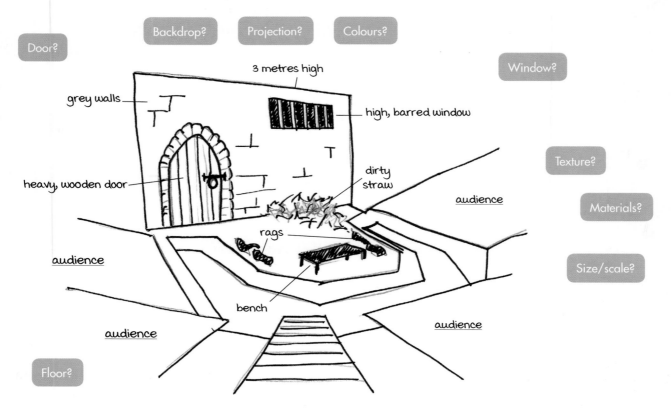

The Crucible – Act IV, Thrust stage (Salem jail cell)

Draw your sketch showing:

▶ the colours and textures (rough, smooth, patterned, irregular) you will use

▶ the materials for the set (or what they will look like, e.g. stone, wood, plaster, metal)

▶ the scale of the set in relation to the size of the actors

▶ any levels (stool, benches, platforms)

▶ where key events like entrances/exits will occur.

Below are three different sample responses to a question about the set in Act 4.

A

Identifies stage configuration and its limitation in terms of scenery

Refers to jail cell, but says 'typical', which may be stereotypical and not entirely clear

As I am working on a thrust stage, I will use only the back wall to show the setting. ❶ I will have a projection ❷ showing a typical jail cell, ❸ with bars on the windows. Everything on the stage will be dark and dirty. It will look very uncomfortable. There will be a stool for characters to sit on.

Uses projection

B

Discusses colour and scale

In order to create the feeling of entrapment, ❹ I will try to make the thrust space seem much smaller than in the previous acts. To accomplish this I will use piles of boxes and rags along the edges, some of which will be hiding characters like Sarah Good at the beginning of the act. ❺ Upstage right there will be a dark-brown, over-sized door, at least three metres tall ❻ and will appear to be very heavy to open. This will make clear how hard it would be to escape.

Explains how it will help the action of the scene

Explains how it will help introduce a character

C

Shows approach to overall design

Explains effect of choices

Comments on overall design

My design will combine both naturalistic and symbolic touches. ❼ The walls will have chains and the high, barred windows will let in little light. The back wall upstage will be a very dark grey, appearing to be made of dark, rough stone with a large ragged splash of red, like blood, on it. ❽

The dark, uneven stones represent the frightening prison and the red splash symbolically suggests the frightening death that awaits them. ❾ The grey and red colour palette will be used throughout my design. ❿ When Proctor exits to his death, the backdrop behind the doorway will be bright red. ⓫

Discusses colours and texture

Shows how design supports the action of the scene

TASK 16

All of the responses above have different strengths. Read through them and decide which one you think best explains their design and why.

TASK 17

Now choose a scene from Act 1, Act 2 or Act 3 and, as a set designer, using the stage configuration of your choice, answer the following:

> You are a designer working on one aspect of design for this extract.
>
> Describe how you would use your design skills to create effects that support the action of this extract and explain why your ideas are appropriate both for **this extract** and the **play as a whole**.

Lighting design

When creating your lighting design you might consider how to create:

▶ time of day and, possibly, season

▶ atmosphere

▶ focus to highlight particular moments

▶ how to help convey the setting, action and characters of a scene (such as a follow spot to focus the audience on a character's journey or backlighting to make them appear mysterious).

Some of your tools are:

▶ colours

▶ angles and intensity

▶ light from onstage sources (**lanterns**, candles, etc.)

▶ use of shadow and silhouette

▶ special effects

▶ use of **blackouts** or **fades**.

SET PLAY 1:
'The Crucible'
by Arthur Miller

1

KEY TERMS:

Lanterns: the equipment used to produce light onstage, such as floods, fresnels or profiles.

Blackout: in lighting, suddenly switching all the lights off.

Fade: in lighting, gradually getting lighter or darker.

TASK 18

Use the mindmaps below to make notes in your notebook on the different lighting demands of Act 1 and Act 4.

ACT 1
- Time of day?
- Season?
- Direction of light?
- Any onstage light?
- Colours?
- Atmosphere?
- Use of shadow?
- Special effects?

ACT 4
- Season?
- Time of day?
- Direction of light?
- Any onstage light?
- Colours?
- Atmosphere?
- Use of shadow?
- Special effects?

Below are some short excerpts from various responses to the demands of lighting **'The Crucible'**.

A

Technical term (footlights) and notes location

In order to capture the eerie quality of the jail, I will use footlights downstage ①. These will cast eerie shadows back onto the faces of the actors and emphasise how tired and desperate they look. ②

Explains effect

B

I want to show how ordinary Act I is in comparison to the others, so I will use soft, slightly yellow light coming in through the bedroom window from a lighting rig in the wings using gels, projecting a light like a lovely spring afternoon.

C

In Act 3, on the moment when Proctor shouts 'Elizabeth, I have confessed it,' I will use a strobe to create a flash of lightning to indicate that this is a moment when everything goes wrong for the Proctors.

D

In Act 4, I will have the actors using lanterns, while much of the stage will be dark. This means that, at certain moments, when they hold the lanterns close to their faces they will be lit and other times in shadows.

E

At the end of Act I, I would have the lights slowly dim from the moment the girls begin naming various women as being with the Devil. I want to create the effect that their naming of people will go on a long time, even after the lights are out.

F

In Act 2, I will have a warm orange light on the fireplace, as that is the source of warmth in the household. Outside the door and window, a blue evening spring light will be streaming diagonally into the room.

G

In Act I, I will have Reverend Hale backlit when he enters the doorway, creating almost a halo around him. I want to give the impression at first that he is a good man of God who is there to help.

H

Act 4 goes from night to morning, so I would have the ghostly, pearly white light, representing moonlight, entering from the barred windows, gradually change to a rosy glow by the end of the play. This light would be shining on Proctor as he exits.

KEY TERMS:

Footlights: lights placed at the front of the stage at the level of the actor's feet, with their light directed upwards.

Rig: what the lights are positioned on (a lighting rig) or 'to rig the lights' is to set them in position.

Strobe: a stroboscopic lamp that produces flashes of light.

TASK 19

Read the excerpts on this page and underline and note any which refer to: colours, angles, special effects, onstage lights, dimming or blackouts. Check that you are confident identifying different ways lighting can be used in your response.

Sound design

When creating your sound design for '**The Crucible**', you will want to consider how to:

▶ create atmosphere

▶ add to the action and emotion of a scene

▶ contribute to the setting and style of the play

▶ fulfil practical needs of the script.

Some choices you can make involve:

▶ live or recorded sound

▶ volume/amplification (use of microphones)

▶ naturalistic or symbolic sound

▶ music.

On the right is a sample of possible sound designer notes for Act 2.

TASK 20

Focus on Act 3, from Abigail's line 'Look out! She's coming down!' and ending with Mary's 'No, I love God.' How could you add extra tension to this scene through your sound design?

Some choices you could make include:

▶ adding recorded music under the scene

▶ having performers onstage or offstage playing instruments to highlight certain moments

▶ adding recorded sound effects such as squealing violins, squawking birds or rushing wind

▶ experimenting with the volume of the sound (suddenly getting louder or softer)

▶ adding either live or recorded drumming or other percussive instruments to highlight key moments.

Experiment with different versions of this scene and then make notes, either in pencil in your script or on the notes you make in your notebook accompanying your script, about which choices you thought were most effective.

> **Opening:**
>
> **Music:** recorded period folk song, 'Greensleeves'. Fades. Same song is picked up by actor playing Elizabeth, who sings it live.
>
> **Sound:** recorded bird song and distant sounds of cattle, projected from upstage speaker.
>
> **Singing:** live (offstage): actor playing Elizabeth singing 'Greensleeves'.
>
> **Sound:** live (offstage): children murmuring as being put to bed.
>
> **Sound:** recorded: outside bird and cattle noises fade to silence.
>
> **Sound:** live: Proctor's footsteps.

PRACTICE QUESTIONS FOR SET PLAY 1

The extracts in the examination paper can be from any section of the play.
You will answer the first three questions and then have a choice between question 4 or 5.

Extract from Act 1:

Focus on the extract from the end of Act 1, TITUBA: 'I don't know, sir, but the Devil got him numerous witches' to 'PARRIS: What woman? A woman, you said. What woman?'

1   You are designing a costume for Tituba to wear in a performance of this extract. The costume must reflect the context of 'The Crucible', set in a Puritan community in the 17th century. Describe your design ideas for the costume.   [4 marks]

2   You are performing the role of Parris.
    Describe how you would use your vocal and physical skills to perform the line below and explain the effects you want to create:

    'What woman? A woman, you said. What woman?'   [8 marks]

3   You are performing the role of Tituba.
    Focusing on the lines from 'Aye, sir, a good Christian woman' to 'Bless Him. Bless Him', explain how you and the actor playing Hale might use the performance space and interact with each other to create tension for your audience.   [12 marks]

AND EITHER

4   You are performing the role of Hale.
    Describe how you would use your acting skills to interpret Hale's character in this extract and explain why your ideas are appropriate both for this extract and the play as a whole.   [20 marks]

OR

5   You are a designer working on one aspect of design for this extract.
    Describe how you would use your design skills to create effects that support the action of this extract and explain why your ideas are appropriate both for the extract and the play as a whole.   [20 marks]

Extract from Act 2:

Focus on the extract from Act 2, from Proctor's 'I am only wondering how I may prove what she told me, Elizabeth' to Elizabeth's 'And I.'

1   You are designing a setting for this extract.
    The set must reflect the context of 'The Crucible' set in a Puritan community in the 17th century. Describe your design ideas for the setting.   [4 marks]

2   You are performing the role of John Proctor.
    Describe how you would use your vocal and physical skills to perform the line below and explain the effects you want to create: [8 marks]

    'I'll not have your suspicion any more.'

3   You are performing the role of John Proctor.
    Focusing on the lines from 'Now look you –' to 'And I'. explain how you and the actor playing Elizabeth might use the performance space and interact with each other to create tension for your audience.   [12 marks]

AND EITHER

4   You are performing the role of Elizabeth.
    Describe how you would use your acting skills to interpret Elizabeth's character in this extract and explain why your ideas are appropriate both for this extract and the play as a whole.   [20 marks]

OR

5   You are a designer working on one aspect of design for this extract.
    Describe how you would use your design skills to create effects that support the action of this extract and explain why your ideas are appropriate both for the extract and the play as a whole.   [20 marks]

SET PLAY 2: 'Blood Brothers' by Willy Russell

Synopsis

'Blood Brothers' was **first performed in 1983** and is set in **Liverpool**. The play opens with a **Narrator** warning the audience that **Mrs Johnstone**, a working-class mother, is 'so cruel' because she had twins and gave one away. Mrs Johnstone sings about her husband who, after she had many children, left her for a younger woman.

Mrs Johnstone has a job cleaning for a middle class couple, the **Lyons**, who are unable to have children of their own. When Mrs Johnstone discovers she is pregnant with twins, **Mrs Lyons** convinces her to give one of the twins to her. Mrs Lyons tells the superstitious Mrs Johnstone that if the boys ever learn they are twins they will both die.

At age seven, the twins, **Edward** and **Mickey**, meet and, unaware of their relationship, become best friends and 'blood brothers'. Edward's and Mickey's upbringings are very different. Edward is protected by Mrs Lyons, whereas Mickey spends his days playing in the streets with his friends, including **Linda**. He is bullied by his older brother **Sammy**, who he both admires and fears.

Mrs Lyons convinces Mr Lyons that they should move away. When Edward comes to say goodbye to Mickey, Mrs Johnstone gives him a locket with a photograph of a young Mickey and her in it.

The first act ends with Mrs Johnstone celebrating the news that they are being rehoused to a council estate in the country, which they hope will be a bright new start for them.

Act 2 begins with Mrs Johnstone singing about the joys of their new life, but also suggesting that they have brought their problems with them. In particular, Sammy has begun to get into trouble with the law. Mickey is now a self-conscious 14-year-old. Linda declares her love for him. Meanwhile, Edward is at a nearby private school where he is suspended after a teacher tries to take his locket from him. Mickey and Linda are also suspended for talking back in class. Linda and Mickey go up to a field, but Mickey finds he can't express himself to Linda and she storms off. Edward arrives and the boys resume their friendship.

Mrs Lyons, who is behaving in an increasingly unstable way, confronts Mrs Johnstone. Mrs Lyons lunges at Mrs Johnstone with a knife, but Mrs Johnstone fights her off. Linda, Mickey and Edward have three idyllic summers together, with both boys attracted to Linda, but neither declaring his love. As Edward prepares to go to university, he encourages Mickey finally to ask Linda out.

Mickey gets a job at a factory. Linda becomes pregnant and she and Mickey get married.

When Edward comes back for the Christmas holidays, he discovers an unhappy Mickey who has been laid off from his job. Edward and Mickey argue. Edward declares his love to Linda and she tells him that she's now pregnant and married to Mickey.

Sammy convinces Mickey to take part in a robbery. Sammy kills the petrol station worker and he and Mickey go to jail. When Mickey leaves jail, he is addicted to pills.

Edward is now a Councillor. With Edward's help, Linda arranges to get a new home and a job for Mickey.

Mrs Lyons shows Mickey that Edward and Linda are meeting in secret. Armed with a gun, Mickey goes to the Town Hall where Edward is speaking at a council meeting. Afraid that Mickey is going to kill Edward, Mrs Johnstone tells him, 'He's your brother.' Mickey is enraged, saying, 'I could have been him!' The gun goes off and kills Edward. The police shoot Mickey. Mrs Johnstone is left mourning her two sons.

 TIP

Although '**Blood Brothers**' is a play with musical numbers, you will not be tested on your knowledge of musical theatre techniques, such as singing or choreography. Instead, focus on how characters are created and the plot is developed.

TASK 1

a   With your group, create ten still images showing what you think are the most important plot points in the play.

b   In a group, discuss and then make a list of what you think are the biggest challenges in performing and designing the musical '**Blood Brothers**'. You might consider costumes, setting, sound and lighting, and the demands on the actors.

For example:

 ◀ Timescale – showing characters getting older.

▶ Making the ending moving/sad.

 ◀ Balancing the comic and serious elements.

 ▶ Showing the time period/context.

Context

Willy Russell has set his play in a **working-class community in Liverpool**, his own hometown. Liverpool was for many decades a thriving port city and supported many industries.

The play spans the 1960s to the early 1980s. In the 1960s, Liverpool became internationally famous for its culture, particularly music by popular groups such as the Beatles. However, in the 1970s and early 1980s, Liverpool suffered a great economic decline (which some blamed on the Prime Minister at that time, Margaret Thatcher), which led to many lost jobs. Russell refers to this in the song 'Take a Letter, Miss Jones' when Mr Lyons fires a number of employees as 'an unfortunate sign of the times'. At some points, the unemployment rate was as high as 50%. The recession heightened the differences between the working class and middle and upper classes.

In '**Blood Brothers**', Linda and Mickey, like Willy Russell himself, appear to attend a secondary modern, a state school for students who did not pass their 11 plus examination – a test that state school children took to establish their academic potential and future schooling. Edward attends a private boarding school, spending term times at school and returning home for the holidays. Russell highlights the contrasts between the two schools by cutting straight from one to the other, showing the differences between the students and the teachers.

In the first act of the play, the Lyons and the Johnstones are shown to be living close to each other despite their different levels of wealth. At the end of the first act, the Lyons relocate to the countryside with Mrs Lyons hoping that a move away from the Johnstones will mean that Edward will not only avoid learning about his true mother, but also that he will mix with what she believes will be a better class of people.

However, the Johnstones, who have probably been living in a small rented terraced house, are moved out to one of the suburban council estates that were being built, not far from where the Lyons now live and where Edward goes to school. The move away from inner-city areas was a government plan aimed at improving the quality of housing for the poor, but many residents missed the sense of community and the convenience of their city homes.

| SET PLAY 2: 'Blood Brothers' by Willy Russell | 2 |

TIP

When you are asked to reflect on the context of '**Blood Brothers**' it is the context of 1970s Liverpool and its working-class community (as represented by the Johnstones) or the middle class (as represented by the Lyons) that you should discuss.

TASK 2

a Look at the photographs of houses on this page. Select which ones best represent your idea of:

  i what the Lyons' house might look like

  ii what the Johnstones' house might look like.

b Carefully read the scenes that take place within the Johnstone and Lyons houses.

  i List which props are mentioned in the text.

  ii What additional props could be added to create the context of homes?

Costume, hair and make-up design inspired by context

In the beginning of Act 2, the teenage Sammy is 16 and getting into trouble with the police. Although he didn't have much money, like many young men at this time, Sammy's fashion choices were influenced by rock bands, such as the Bay City Rollers, and other well-known figures, such as the footballer George Best. In some working-class communities there was a revival of Teddy Boy clothing, with exaggerated 1950s big jackets, rolled jeans and heavy shoes or boots. As a designer, how would you costume **Sammy** for the scene in Act 2 when he gets into trouble with the bus conductor? Consider:

▶ how the costume will reflect his personality
▶ how the costume will reflect the play's context.

 TIP

It is important to explain why you have made your design choices. For example, have you chosen bright colours to suggest he has an outgoing personality, or chosen heavy boots, which might make him seem more dangerous or threatening? Does he take care with his appearance or model himself on people he admires?

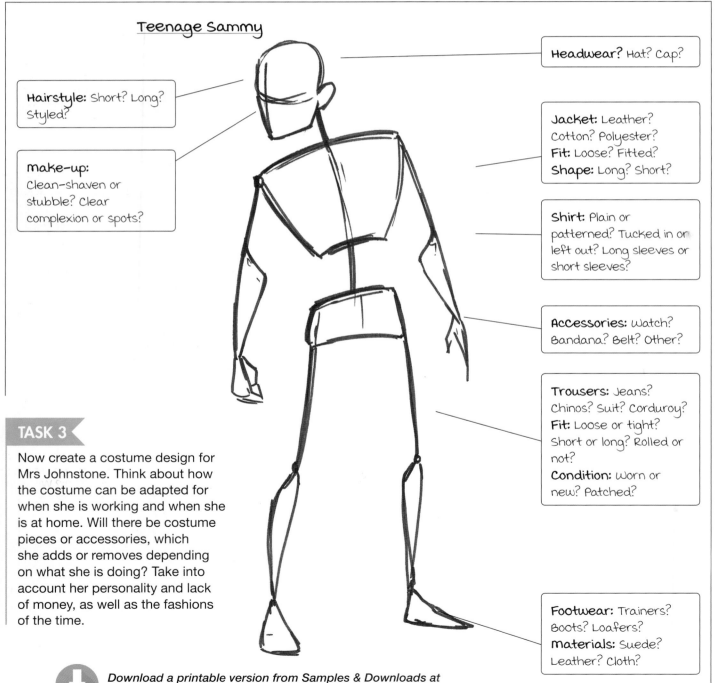

Teenage Sammy

Hairstyle: Short? Long? Styled?

make-up: Clean-shaven or stubble? Clear complexion or spots?

Headwear? Hat? Cap?

Jacket: Leather? Cotton? Polyester? **Fit:** Loose? Fitted? **Shape:** Long? Short?

Shirt: Plain or patterned? Tucked in or left out? Long sleeves or short sleeves?

Accessories: Watch? Bandana? Belt? Other?

Trousers: Jeans? Chinos? Suit? Corduroy? **Fit:** Loose or tight? Short or long? Rolled or not? **Condition:** Worn or new? Patched?

Footwear: Trainers? Boots? Loafers? **materials:** Suede? Leather? Cloth?

TASK 3

Now create a costume design for Mrs Johnstone. Think about how the costume can be adapted for when she is working and when she is at home. Will there be costume pieces or accessories, which she adds or removes depending on what she is doing? Take into account her personality and lack of money, as well as the fashions of the time.

Download a printable version from Samples & Downloads at www.illuminatepublishing.com.

Set design inspired by context

The set must be flexible enough to accommodate a number of different locations, while having enough detail to convey the context of the play.

In the first act there is the opportunity to show both the exteriors and interiors of the Johnstones' and Lyons' homes in Liverpool. Often, productions show the two exteriors of the homes at the same time at the beginning of the play, highlighting the contrasts between the two.

 TIP

It is important to know that you do not have to create the exterior of the homes in your set at all. However, this is a useful exercise to begin thinking about the differences between the families and their homes.

TASK 4

Note the differences between the exteriors of the two homes, using the following questions to help you:

WHOSE HOME? Johnstone – working-class, poor, rented, small terraced home
FEATURES

1. If there is a street sign outside the house, what might the street name be?
2. What are the main colours used?
3. What materials are the walls made of? (Brick? Stone? Wood? Concrete?)
4. What condition are the walls in? (Paint peeling? Graffiti? Other signs of wear?)
5. What are the size, shape and colour of the doors and windows?
6. Is there any way of indicating how many children live in the house?
7. In what period do you think the home was originally built?

WHOSE HOME? Lyons – middle class, private home
FEATURES

1. If there is a street sign outside the house, what might the street name be?
2. What are the main colours used?
3. What materials are the walls made of? (Brick? Stone? Wood? Concrete?)
4. What condition are the walls in? Are there any special features that make the home seem prosperous? (Columns? Steps?, Balcony? Window boxes?)
5. What are the size, shape and colour of the doors and windows?
6. Are there any external features such as a garden, pathway or plants?
7. In what period do you think the home was originally built?

 TIP

When considering how you will design your set, it is important to know that you will rarely use the actual materials of the buildings, but instead create the set out of materials that have the appearance of those materials. For example, if you want one of the homes to be built of brick, you would use painted wood or a canvas backdrop to indicate that. If you want an ornate street lamp, you would use a lighter material and paint it to make it look like metal.

📈 CHALLENGE

Research online the furniture from the time. Based on your research, draw sketches of key furniture items, such as the Lyons' dining table or Mrs Johnstone's kitchen table, which you believe would be appropriate for your design. Explain how they could be used in a scene.

 TIP

Consider how you will accomplish the quick scene changes. For example, how will you move on Mrs Johnstone's kitchen set (page 75) and then remove it (page 79)? Will you use **trucks**? Casters on the furniture? **Fly** the set pieces in? Have actors carry or push the set pieces on/off?

KEY TERMS:

Truck: a platform on wheels upon which scenery can be mounted and moved.

Fly: raising and lowering scenery or other items onto the stage using a system of ropes and pulleys.

Writing about your design ideas

Question 1 will ask you to consider an aspect of design for the play in relation to its context. Below is a student's plan for the following question:

TIP

It is important to know that there are many other interpretations of how Mrs Johnstone might be costumed.

You are designing a costume for Mrs Johnstone to wear in a performance of this extract (from 'Hello Mrs Johnstone' to 'O, I see …' from the first act). The costume must reflect the context of '**Blood Brothers**', set in a working-class community in the 1970s. Describe your design ideas for the costume.

1 Understanding of the character in the play:

Mrs Johnstone is a working-class, single mother who works as a cleaning woman to support her family.

2 Period:

Colours and fabrics: 1970s bright prints, inexpensive fabrics, such as polyester and cotton. Knee-length dress as appropriate for the 1970s.

3 Occupation/role:

She would wear an apron or tabard to protect her clothes. She is a cleaning woman, so clothes need to be practical and hard-wearing. Her hair would be pulled back so it doesn't get in her way. Her shoes are well-worn flats, which need to be replaced, but she can't afford to yet.

4 Character shown through costume:

She is naturally cheerful and tries to make the best of bad situations, so, even though she doesn't have much money, her dress, though worn, would be neat. The dress might be brighter than the drab tabard over it. She has put on weight since having children, so the fit of her clothes would be shapeless to suggest this. Her simple clothes should contrast with Mrs Lyons' more expensive outfits.

TIP

It is important that you justify your ideas. Explain why you are making these specific choices, don't just describe what they will look like. What do we learn about the Narrator's role in the play and what effect do you want them to have?

1 Understanding of the character in the play:

2 Period:

3 Occupation/role:

4 Character shown through costume:

TASK 5

Using the above plan as a guide, create your own plan for the character of the Narrator in answer to the following question:

You are designing a costume for the Narrator to wear in a performance of this extract from the first act (from the opening 'So did y'hear the story of the Johnstone twins' to 'How she came to play this part'). The costume must reflect the context of '**Blood Brothers**', set in Liverpool in the 1970s. Describe your own design ideas for the costume.

Practical exploration of the play's style and themes

When writing about performing roles in the play, you must demonstrate that you understand the characters and how they interact. You need to use the performance space to show your understanding of the play. Below are two themes from the play that you can explore practically to develop your understanding of it and the characters, and how it can be performed.

Childhood

Throughout the play we see Mickey, Linda and Edward grow from young children into adults. These roles are usually cast with adult actors who have to play the different ages though their use of body language, facial expression and vocalisation. To help you develop ways of performing and interacting, try the exercises in Task 6.

TASK 6

a   Start by playing 'It' or 'Tag'. When someone is tagged they have to freeze. Think about how you use your bodies, how much energy you expend, how you avoid getting tagged and what each other's facial expressions are like when playing.

b   Play 'Cops and Robbers' by dividing your group into criminals who have got away with a crime and 'cops' who pursue and arrest them. Have one person be the 'Sammy' of the group who tells everyone else what their roles are and dictates when the game begins and ends. Discuss what it was like having Sammy as a leader.

c   Study photographs of children and note the following about them:

▶ facial expressions

▶ proximity to each other

▶ use of levels.

Choose one photograph and create a still image based on it, do your best to capture the children and their proximity to each other. Then create a series of still images showing the relationships between the children. For example, who is the leader? Who wins? How do the others react?

d   Now read from the stage directions of '**Blood Brothers**', '*They all laugh at* MICKEY' (page 41) to Linda's 'I hate them!' How can you use your vocal skills to show the youthfulness of the characters and the comedy in the situation? Try the following:

▶ Speaking with a higher pitch.

▶ Over-enunciating unfamiliar words.

▶ Speaking energetically and with enthusiasm.

▶ Exaggerating the characters' Liverpool accents.

▶ Using a quick pace and sudden pauses.

Note in your scripts, using pencil, or in your notebooks any changes in your voice that are helpful for showing the characters' ages and personalities.

d   Create four still images showing the characters' movements during this extract. It is important to include their use of facial expressions and gestures. Take a photograph of the images or quickly sketch and label them.

▲ *Observe the children's facial expressions and body language to inform your own still images.*

 TIP

For comedy, you might look for sudden changes in status; unexpected movements or gestures; a quick pace or use of exaggeration.

 CHALLENGE

Now write bullet notes in your notebook on the following task:

> You are performing the role of **Linda** in the extract on the previous page.
>
> Explain how you and the actors playing the other children might use the performance space and interact with each other to create comedy for your audience.

THEATRE MAKER ADVICE

Mark Hutchinson, actor

Playing Eddie at four different stages is a challenge, costumes obviously help, but I also decided to change my hairstyle three times in the show:

- tidy side parting for 7
- centre parting for Act 2 teenager
- completely gelled back for the scenes when he is a councillor.

Vocally, a brighter, open, slightly higher, but not too high tone, to suggest age and innocence, slightly lower and awkward for teenager, and older, louder and very assured for the councillor.

Physically, I decided, Eddie was a very still child, an only child brought up by strict parents, so very still as a seven-year-old, with very proper posture and a very calm physicality, very different from Mickey and the other children. I play him more physically awkward as a teenager, and then very confident as an adult.

Status

One of the main themes in the play is status. Although Edward and Mickey are twins, they have different opportunities in life because of the families in which they are raised. Willy Russell emphasises this in several scenes by contrasting how the boys are treated by others. For example, the policeman is much harsher with Mrs Johnstone than he is with the Lyons about the boys' misbehaviour; the two schools offer different opportunities; Edward goes to university, while Mickey loses his job at the factory; and, at the end, Edward is a respected Councillor, while Mickey only has a home and a job because of Edward's help.

To explore this theme try Task 7.

> **KEY TERM:**
>
> **Diction:** how clearly and precisely words are spoken.

TASK 7

a Use any props and costumes you can find and put them either into a pile labelled 'Johnstone' or a pile labelled 'Lyons'. Discuss how you made your choices. For example, were you influenced by the fabrics, style or condition of the item? What do you learn about how we judge people's status by what they wear and what they own?

b Focus on the scene when Edward and Mickey at age seven meet in the first act. Concentrating on your vocal skills, explore how you can contrast their different upbringings. Experiment with the following:

▶ Use of dialect – would one of the boys have a stronger working-class Liverpool accent?

▶ Use of volume – would one of the boys speak more softly?

▶ Use of pace – would the boys speak at different paces? Is one more impulsive and one more thoughtful?

▶ Enunciation – does one speak with a clearer **diction**? Does one use more slang?

▶ Use of inflection or intonation – can comic effects be created through vocal tone or emphasis?

Note in your script, using a pencil, or in your notebook any discoveries you make.

c Focus on the policeman scenes in the first act, when he visits Mrs Johnstone and then the Lyons. Create two still images showing the difference in the policeman's attitude towards each family. Either take a picture or draw a sketch for each still image and label how it shows the different status of the families.

Interpretation of character

You will need to show how you can interpret a character. This means that you understand the character's motivations and goals, and the obstacles they face. Then you must be able to use your vocal and physical skills to portray the character and create particular effects for the audience, such as tension, comedy, surprise, pity or sorrow.

Look below at one interpretation of the character of **Linda** as a 14-year-old in the second act, in the scene in the field with Mickey (your interpretation may differ).

SET PLAY 2:
'Blood Brothers'
by Willy Russell

2

FACTS:

Background: *a working-class, 14-year-old*

Job: *student, attending a secondary modern*

Interpretation:

PHYSICAL APPEARANCE:

I imagine Linda to be active and attractive.

HAIR:

Freshly washed hair, tied up in a high ponytail.

BODY LANGUAGE:

She is physically confident. She pretends she is helpless in the field scene, but it is an act. She stands her ground and can stick up for herself. She looks for any excuse to touch and flirt with Mickey.

MAKE-UP:

Emphasises her fresh-faced youth. 1970s make-up often used pink tones with shiny cheeks, aiming for a healthy, natural look. Peach- or berry-coloured lip gloss. Eyeliner, cream eye shadow and mascara, perhaps applied heavily as make-up is a new skill for her.

VOICE:

Speaks with a working-class Liverpool accent. She speaks loudly as doesn't care who hears her. She sometimes teases Mickey, so has a playful tone and laughs a lot.

COSTUME:

School uniform (white blouse, grey skirt) which she has adjusted to fit her sense of fashion. She has rolled the waistband over to make her skirt very short. Mini-skirts were popular at this time, so she would be imitating people she'd seen in magazines, and would be turning her knee-length skirt into a mini. Her green school tie is knotted and shortened as an act of rebellion. She takes off her grey school jumper and ties it around her waist when trudging up the hill. She is wearing non-school regulation high heels with flesh-coloured tights.

EFFECT ON AUDIENCE:

The audience should see a startling transformation from the tomboyish seven-year-old to this attractive, confident teenager. She is beginning to be aware of her effect on boys, but still has the outspokenness and protectiveness of Mickey that was apparent when she was a child.

> ## TASK 8
>
> Using your own understanding of the characters in the play and how they could be interpreted, create an interpretation on paper of Edward, Mickey, Mrs Lyons, Mrs Johnstone or the Narrator, using the following headings: Age, Job/Education, Physical appearance, Voice, Body language, Costume, Hair, Make-up. In this instance, think about total characterisation, which includes facts about the characters and their appearance as well as how they could be interpreted through acting, costume and make-up choices. This will help you to think about all aspects of interpreting the character, even when writing about acting or design.

Performing choices

In question 2, you will be asked to discuss in detail how you would perform a particular line as a given character.

For example:

KEY TERM:

Received pronunciation: how clearly and precisely words are spoken.

You are performing the role of _____ .

Describe how you would use your vocal and physical skills to perform the line below and explain the effects you want to create.

Sample:

MRS LYONS: Act 1: 'Do you go to the same school as Edward?'

In this scene, Mickey has turned up unexpectedly at the Lyons house and Mrs Lyons is immediately suspicious of him. I want to establish that Mrs Lyons is not welcoming to Mickey and wants to discover who he is. ❶ Playing Mrs Lyons, I would hold myself very stiffly and formally, making no gestures of welcome to Mickey. ❷ I would look down at him and examine him, noting that his clothing and accent are not what I would expect of Edward's friends. ❸ I don't have a strong Liverpool accent; instead I speak received pronunciation, which indicates my background and education. My voice is well-modulated, not rude, but I would use a slightly cold tone. ❹ I would emphasise the word 'you' as there is a sense of disbelief that Mickey could go to the same school as Edward. ❺ I would say Edward's name warmly and protectively, as I think of him as my boy. I would speak slowly and clearly, determined to get an answer. ❻ At the end of the line, I would look between the boys, beginning to realise who Mickey is. ❼ I would then move closer to Edward, blocking Mickey from him, my facial expression beginning to show my alarm. ❽

Effect — ❶

Physical skills — ❷

Physical skills — ❸

Vocal skills — ❹

Vocal skills — ❺

Vocal skills and effect — ❻

Physical skills and effect — ❼

Physical skills and effect — ❽

> **TASK 9**

Experiment with different ways of using your vocal and physical skills for each of the following lines:

> **MRS LYONS:** Give one of them to me.
>
> **MRS JOHNSTONE:** Well, I ... I just ... It's ... couldn't I keep them for a few more days, please, please, they're a pair, they go together.
>
> **EDWARD:** Well, my mummy doesn't allow me to play down here actually.
>
> **MR LYONS:** Mummy will read the story Edward. I've got to go to work for an hour.
>
> **LINDA:** Well, he is. An' what do you care if I think another feller's gorgeous, eh?
>
> **NARRATOR:** And who'd dare tell the lambs in spring / What fate the later seasons bring?
>
> **MICKEY:** You don't understand anything, do ye? I don't wear a hat that I could tilt at the world.

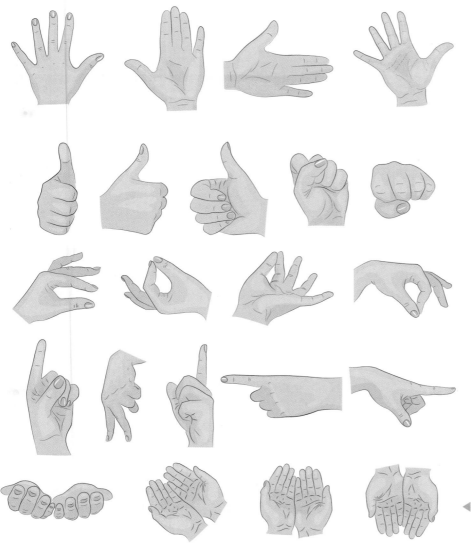

SET PLAY 2:
'Blood Brothers'
by Willy Russell

2

 TIP

It is important that you write in the first person ('I') so you can fully imagine your own performance of the role. Don't only describe the vocal and physical skills you will use, but also think about how your choices will add to the audience's understanding of the play's meaning, the character and the character's relationship with others.

> **TASK 10**

a   Make notes on the following:
  ▶ Vocal skills: ▶ Physical skills:
  ▶ Effects achieved:

b   Then, using the example answer on the previous page as a guide, write an answer to the same question referring to each of the characters and lines.

c   Check your work by writing 'V' next to each vocal skill, 'P' next to each physical skill and 'E' next to an effect. Make sure that you have answered this question fully.

◀ *When thinking about physical skills consider your use of gestures.*

Character revision sheet

Below is an example of a character revision sheet based on the character of **Mrs Lyons**, which has been partially completed. Copy the grid and complete it.

Character and importance to the play	Mrs Lyons
What do they want?	She wants a baby. She wants a perfect, happy home.
What obstacles do they face?	She and her husband can't have children. Fear that Mrs Johnstone will reclaim Edward.
What are their key scenes?	Act I: Discovering Mrs Johnstone is pregnant. Act I: Asking Mrs Johnstone to give a baby to her. Act I: Coming to collect the baby. Act I: Fires Mrs Johnstone. Act I: Mickey comes to their house. Mrs Lyons hits Edward. Act I: Increasingly paranoid. Suggests they move. Act I: Move to new home. Act 2: Dancing with Edward. Act 2: Finds Edward's locket. Act 2: Attacks Mrs Johnstone.

How might they be costumed?

Draw a simple sketch or write a description of it. Consider:
- colours
- fabrics
- shape and fit
- character's personality and status

How might their hair and make-up be done?

Draw a simple sketch or write a description of it. Consider:
- style and colour of hair
- type of make-up (realistic or fantasy; colours; how it is appropriate for character, setting and period)

How might they use body language?
- posture
- gait (the way they walk)
- facial expression

How might they use their voice?

Emotional range (angry, sad, happy, irritated, desperate, dominating, etc.)
Pitch and volume (how low or high; how loud or soft)
Accent or other distinctive vocal features

Choose one important line and analyse how they might say it.

Act 2: 'Are you always going to follow me?'

> **TASK 11**
>
> Using the above grid for guidance, create similar revision sheets for all major characters including: Mrs Johnstone, the Narrator, Mickey, Edward, Linda and Mr Lyons.

 Download a printable version from Samples & Downloads at www.illuminatepublishing.com.

Using the performance space and interaction with others

There are opportunities to explore the space and interaction with others in a number of different ways in the play. There are large ensemble scenes and intimate two-person scenes. Some productions may choose to perform the play very naturalistically, while others rely on the conventions of musical theatre, such as group movement or dancing. Many productions combine both naturalistic and stylised acting. Willy Russell also provides additional challenges by having some scenes overlapping or **cross-cutting**. When you are writing about how you will use the performance space and interaction with others, make sure you focus on the effects you wish to achieve, such as tension, surprise, humour, pity or sorrow, and how you will achieve them.

> **KEY TERM:**
>
> **Cross-cutting:** alternating between two different scenes.

TASK 12

Focus on the scene between Mickey and Linda in Act 2, which begins: 'Mickey, Mickey, come on, you'll be late …' to Mickey's exit with the pills.

a Read the scene, taking particular notice of any stage directions.

b Agree what stage configuration you are going to use: end on, theatre in the round, thrust, promenade, proscenium or traverse. Mark where the entrances will be and any pieces of furniture.

c Decide what effects you wish to achieve in this scene. To help you do this, answer the following questions about the various issues:

> ▶ Mickey's character after leaving prison. How have his mental state and dependency on drugs affected his movement, facial expressions and entire personality?

> ▶ Linda's reaction to him. Linda has always loved Mickey and is now his wife. However, he is very changed. How does she look at him? What are her motivations in this scene?

> ▶ Use of props. How does he feel about Linda handing him his lunch? How important is it to Mickey that he finds his pills? Where does he look for his pills?

> ▶ Turning point. What convinces Linda to give him her bag so he can find his pills?

> ▶ Use of subtext. Are there any instances when you believe characters are not saying entirely what they are thinking or feeling? How could that be conveyed?

d How will you use stage space? Try the following:

> ▶ Mickey's entrance:

>> ▶ Mickey enters quickly, avoids eye contact with Linda. Begins looking immediately for pills around the flat.

>> ▶ Mickey enters slowly, with careful movements. He goes to where his pills are usually kept. Freezes momentarily confused when they aren't there.

>> ▶ Mickey enters putting on his jacket. His hands are visibly shaking and he struggles to get his jacket on. He pushes aside Linda's hand offering the lunch bag.

> ▶ Linda's reaction:

>> ▶ Linda follows Mickey around the room, like a mother dealing with an uncooperative toddler.

>> ▶ Linda smiles brightly, trying to pretend that everything is all right. She continues to get ready to go out herself, putting on her earrings and chatting casually to him.

>> ▶ Linda tries to block him from finding the pills and hides her bag. She clearly feels worried and guilty, finding it hard to meet his eyes.

e Continue working through the scene, experimenting with different staging configuration ideas. When you have finished, answer the following question:

> You are performing the role of **Mickey**.
>
> Focusing on the lines 'I didn't sort anything out, Linda' to 'Now give me the tablets … I need them', explain how you and the actor playing Linda might use the performance space and interact with each other to create tension for the audience.

Answering a question about character interpretation

If you choose to answer question 4, you will need to write about how you would use your acting skills to interpret a character both in the extract provided and in the **play as a whole**.

An example of this sort of question might be:

> You are performing the role of **Mrs Johnstone**.
>
> Describe how you would use your **acting skills** to interpret Mrs Johnstone's character in this extract (Act 1, lines 'MRS JOHNSTONE: I had it all worked out' to 'Give one to you?') and explain why your ideas are appropriate both for **this extract** and the **play as a whole**.

Below is a sample student plan for this question.

This extract:

1 Character of Mrs Johnstone and reasons for making acting choices:

working-class, superstitious, single mother, struggling financially. Worried about managing with two more babies, afraid social services will take her children. Wonders if one of the twins will have a better life with the Lyons.

2 Acting skills: vocal:

Liverpool accent. Informal diction. Mrs Lyons is her boss so I will speak with a respectful tone to her. Tries to please. Anger on the word 'they' about all those officials who want to take children and don't give me the support I need. Emotional on lines like 'Kids can't live on love alone'. A shocked pause before saying 'Give one to you?' to show I can't believe what I am hearing.

3 Acting skills: physical:

Heavily pregnant, but still have to work. Movements are automatic as I speak thoughts aloud, I continue to dust. When I clean something low, I struggle a bit getting up again. Touch my belly when I say, 'I'll even love these two ...' to show I am already attached to the babies.

Rest of play:

1 Character of Mrs Johnstone and reasons for making acting choices:

She is a warm, relatable person, but haunted by her decision to give up one of her sons. In her two scenes alone with Edward, her love for him is apparent and, in the final scene, she rejects her own superstition in an effort to save him and Mickey.

2 Acting skills: vocal:

In scene with Edward towards the end of Act 1, speak softly and affectionately. Don't want their conversation to be overheard. Comforts him when he's crying, 'Shush, shush'. Laughs on, 'God help the girls when you start dancing.' At the end of the play, voice is loud and desperate: 'Mickey. Don't shoot.'

3 Acting skills: physical:

Physically affectionate with children, hugs and teases them. Always busy, cleaning, cooking, looking after others. Towards end suggest weariness in some movements (slow to rise from chairs, more hesitant) but still strong. Fights off Mrs Lyons and rushes to town council.

 TIP

It is important to include both vocal and physical skills in your answers. Note key moments when these skills can be discussed.

1 Character of the Narrator and reasons for making acting choices:

2 Acting skills: vocal:

3 Acting skills: physical:

TASK 13

Using the above plan as a guide, create your own plan in answer to the the following question:

> You are performing the role of the **Narrator**.
>
> Describe how you would use your **acting skills** to interpret the Narrator's character in Act 2, from their entrance on page 100 to Edward's line: 'Hey' on page 101, and explain why your ideas are appropriate both for **this extract** and the **play as a whole**.

Design choices

If you choose to answer question 5, you will be thinking as a designer and commenting on one aspect of design.

For example:

> You are a designer working on one aspect of design for this extract.
>
> Describe how you would use your design skills to create effects that support the action of this extract and explain why your ideas are appropriate for **this extract** and the **play as a whole**.

You may choose to focus on set design, costume design, lighting design, sound design or puppet design. Whichever you choose, you must explain why your ideas are appropriate to the play as a whole. You might refer to:

▶ how your design helps to show the action of the play and the nature of the characters

▶ how your design for the extract is consistent with the design requirements of the rest of the play (for example, don't suddenly change the style of the production)

▶ how you have used design methods that fit in with the mood or atmosphere of the play

▶ props, anything that the actors may carry on stage.

'Blood Brothers' is usually performed and designed with a combination of naturalistic and stylised musical theatre features. The presence of the Narrator and the use of song tell the audience that this won't be an entirely naturalistic production. There are rapid, fluid transitions from one scene to another. Many productions move various pieces of scenery on and off a basic set. Some productions use scaffolding in the set to provide extra levels, such as a platform from which the Narrator may watch and comment on the action. Some use the ensemble to change the set, which is presented in a minimalistic and symbolic way using just a few key props and set pieces. Others create highly realistic interiors for both the Johnstone and Lyons households in order to highlight the differences in their social classes.

Most productions employ multi-roling (Willy Russell even has a joke in the script about the milkman giving up his job to become a gynaecologist), so the costume designer must create costumes that can quickly be changed into in order to indicate the new role an actor is playing.

Music is central to the play, but additional sound effects to create comedy or tension can be added. Lighting effects can be used to pick out key moments or to emphasise the passing of time. Whatever design choices you make, you must make sure that they show your understanding of the play and its needs.

Costume design

For the costume design, you might consider:

▶ style, cut and fit

▶ colour, fabric, decorative features

▶ condition (worn or new; neat or wrinkled; clean or stained, etc.)

▶ footwear/headgear

▶ accessories

▶ status or social role of character

▶ make-up and hairstyle.

▲ *The choice of fabric, including colour, texture and pattern, is important.*

Below is an extract from a sample response for a question based on Mr Lyons in Act 1, in his scene with Mrs Lyons, beginning 'Oh Richard, Richard', describing how a costume designer would use their skills to create effects that support the action of this extract and the rest of the play.

Understanding of action of scene

Discusses colour and fabric and effect achieved

Shows how accessories can create effect

Accessory reveals aspect of character

Condition of footwear and effects achieved

Some mention of hair/make-up, although this could be more developed

Insight into action of scene

How costume helps to convey action in the rest of the play

How costume would be altered for his role in the rest of the play

In this scene, I would have Mr Lyons dressed as if he's just come in from work to find his wife once again distressed. ① He has an important job in manufacturing, so I would dress him in a conservative grey, pin-striped wool suit, with a matching waistcoat and a white shirt and a conservative navy-blue tie. ② There is nothing particularly fashionable about his clothing, he would blend in with the crowd, but small details, like wearing gold cufflinks and a good watch, would show his relative wealth. ③ I imagine he has just come in from work, so I would have him enter carrying a newspaper and a brown leather briefcase. He wears dark-rimmed spectacles to read, but these will be in his pocket at the beginning of the scene. ④ His shoes are dark, leather and well-shined. Everything about him suggests competence and order, which reinforces why he is so annoyed to find his wife coping so poorly. ⑤ He would like to be met with a drink, but instead immediately has to begin solving problems. In my interpretation, Mr Lyons is a little older than his wife, so I would use make-up to indicate that his hair is greying at his temples. ⑥ His appearance in this scene would stress how important his work is to him and how he is not totally comfortable at home. ⑦

In the rest of the play, he would wear variations of this outfit for most scenes. When playing with Edward he would take off his jacket. With Miss Jones, he would be at his most formal, wearing his glasses and very neatly presented to show his power and his apparent lack of concern for his employees. ⑧ One moment of contrast in his outfit might occur towards the end of Act 2, when the family has moved to the country. In order to show how they have changed from city dwellers to country people, I would costume him in a green waxed jacket with a warm plaid flannel lining and black wellington boots. ⑨ However, for most of the play, he presents authority and his costume must indicate that.

TASK 14

Draw sketches showing Mickey's and Edward's contrasting costumes, make-up and hair for Act 1 at their first meeting, when they are aged seven. Label the sketches, showing the differences between the costumes. It is important to consider: fabrics, condition of clothing, colours, shape and fit.

TASK 15

Write an answer to the following question as a costume designer.

> Focus on Act 1, from 'MRS LYONS: Hello, Mrs Johnstone ...' to 'MRS LYONS: Oh, I see ...'
>
> You are a designer working on one aspect of this extract.
>
> Describe how you would use your design skills to create effects that support the action of this extract and explain why your ideas are appropriate both for **this extract** and the **play as a whole**.

After you have completed your work, check to make sure you have:

✓ Referred to fabric, colours, shape/fit, condition.

✓ Included headwear/footwear, if appropriate.

✓ Considered make-up and hairstyle.

✓ Explained how the use of costume helps the action of the extract.

✓ Related your answer to the play as a whole.

Set design

For the set design, you might consider:

▶ stage configuration

▶ if you will use one main set to represent all locations or if you will have a number of different sets

▶ the scale (how large) your set will be

▶ if there will be any levels, ramps or stairs

▶ the entrances/exits

▶ if there will be backdrops, flats or projections

▶ the colour palette you will use

▶ how the materials, textures and shapes will help to create a suitable setting

▶ which props are needed.

TASK 16 CONTINUED ON PAGE 68

You have been asked to design the set for the opening of Act 1 for the stage configuration of your choice. Consider how you will use the set to:

▶ establish role and importance of the Narrator

▶ establish the Liverpool, 1970, working-class setting

▶ create interest in Mrs Johnstone's story.

TIP

You might want to consider the following:

● the characters' relative wealth

● their relationship as employer and employee

● what we learn about their character.

TASK 16 ◄ CONTINUED

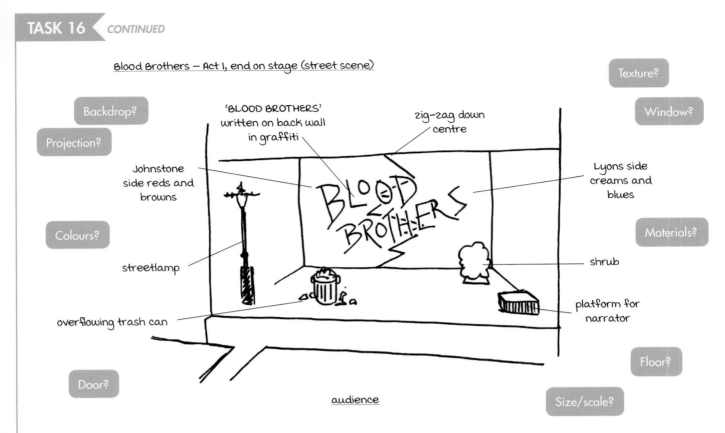

Blood Brothers – Act I, end on stage (street scene)

Backdrop?
Projection?
Colours?
Door?

'BLOOD BROTHERS' written on back wall in graffiti
Johnstone side reds and browns
streetlamp
overflowing trash can

zig-zag down centre
Lyons side creams and blues
shrub
platform for narrator

Texture?
Window?
Materials?
Floor?
Size/scale?

audience

Draw a sketch showing:

▶ the colours and textures (rough, smooth, patterned, irregular) you will use

▶ the materials for the set (or what they will look like, i.e. stone, wood, plaster, metal)

▶ the scale of the set in relation to the size of the actors

▶ any levels (balconies, scaffolding, upper windows, platforms)

▶ where key events such as entrances/exits will occur.

Below are excerpts from three different sample responses to a question about the set at the beginning of Act 1.

A

Establishes 1970s setting and style of design

Discusses scale and how set will be used

I am creating an abstract, non-naturalistic setting for the play, so will use large, metal scaffolding. In the upstage centre section of the scaffolding there will be a large screen upon which different images of Liverpool in the 1970s will be projected as the audience walks in and while the overture plays. ❶ It will freeze on an image of boy twins and the caption: The Johnstone Twins. Upstage left is a smaller platform about two metres high which can be accessed by ladders. The Narrator will make his first appearance there. ❷ Downstage centre, Mrs Johnstone will appear, unaware of the narrator above her. I think this will create suspense and interest for the audience who will wonder about the connection between the two characters and the projected image. ❸

Considers effect of design choices

Explains how homes will
contrast

B

I want to highlight the theme of social class, so my initial set
will show the exterior of the Lyons' home stage left and the
Johnstones' home stage right. ④ Both will use painted canvas
sets. The colours for the Lyons' house will be creams and
blues, while the Johnstones' house will be painted dark red
brick. ⑤ There will be white columns either side of the front
door of the Lyons' home and an overflowing trash bin in front
of the Johnstones', in order to show the difference in their
social class. ⑥

Explains intentions of
design

Provides details to establish
characters

Discusses use of levels

C

I think the Liverpool street is an important aspect of the
set, so the first image the audience will see will be painted
flats that create a brick wall with graffiti written on it
and posters advertising rock groups from the 1970s. ⑦ The
stage will be made of a series of ramps that lead up to a
central circular acting area. The Narrator will make his first
appearance in this highest, most prominent area, appearing
in the light of a streetlamp, which makes him look mysterious
and important. ⑧ The wall will be mounted on trucks that
part to reveal the two contrasting homes. ⑨

Establishes 1970s setting

Explains how set can be
changed to help action of
play

TASK 17

All of the responses above have different strengths. Read through them and, with a
partner, discuss which design in your opinion is best at establishing the location, period
and mood of the opening. Draw a sketch showing your own ideas about how the play's
opening set would look.

TASK 18

You are now going to create a design for the end of Act 1 set using the stage
configuration of your choice. At this point, the characters have moved to the country.
How can the set design represent this change? Think about:

▶ entrances/exits and areas for key moments   ▶ how to create atmosphere

▶ use of backdrops, projections or set furniture   ▶ scale.

TASK 19

Now, writing as a set designer and using the stage configuration of your choice, choose
any setting from either Act 1 or Act 2 and answer the following:

> You are a designer working on one aspect of design for this extract.
>
> Describe how you would use your design skills to create effects that support the action of this
> extract, and explain why your ideas are appropriate both for **this extract** and the **play as a whole**.

Lighting design

When creating your lighting design you might consider how to create:

▶ time of day and, possibly, season

▶ atmosphere or mood

▶ highlight particular moments

▶ how to help convey the setting and action, or enhance the impact of a character (such as a follow spot to focus the audience on a character's journey or backlighting to make them appear mysterious).

Some of your tools are:

▶ colours

▶ angles and intensity

▶ light from onstage sources (lamp-posts, lamps, neon signs)

▶ use of shadow and silhouette

▶ special effects

▶ use of blackouts or fades.

TASK 20

Use the mindmaps below to make notes in your notebook on the different lighting demands of Act 2, showing the three summers of the teenage Mickey, Edward and Linda, starting with 'There's a few bob in your pocket' and ending with 'Where's Mickey?'

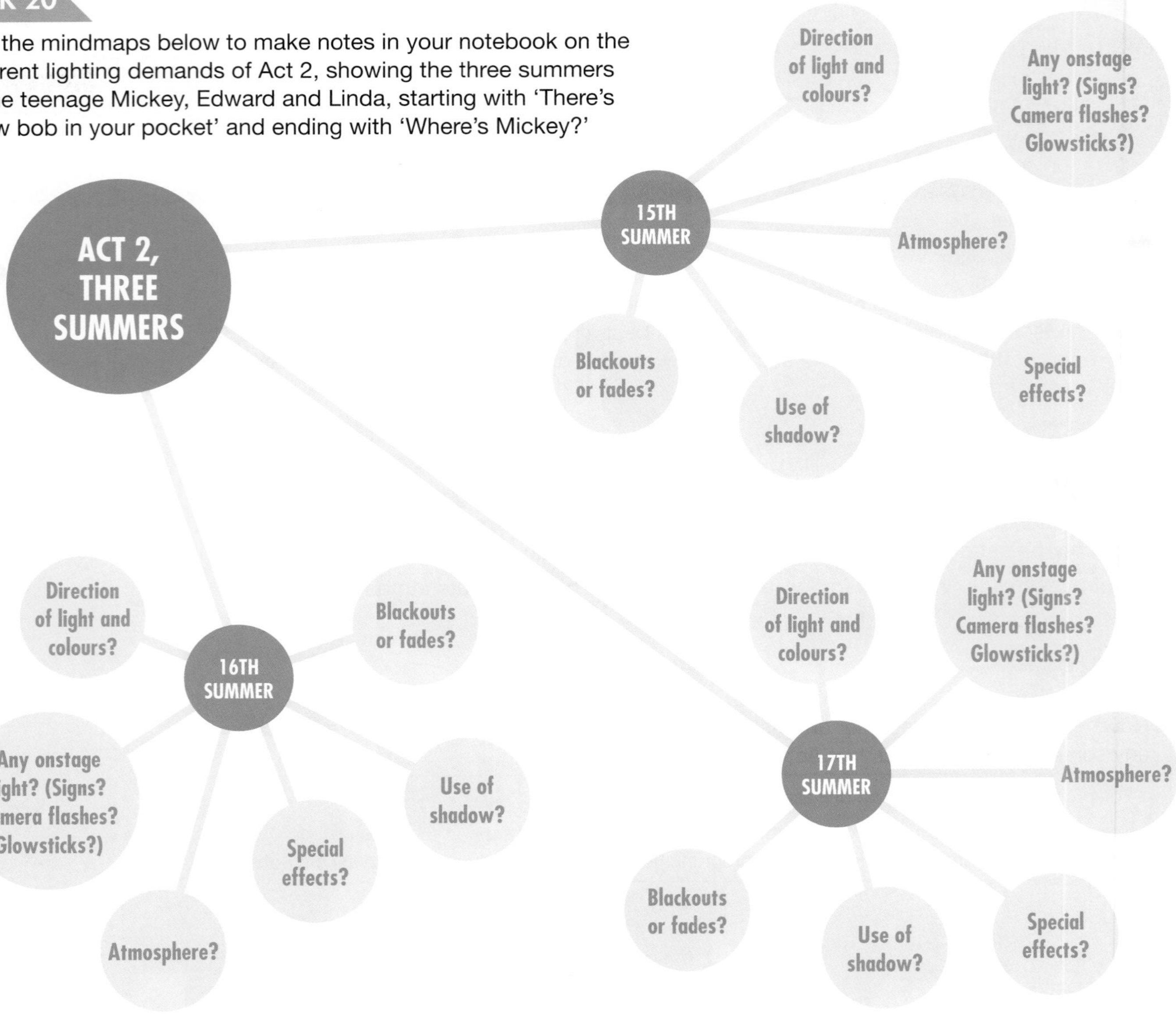

Below are some short excerpts from various responses to the demands of lighting in other scenes from the play '**Blood Brothers**'.

A

Shape and colour

Reason for choice and effect created

When Mrs Johnstone first enters, I will have her appear in a pool of blue light. ❶ This will emphasise the sad nature of her story and make the beginning feel like a mysterious dream. ❷

B

I want the Narrator to appear like a harsh judgemental character. I will use some low-angled lights that will cast shadows on his face, making him appear gaunt and frightening.

C

At the end of the Marilyn Monroe song, I will have the rosy bright light from the profile spots, fade to a cooler, more ordinary daylight, to show the contrast between Mrs Johnstone's dreams and reality.

D

During the Narrator's 'Shoes upon the table' I will have the lighting become more intense and harsh. He will be lit from the front, casting large looming shadows behind him. On the final 'He's knocking on the door' there will be a brief blackout and, when the lights come back on, the Narrator has disappeared.

E

To indicate Mickey's mental state when he is looking for Edward towards the end of Act 2, I will have flashing red lights, showing his anger. These will be replaced by blue flashing lights when the police appear.

TASK 21

Read the excerpts above and underline in pencil any references to: colours, angles, special effects, onstage lights, dimming or blackouts.

Sound design

'**Blood Brothers**' offers many opportunities for sound design, not only because it is a musical, but also because there are moments when tension or a character's psychological state might be emphasised through the use of sound.

Sound design can help to:

establish location   enhance the atmosphere

aid a transition from one scene to another   highlight a particular moment or character

> ### KEY TERM:
>
> **Soundscape:** drama technique where performers use their voices (and sometimes other items) to create sounds to enhance the mood or theme of a piece of drama.

TASK 22

Focus on Act 2 from 'MRS LYONS *enters and goes to* MICKEY' to the Narrator's 'There's a mad man / there's a mad man.'

a   In a group, using materials you can find and your own voices, create a **soundscape** to accompany this scene. Consider:

  ▶ Volume: when will the sound get louder and when will it be softer?

  ▶ Type of sound: will it be gentle and tuneful or harsh and discordant?

  ▶ Character and action: will there be different sounds/instruments to accompany certain characters or actions?

b   Discuss how you could use either live or recorded sound effects/music to accomplish the effects that you want.

c   Make notes, either in pencil in your script or in your notebook, to explain your discoveries.

When creating your sound design you should annotate your script with your ideas, including:

▶ Live or recorded?

▶ Produced onstage or offstage?

▶ Volume/amplification.

Here is an example:

Recorded sound of bus

Live sound of police whistles from onstage

Sudden silence

❶ Sammy leaps from the 'bus' ❷ and is pursued by two policemen. ❸ The 'bus' pulls away ❹ leaving mickey and Linda alone on the pavement. ❺

Recorded sound of screeching stop. Comically loud

Recorded sound of bus pulling away. Volume decreases as it goes into the distance

TASK 23

At the end of Act 1, the Johnstones move from the city to the country. Focusing on the script from Mickey's 'It's like the country, isn't it, Mam?' to the end of the act, annotate your script, in pencil, showing how you would use sound design to show the change in location and mood.

PRACTICE QUESTIONS FOR SET PLAY 2

You will answer the first three questions and then have a choice between question 4 or 5.

Extract from Act 2:

Focus on the scene between Mrs Lyons and Mrs Johnstone in Act 2 starting with:

'MRS JOHNSTONE: Hello' and ending with 'MRS LYONS: Is it money you want?'

1   You are designing a setting for a performance of this extract. The setting must reflect the context of 'Blood Brothers', set in a working-class community in the 1970s. Describe your design ideas.   [4 marks]

2   You are performing the role of Mrs Lyons.
    Describe how you would use your vocal and physical skills to perform the line below and explain the effects you want to create:

    'Are you always going to follow me?'   [8 marks]

3   You are performing the role of Mrs Lyons.
    Focusing on the lines from 'No, I took him' to 'Is it money you want?', explain how you and the actor playing Mrs Johnstone might use the performance space and interact with each other to create tension for your audience.   [12 marks]

AND EITHER

4   You are performing the role of Mrs Johnstone.
    Describe how you would use your acting skills to interpret Mrs Johnstone's character in this extract and explain why your ideas are appropriate both for this extract and the play as a whole.   [20 marks]

OR

5   You are a designer working on one aspect of design for this extract.
    Describe how you would use your design skills to create effects that support the action of this extract, and explain why your ideas are appropriate both for this extract and the play as a whole.   [20 marks]

Extract from Act 1:

Focus on the scene between Mickey and Edward in Act 1, from:

'MICKEY: It's cos he's got a plate in his head' to 'EDWARD: Well, I'm nearly eight, really.'

1   You are designing a costume for Mickey to wear in this extract. The costume must reflect the context of 'Blood Brothers', set in a working-class community in the 1970s. Describe your design ideas for the costume.   [4 marks]

2   You are performing the role of Mickey.
    Describe how you would use your vocal and physical skills to perform the line below and explain the effects you want to create:

    'I'm older than you. I'm nearly eight.'   [8 marks]

3   You are performing the role of Mickey.
    Focusing on the section from 'I don't think so' to 'I suppose, I suppose if y'looked under his hair', explain how you and the actor playing Edward might use the performance space and interact with each other to create comedy for your audience.   [12 marks]

AND EITHER

4   You are performing the role of Edward.
    Describe how you would use your acting skills to interpret Mickey's character in this extract and explain why your ideas are appropriate both for this extract and the play as a whole.   [20 marks]

OR

5   You are a designer working on one aspect of design for this extract.
    Describe how you would use your design skills to create effects that support the action of this extract and explain why your ideas are appropriate both for this extract and the play as a whole.   [20 marks]

3   SET PLAY 3: 'The 39 Steps' by John Buchan and Patrick Barlow

Synopsis

The play is set in **1935**, in pre-World War II **London**. A restless **Richard Hannay** decides to attend a show at a Music Hall. A beautiful woman, **Annabella,** sits next to Hannay. She interrupts **Mr Memory**'s act by shooting a gun into the air. In the chaos that follows she asks Hannay if she can come home with him.

Poster for the Alfred Hitchcock film of The 39 Steps.

At his flat, she confesses to being a secret agent and claims that two men are pursuing her. She asks if he has heard of the 'Thirty-Nine Steps' and tells him that she must visit a man in Scotland at a place called '**Alt-na-Shellach**'. She is searching for a foreign agent who is missing part of his little finger and who is on the verge of obtaining vital secret information.

Later that night, she dies in Hannay's apartment. Hannay decides to take up her cause in order to prevent the secret leaving the country. The next morning, after he leaves, his cleaning woman discovers Annabella's body.

On the train to Edinburgh, Hannay discovers that he is a wanted man. The police are searching the train. To escape detection, Hannay kisses a passenger, **Pamela**. He jumps from the train onto the Forth Bridge to avoid being arrested.

Hannay stays at a cottage owned by a **Crofter** and his beautiful wife, **Margaret**. At midnight, Margaret wakes Hannay up to tell him the police are coming for him. Her jealous husband threatens him. Margaret helps him to escape and they kiss passionately.

Hannay arrives at Alt-na-Shellach, the house owned by **Professor Jordan**. **Mrs Jordan** says that they are having a party and asks him to wait for the Professor. Hannay relays as much of Annabella's message as he can to the Professor. The Professor reveals that he is missing a little finger and pulls a gun on Hannay. The Professor is a German agent and tries to recruit Hannay to his cause. Hannay says he despises him. The Professor shoots him.

Act 2 begins in a Sheriff's office with Hannay explaining what happened and how a hymn book that Margaret gave him stopped the bullet from killing him.

A Chief Inspector tries to arrest Hannay but he escapes. Hannay enters a political campaign meeting and gives a speech as if he was a candidate. Pamela enters and identifies him to the Inspector. Pamela and Hannay are then abducted by two henchmen. When the car stops in a field, Hannay forces Pamela, who is handcuffed to him, to escape with him.

They pretend to be a married couple and get a room at the McGarrigle Hotel. When Hannay falls asleep, Pamela slips her hand out of the handcuff. She leaves, but returns the next morning when she discovers that he has been telling her the truth and that the 'policemen' who arrested them were working for the foreign agent. She has discovered that the foreign agents are going to pick someone up from the London Palladium theatre.

Hannay and Pamela rush there to see the Mr Memory act. Hannay realises that the secret they want is in Mr Memory's memory. Hannay shouts 'What are the Thirty-Nine Steps?' and Mr Memory begins to recite that it is an organisation of spies. Professor Jordan shoots Mr Memory. Backstage, a dying Mr Memory reveals the secret formula he had memorised to be taken out of the country.

The play ends with Hannay and Pamela together in his flat preparing to celebrate Christmas.

TASK 1

a After reading the synopsis above, in your group choose ten important plot points and create a still image for each. Discuss which moments you think are the most exciting and dramatic.

b Then create a bullet point list of some of the performance and design challenges in putting **'The 39 Steps'** onstage. It is important to consider: lighting, sound, costume and setting.

  You might begin by:

  ▶ creating the period setting

  ▶ differentiating between the many characters

  ▶ quick costume changes

  ▶ showing the many different locations.

Context

The novel *The 39 Steps* by John Buchan was the basis for a popular 1935 Alfred Hitchcock film. Both the novel and film, in turn, provided inspiration for this stage adaptation by Patrick Barlow, which is an affectionate **parody** of many of the conventions of period action thrillers.

The context you need to understand is the 1930s. The play is set in England and Scotland in August 1935, and it reflects the sense of growing unease about the threat of fascism in Europe. In particular, there is concern about unrest in Germany and a sense that Britain may be in danger. Both Annabella and Professor Jordan are German characters, one representing the fight for good and the other evil.

> **KEY TERM:**
>
> **Parody:** an exaggerated imitation for comic effect.

The 1930s were also a time of rapid technological development in Britain. It was a time of scientific discovery, which makes the secret formula involving the design of a new engine particularly valuable, as it would give the owner an international advantage. There was a greatly increased use of electrical lighting and motor vehicles.

For entertainment, radios and gramophones (record players) were popular, as well as going to the cinema and theatre. There was, of course, no television or internet, so newspapers and radio were the primary sources of news.

Hannay claims to be bored, having returned to London from more exotic adventures, but he does enjoy some of the distractions of London such as the theatre. In contrast, the Scottish Crofter's cottage, where Margaret and her husband live, seems very rustic and isolated, almost like something from the previous century. Alt-Na-Shellach, the Scottish highlands estate of Professor Jordan, would be a far more luxurious setting. It might be an older building or it could reflect more modern architectural and interior design ideas.

Art Deco, a popular arts movement of this time, used geometric designs and bold colours, influenced fashionable architecture and the design of household objects.

▼ *A fashionable woman in 1930s clothing.*

An art deco interior ▲

There was greater independence and freedom for women during this period than previous decades, with more opportunities for education and employment. This is reflected in the independent-spirited female characters such as Pamela and Annabella. Roughly one-third of women in Britain worked outside the home, although that number was greatly reduced among married women.

Margaret is an example of a woman who is entirely reliant on her husband. The differences between the women and their roles in society would be reflected by their costumes.

▲ *The inhabitants of a simple crofter's cottage.*

TASK 2

Using the images on this page and your own internet research, sketch a design or write a paragraph showing how you believe the characters of Pamela and Margaret might be costumed.

Costume, hair and make-up design inspired by context

TASK 3

Use your understanding of the play's context and the prompts below to design a costume for **Annabella** for Act 1. She is described in her first entrance as wearing a '*plunging black 1930s evening gown*'.

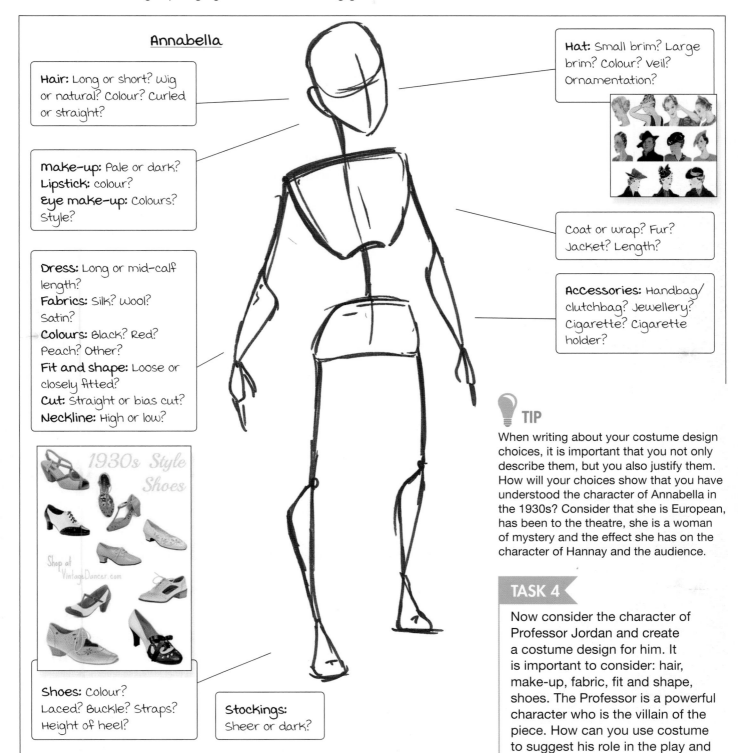

Annabella

Hair: Long or short? Wig or natural? Colour? Curled or straight?

make-up: Pale or dark? **Lipstick:** colour? **Eye make-up:** Colours? Style?

Dress: Long or mid-calf length? **Fabrics:** Silk? Wool? Satin? **Colours:** Black? Red? Peach? Other? **Fit and shape:** Loose or closely fitted? **Cut:** Straight or bias cut? **Neckline:** High or low?

Hat: Small brim? Large brim? Colour? Veil? Ornamentation?

Coat or wrap? Fur? Jacket? Length?

Accessories: Handbag/clutchbag? Jewellery? Cigarette? Cigarette holder?

1930s Style Shoes
Shop at VintageDancer.com

Shoes: Colour? Laced? Buckle? Straps? Height of heel?

Stockings: Sheer or dark?

TIP

When writing about your costume design choices, it is important that you not only describe them, but you also justify them. How will your choices show that you have understood the character of Annabella in the 1930s? Consider that she is European, has been to the theatre, she is a woman of mystery and the effect she has on the character of Hannay and the audience.

TASK 4

Now consider the character of Professor Jordan and create a costume design for him. It is important to consider: hair, make-up, fabric, fit and shape, shoes. The Professor is a powerful character who is the villain of the piece. How can you use costume to suggest his role in the play and the effect his presence has on the audience?

TIP

When considering how to design your set, it is important to know that you will rarely use the actual materials of the time, but instead you will create the set out of materials that have the appearance of those materials. For example, you may use gold paint to suggest gilt in the theatre; painted wood to give the appearance of marble or stone at Alt-na-Shellach; or boxes with added details to suggest train seats. Due to the many quick changes of the set, you will have to think how to represent quickly and simply the different locations.

Setting design inspired by context

One of the challenges of designing '**The 39 Steps**' is that it must show many different settings, from Hannay's flat to a Music Hall; from a Crofter's cottage to a fast-moving train. As a designer, you will need to consider how your design will:

▶ serve the practical needs of the play

▶ show the period setting

▶ suggest the atmosphere and role of the setting.

After choosing your stage configuration, use the chart below, listing some of the main settings of the play, to begin formulating your ideas for your set design (the requirements have been started for you, but you may discover additional aspects of the set or props that you wish to include).

LOCATION: Cockney Music Hall

REQUIREMENTS: Stage area. Theatre box with at least two chairs.

DESIGN CHOICES:

1 How can you show the difference between the stage and theatre box areas, making clear that Hannay and Annabella are in the audience?
2 What props can you use to show that this is a Music Hall?
3 What colours would you use for the theatre?
4 How can you create the impression of a Music Hall that can quickly be moved on and off stage?

LOCATION: Edinburgh train

REQUIREMENTS: Seats. Windows. Compartment. Outside of train.

DESIGN CHOICES:

1 How can you suggest that this is a 1930s train rather than one from the present day?
2 How will your design show the different sections of the train, including the outside of the train?
3 How can you represent train seats without actually having the full interior of a train onstage?

LOCATION: Crofter's cottage

REQUIREMENTS: Armchair. Table. Three chairs. Window.

DESIGN CHOICES:

1 The cottage is described as 'miserable'. How can your design emphasise that this is a poor and old-fashioned home?
2 What will the dominant colours and textures be?
3 Where would you position the furniture, window and door in order to achieve the best effect in the scene when the Crofter spies on Hannay and Margaret in Scene 13?

LOCATION: Hannay's apartment

REQUIREMENTS: Armchair. Lamp. Table. Bottle of Scotch. Glass. Telephone. Window. Blinds.

DESIGN CHOICES:

1 What details can you use to suggest the 1930s period?
2 What colour palette might you use?
3 What textures might you use for the fabrics or walls?
4 What props can you add to give the audience an impression of Hannay's character?

LOCATION: Alt-na-Shellach

REQUIREMENTS: Door. Professor's study. Armchair.

DESIGN CHOICES:

1 How will this room suggest that the Professor is powerful and successful? Are there any 1930s props or use of materials in the set that will add to the impression of his power?
2 Where will you position the furniture and doors in the study?

CHALLENGE

Research online the furniture from the time. Based on your research, draw sketches of key furniture items, such as Hannay's drinks cabinet or the Professor's armchair that you believe would be appropriate for your set design.

TASK 5

You are designing a setting for Scene 3 (Hannay's flat) of '**The 39 Steps**'. The setting must reflect the 1930s period setting of '**The 39 Steps**'. Describe your design ideas for the setting.

You may wish to include:

▶ How the set depicts the 1930s period.

▶ What it suggests about the character of Hannay.

▶ How it meets the needs of this scene.

▶ How the set practically functions in terms of how it is used and brought in/removed.

Writing about your design ideas

Question 1 will ask you to consider an aspect of design for the play in relation to its context. Below is a student's plan for the following question.

You are designing a costume for Hannay to wear in a performance of this extract from **Scene 21**. The costume must reflect the 1930s period setting of 'The 39 Steps'. Describe your design ideas for the costume.

1 Understanding of the character in the play:

Richard Hannay is a dashing, cultured, resourceful man. Although he may be a bit rumpled as he has been on the run, he needs to look presentable enough to be believable as the candidate he pretends to be in this scene.

2 Period: colours, fabrics, shape and fit:

1930s men's fashions often emphasised shoulders and tapered to waist. muted colours of tans and greys. His jacket is a light-coloured Harris Tweed (mentioned in Scene 14). Trousers were loosely cut and high-waisted. He may still have the dark overcoat given to him by Margaret, but as it is rough, might hold it rather than wear it in this scene. He would hold his brown fedora hat in his hand as he spoke.

3 His relationship to society:

He makes a positive first impression so no-one suspects him of being on the run. His clothing would indicate that he is fashionable and up-to-date. There would be a contrast between him and the country characters.

4 Character shown through costume, hair and make-up:

Hannay knows he is attractive. He is well-groomed, with a small, tidy moustache. His hair is cut short and a pomade such as Brylcreem would be use to style his hair neatly back from his face.

▲ *An example of handwoven Harris Tweed fabric.*

> **KEY TERM:**
>
> **Harris Tweed:** a high-quality, handwoven, woollen cloth.

 TIP

It is important to know that there are other interpretations of how Richard Hannay might be costumed in relation to the play's context.

 TIP

It is important that you justify your ideas. Explain why you are making these specific choices, don't just describe what he will look like. How does the Crofter's job and isolated position affect the costume he might wear or his hair and make-up?

1 Understanding of the character in the play:

2 Period:

3 His relationship to society:

4 Character shown through costume, hair and make-up:

TASK 6

Using the above plan for Hannay as a guide, create your own plan for the character of the Crofter in answer to the following question:

> You are designing a costume for the Crofter to wear in a performance of Scene 12. The costume must reflect the 1930s setting of 'The 39 Steps'. Describe your own design ideas for the costume.

▲ *Cartoon showing a stereotypical hero, villain and damsel in distress – with horse.*

> **KEY TERM:**
>
> **Stock gestures:** stereotypical gestures to signal certain emotions, such as shaking a fist to show anger.

Practical exploration of the play's style and themes

Style and themes

When writing about performing roles in the play, you must demonstrate that you understand the characters and how they interact. You need to use the performance space to show your understanding of the play. Below are some exercises to help develop your understanding of the play, its characters and its style.

Melodrama and Good versus Evil

'**The 39 Steps**' uses many of the conventions of **melodrama** with its hero, Hannay, overcoming the evil villain, Professor Jordan, while also winning the love of a good woman. Melodrama often relies on a series of easily recognised gestures to suggest the nature of the characters, such as a villain twirling his moustache to show that he is evil or a hero striking a powerful chest out, hands-on-hips pose to show his determination to succeed or the damsel in distress who might fall to her knees and hold her clasped hands before her in a pleading gesture.

TASK 7

a Working in your group, agree one exaggerated **stock gesture** for the following characters:
  - ▶ Professor Jordan
  - ▶ Margaret
  - ▶ Richard Hannay
  - ▶ Annabella
  - ▶ the Heavies from Scenes 22–24.

b Have everyone in the group take a turn at doing the stock gesture for each character, quickly transforming from one character to the next with clear, exaggerated use of body language and gesture.

c When each heroic character appears, have the rest of the group cheer them. When a villainous character appears, the rest of the group should boo them.

d Take a photograph or draw a sketch of the stock gestures and note where in the script these positions could occur.

Multi-role

The play was originally conceived as having multi-role as its performance style, with all the actors, except the one playing Richard Hannay, playing a number of roles. This is particularly true of the actors called 'Clown 1' and 'Clown 2' who play many roles, sometimes changing parts mid-scene.

This requires the actors to be able to change physically and vocally to show that they are new, as there is often only time for the most minimal of costume changes.

The following tasks should help you to become more confident about multi-roling.

▶ For more about melodrama see page 199.

TASK 8

The hat game:

a Put a wide assortment of hats in a pile.

b The first two actors randomly pick two hats from the pile and begin a scene that fits those two hats. For example, someone might have a policeman's hat and arrest someone who is wearing a balaclava.

c As the scene goes on have two people on the side hand them new hats. The actors must suddenly change their characters and the scene to fit their new hats. So the policeman's hat might be replaced by a flowery bonnet and the balaclava with a cowboy hat, which should inspire two new characters and a fresh interaction.

d Keep changing hats until a variety of different characters and scenes have been introduced.

e Then switch in new actors and start the game over again.

TASK 9

Applying multi-roling to the Clowns.

a Working with a partner, create a series of still images to show the following different transitions:

Student 1:	Student 2:
Mr Memory	Compere
Mrs Higgins	Milkman
Salesman 1	Salesman 2
Paperboy	Policeman
Salesman 1	Porter
Paperboy	Policeman
Salesman 1	Porter
Mrs Higgins	

b Find one prop or piece of costume for each of the characters (such as an apron for Mrs Higgins and newspapers for the paperboy).

c Improvise a short scene in which you play all the characters listed in part a, changing vocally and physically for each, and using an appropriate prop or piece of costume.

d Then write short vocal and physical notes in your notebook for each of these characters such as:

Mr Memory: voice: Cockney accent, pompous, resonant voice. Physical: well-rehearsed gestures, touches forehead to indicate his brilliant memory. Prop or costume: bowtie.

e For question 2, you will be asked to describe how you would use your vocal and physical skills to perform certain lines. Choose one line from one of the following characters and write a short paragraph describing how you would use your vocal and physical skills to perform the line and explain the effects you want to create: Mr Memory, Compere, Salesman 1, Policeman, Mrs Higgins. It is important that you use any discoveries you made through the multi-roling exercise and your subsequent notes.

SET PLAY 3:
'The 39 Steps' by John Buchan and Patrick Barlow

3

REFLECTION

Discuss what techniques the actors used to successfully convey their new characters. Did they change the pitch, volume or tone of their voices? Did they change accents? How did their body language change? Did they move more slowly or quickly? How did they use gestures or proximity?

TIP

'**The 39 Steps**' offers many opportunities to explore different **accents**. In some cases, performers are playing several different characters so must make the characters clear through differentiating them vocally as well as physically. For example, how might Mrs McGarrigle's Scottish accent differ from Mr Memory's London performer's voice? How might the German accents of Annabella and the Professor be suggested? How do different characters' occupations suggest the ways they speak, such as the policemen, the milkman and the housekeeper? As it is a comedy, you might even think of ways of exaggerating the accents for comic effect.

CHALLENGE

Watch British films from the 1930s and 1940s (many of which are available online) to gain a greater understanding of the accents of the time. The 1938 film *Pygmalion* shows Henry Higgins teaching a cockney flower-seller how to speak with an upper-class accent. The 1945 film *Brief Encounter* depicts a combination of working-class and upper-middle-class accents. Other sources of period voices can be found on the British Pathé website, which has period newsreels from the time. For inspiration for parodies of the accents from this period, the comedian Harry Enfield has a number of short comedy sketches about the 1930s, in which he plays Mr Cholmondley-Warner, which are available online.

Interpretation of character

You will need to show how you can interpret a character. This means that you understand the character's motivations and goals, as well as the obstacles they face. Then you must be able to use your vocal and physical skills to portray the character and create particular effects for the audience, such as tension, comedy, romance, surprise, pity or sorrow. In this instance, think about total characterisation, which includes facts about the characters and their appearance as well as how they could be interpreted through acting, costume and make-up choices. This will help you to think about all aspects of interpreting the character, even when writing about acting or design.

Look below at one interpretation of the character of **Professor Jordan** (your interpretation may differ on some points). In this instance, think about total characterisation, which includes facts about the characters and their appearance as well as how they could be interpreted through acting, costume and make-up choices. This will help you to think about all aspects of interpreting the character, even when writing about acting or design.

> ### TASK 10
>
> Using your own understanding of the characters in the play and how they could be interpreted, create an interpretation of Pamela using the following headings: Age, Physical appearance, Voice, Body language, Costume, Hair, Make-up, Effect on audience. In this instance, think about total characterisation, which includes facts about the characters and their appearance as well as how they could be interpreted through acting, costume and make-up choices. This will help you to think about all aspects of interpreting the character, even when writing about acting or design.

Interpretation:

FACTS:
Background: *educated, speaks English well, but is German and his accent emerges at times. Has a wife and daughter. Lives in a Scottish Highlands estate: Alt-na-Shellach*
Job: *professor and a secret agent for the Germans*

PHYSICAL APPEARANCE:
I imagine Professor Jordan to be tall and broad shouldered (a padded jacket could emphasise this).

HAIR:
Short, perhaps balding or greying at temples.

COSTUME:
Elegant velvet dinner jacket, silk cravat, black pleated tuxedo trousers. Possibly a monocle or spectacles? Pocket handkerchief in jacket pocket.

VOICE:
Speaks in a well-modulated and educated English accent, but his German accent begins to emerge when he speaks of his homeland. He can speak in a cruel, sarcastic way, especially when he tries to provoke Hannay on lines such as 'When have you ever loved anyone?' When angered, he shouts.

BODY LANGUAGE:
Dominating presence. Initially sitting in armchair, poised and confident, legs crossed, watching Hannay with apparent amusement. Smiling. When he makes Hannay sit down, he dominates and towers over him. Moves close to Hannay and blows smoke in his face. He taunts Hannay when showing his missing finger. Handles props like a gun or a cigarette lighter with equal elegance. He isn't used to being defied so explodes with anger.

PROPS:
Gun, cigarette case, cigarette holder.

EFFECT ON AUDIENCE:
Professor Jordan is the villain of the piece. From his first appearance he should provide a source of tension. He attempts to control Hannay and from the moment he pulls a gun on him clearly poses a threat. He tries to win Hannay over through flattery and threats, finally resorting to shooting him. The audience should be intrigued by him, but also thoroughly dislike him and want him to be defeated.

Performing choices

SET PLAY 3:
'The 39 Steps' by John Buchan
and Patrick Barlow

3

In question 2, you will be asked to discuss in detail how you would perform a particular line as a given character.

For example:

You are performing the role of _____.

Describe how you would use your vocal and physical skills to perform the lines below and explain the effects you want to create.

Sample:

> **HANNAY: Scene 1:** And I thought – who the bloody hell cares frankly?

Understanding of play and character

In this opening scene of the play, I want to create through my vocal and physical choices the period and Hannay's role as the hero. **1** He is frustrated and restless, so I need to show that. I am speaking directly to the audience, so will make eye contact with them. **2** I am elegant and graceful, holding a glass of Scotch in one hand and gesturing with the other. I am seated in an armchair with my legs crossed with exaggerated casualness. **3** I would start the sentence casually, speaking in a clipped upper-class accent 'And I thought' but would then change my tone on 'bloody hell' hoping to surprise the audience with my bitterness. **4** I would pause at the end of the line, looking directly at the audience. I would hold out an upturned hand to them, as if to say, 'do you care?' **5** I would then stand and pace around the room to show how close I am to doing something drastic. **6**

Physical skills and intention

Physical skills

Vocal skills and intended effect

Physical skills

Physical skills and effect

TIP

It is important that you write in the first person ('I') so you can fully imagine your own performance of the role. Don't only describe the vocal and physical skills you will use, but also think about how your choices will add to the audience's understanding of the play's meaning, the character and the character's relationship with others.

TASK 11

Experiment with different ways of using your vocal and physical skills for each of the following lines:

ANNABELLA: Scene 3: 'Very well. Have you ever heard of the – Thirty-nine Steps?'

MILKMAN: Scene 5: 'Cor blimey! I wouldn't be in your shoes!'

PAMELA: Scene 9: 'This is the man you want Inspector!'

MARGARET: Scene 14: 'You must go now while there's still a chance!'

PROFESSOR JORDAN: Scene 18: 'Oh, we will give you love, Hannay.'

MRS MCGARRIGLE: Scene 26: 'You can be certain that at the McGarrigle Hotel a warm McGarrigle welcome awaits ye.'

MR MEMORY: Scene 31: 'Will it be all right me telling you, sir?'

TASK 12

a Make notes on the following:
   ▶ Vocal skills:
   ▶ Physical skills:
   ▶ Effects achieved:

b Using the example above as a guide, write an answer to the same question referring to each of the characters and lines.

c Check your work by writing 'V' next to each vocal skill, 'P' next to each physical skill, and 'E' next to an effect. Make sure that you have answered this question fully.

Character revision sheet

Below is an example of a character revision sheet based on the character of **Pamela**, which has been partially completed. Copy the grid and complete it.

Character and importance to the play	Pamela
What do they want?	She is the love interest in the play.
What obstacles do they face?	She helps Hannay defeat the villains.
What are their key scenes?	Scene 9: Kiss on the train. Scene 21: Candidate's speech. Scene 22: Identifies Hannay to the Heavies. Scene 23: In car with Hannay and the Heavies. Scene 24: Escaping across moors handcuffed to Hannay. Scene 25: Argues with Hannay on moors. Scene 26: Checks into McGarrigle Hotel. Scene 27: Hotel bedroom with Hannay. Scene 29: Returns to room knowing that Hannay has been telling the truth. They argue. Scene 30: Joins Hannay at London Palladium. Scene 32: They part outside London Palladium. Scene 33: Returns to Hannay. End of play.

How might they be costumed?

Draw a simple sketch or write a description of it. Consider:
- colours
- fabrics
- shape and fit
- character's personality and status

How might their hair and make-up be done?

Draw a simple sketch or write a description of it. Consider:
- style and colour of hair
- type of make-up (realistic or fantasy; colours; how it is appropriate for character, setting and period)

How might they use body language?

- posture
- gait (the way they walk)
- facial expression

How might they use their voice?

Emotional range (angry, sad, happy, irritated, desperate, dominating, etc.)
Pitch and volume (how low or high; how loud or soft)
Accent or other distinctive vocal features

Choose one important line and analyse how they might say it.

Scene 27: 'I imagine murderers have terrible dreams.'

TASK 13

Using the grid above for guidance, create similar revision sheets for all major characters including: Richard Hannay, Margaret, Crofter, Annabella, Professor Jordan and Mr Memory.

Download a printable version from Samples & Downloads at www.illuminatepublishing.com.

Using the performance space and interaction with others

SET PLAY 3:
'The 39 Steps' by John Buchan
and Patrick Barlow

3

There are opportunities to explore the space and interaction with others in a number of different ways in the many settings of the play. There are intimate romantic scenes, moments of knockabout comedy and also dramatic escapes. When writing about how you will use the performance space and interaction with others, focus on the effects you wish to achieve, such as tension, romance, surprise, comedy or pity, and how you will use your skills to achieve them.

**Jonathan Brody,
performer**

THEATRE MAKER ADVICE

I've done two different productions of '**The 39 Steps**' and both times it was imperative to drill the timing of the physical and comic bits with the other Clown. Practice really does make perfect. The hat business in the scene on the train platform alone required daily drills set aside during the rehearsal period and we'd do it often before performances as well. The shifting back and forth between 'The Heavies' and the McGarrigles requires precision timing as well.

Because of the minimal set pieces and furniture, many scenes require creative use of the space. The train scene, using only four trunks, is a prime example. A combination of mime (to convey the doors and windows), specific body position and movement (to delineate the train compartments, cramped quarters and train movement) and physical blocking with creative use of space (to make clear when we were in the train, scaling the sides or on top of the cars) are all required to make this sequence a success.

TASK 14 CONTINUED ON PAGE 86

Closely read Scene 27 (Hotel Bedroom), taking particular notice of any stage directions.

a Agree what stage configuration you are going to use. Mark where the entrances will be and any furniture.

b Decide what effects you wish to achieve in this scene. To help you do this, answer the following questions:
  ▶ How will you create the comedy of Mrs McGarrigle and her misunderstanding of the situation?
  ▶ How will you deal with the staging configuration complications of Hannay and Pamela handcuffed together?
  ▶ How will you create the sense of growing attraction and romantic tension between Pamela and Hannay?
  ▶ How might props add to the comedy of the scene?

c How will you use stage space? Try the following:
Mrs McGarrigle's re-entry with the tray of food:
  ▶ Hannay quickly pulls Pamela onto his knee. He looks happily up at Mrs McGarrigle while Pamela glares at him.
  ▶ Pamela refuses to sit on his knee. He forces her to and both look up with forced smiles at Mrs McGarrigle.
  ▶ Hannay pulls Pamela onto his knee. She gets up. Then changes her mind and sits down. Gets up again.
    As Mrs McGarrigle enters, he pulls on the handcuff and she falls onto him. Both laugh as if they were cuddling.
Mrs McGarrigles's reaction:
  ▶ She enters with so much food that she doesn't see them. When she does she's embarrassed and backs out.
  ▶ Giggling, she hides her eyes. She tries to find a place to put down the tray without making eye contact.
  ▶ She secretly wants to catch them as she enjoys helping romantic couples, so bustles around, encouraging them.

TASK 14 ◄ *CONTINUED*

d Continue through the scene, experimenting with different staging configuration ideas. Then answer the following:

> You are performing the role of **Pamela**.
>
> Focusing on the lines 'Actually, I will take my shoes off' to 'Well come along', explain how you and the actor playing Hannay might use the performance space and interact with each other to create romantic tension for the audience.

TIP

It is important that you include both vocal and physical skills. Highlight key moments when these skills can be discussed.

Answering a question about character interpretation

If you choose to answer question 4, you will need to write about how you would use your acting skills to interpret a character both in the extract provided and in the play as a whole.

An example of this sort of question might be:

> You are performing the role of **Margaret**.
>
> Describe how you would use your **acting skills** to interpret Margaret's character in this extract (Scene 14, from 'Och, I dinna trust him!' to 'I'll never forget you for this!') and explain why your ideas are appropriate both for **this extract** and the **play as a whole**.

Below is a sample student plan for this question.

This extract:

1 Character of Margaret and reasons for making acting choices:

A pretty Scottish girl from Glasgow. Married to a jealous man. Lives in an isolated place. Attracted to Hannay. Risks husband's anger by helping him.

2 Acting skills: vocal:

Scottish accent, softly spoken. Exclaims 'Och' in shock and pauses after 'Listen!' which builds suspense when listening for husband. Speaks quickly with urgency knowing Hannay must escape. After a series of short, quickly whispered lines, tone changes on 'Don't joke I beg of you', which is said passionately. Says name, 'Margaret' with a simple sincerity.

3 Acting skills: physical:

Movements indicate the tension of the situation. Leans against the door to listen and rushes back to Hannay. Moves quickly, forcing Hannay into husband's overcoat. Movements change from brusque efficiency when Margaret 'melts' into him. Leans into Hannay and maintains eye contact. Positioned very close, with Hannay's arms around her. After the second kiss, with difficulty, forces herself away from him and steps back.

Rest of play:

1 Character of Margaret and reasons for making acting choices:

Margaret is a dreamy character who has little romance or excitement in her life. She is also shy and unaware of the effect she has on others.

2 Acting skills: vocal:

Speaks in a quiet, respectful way, calling Hannay 'Sir'. Scottish accent is clear from her use of 'ye'. More vocally expressive and enthusiastic when describing Glasgow on a Saturday night.

3 Acting skills: physical:

In Scene 12, on first entrance, Margaret is shy, so dips her head and blushes. Used to doing chores, so may enter carrying a bucket or broom. An immediate attraction between Margaret and Hannay, causing them to suddenly look away from each other. In Scene 13, Margaret can barely meet his eyes, and instead busies herself with making supper. Aware of Hannay staring at her, which makes her movements more self-conscious. Assumes 'dreamy faraway' expression when speaking about Glasgow. Throughout Scene 13, their attraction grows, but is comically interrupted by her husband.

TASK 15

Using the plan on the previous page as a guide, write your own plan in answer to the following question:

> You are performing the role of **Hannay**.
>
> Describe how you would use your acting skills to interpret Hannay's character in Scene 19 from the Sheriff's 'Some of those hymns are terrible hard to get through' to Hannay's 'MURDERER' and explain why your ideas are appropriate both for **this extract** and the **play as a whole**.

Design choices

If you choose to answer question 5, you will be thinking as a designer and commenting on one aspect of design. For example:

> You are a designer working on one aspect of design for this extract.
>
> Describe how you would use your design skills to create effects that support the action of this extract and explain why your ideas are appropriate for **this extract** and the **play as a whole**.

You may choose to focus on set design, costume design, lighting design, sound design or puppet design. Whichever you choose, you must explain why your ideas are appropriate to the play as a whole. You might refer to:

▶ how your design helps to show the action of the play and the nature of the characters

▶ how your design for the extract is consistent with the design requirements of the rest of the play (e.g. don't suddenly change the production's style)

▶ how you have used design methods that enhance the play's mood

▶ props, anything that the actors may carry on stage.

'The 39 Steps' makes particular demands on the designer because of the many different settings and the large number of characters, with actors often being required to change rapidly from one character to another.

Some productions use trucks to quickly wheel on important pieces of scenery. Others make a particular feature of creating different settings with only minimal props, for example boxes and chairs used in a variety of ways in different scenes. Some productions rely heavily on lighting to create the different settings, such as a **spotlight** on Mr Memory for the theatre scenes, or coloured side lighting to make the dry ice or smoke machines' effects murky for the Scottish moors.

Use music to underscore the melodramatic qualities of the play, for example by having romantic music playing in romantic scenes or wild dance music during the offstage party at Alt-na-Shellach. Sound effects, such as the wind on the moors or 'canned laughter' (recorded sounds of people laughing) in the theatre scenes will add to the atmosphere.

The costume design should reflect the style of the piece and the demands of creating vivid characters. While Hannay probably will wear the same costume (except when he adds an additional item to disguise himself) all the other performers will have to undertake quick changes.

The actor playing Pamela must convincingly play a range of characters, from a mysterious and glamorous German spy to a simple Scottish woman.

SET PLAY 3:
'The 39 Steps' by John Buchan and Patrick Barlow

3

TIP

When writing your response as a performer, write in the first person. So 'I would move more quickly here' rather than 'Hannay would move more quickly here'. That will help you to fully imagine yourself playing the role.

1 Character of Hannay and reasons for making acting choices:

2 Acting skills: vocal:

3 Acting skills: physical:

KEY TERM:

Spotlight: lamp projecting a narrow intense beam of light directly onto a performer or area of the stage.

Costume design

For the costume design, you might consider:

- ▶ style, cut and fit of costume
- ▶ colour, fabric, decorative features
- ▶ condition (worn or new; neat or wrinkled; clean or stained, etc.)
- ▶ footwear/headgear
- ▶ accessories
- ▶ status or social role of character
- ▶ make-up and hairstyle.

Below is an extract from a sample response for a question based on Pamela in Scene 9.

> **KEY TERM:**
>
> **Silhouette:** the outline or shape created by a costume on a figure.

In this scene, I would have Pamela's costume show her independent, practical nature, while also emphasising her beauty. I would costume her in a soft wool, navy suit, with a long, lean line, as was popular in the 1930s. ❶ The skirt would be close-fitting and mid-calf length. The jacket would have shoulder pads to exaggerate slightly her shoulders and give the outfit a tailored, business-like appearance. ❷ It would dip in at her waist and flare out at her hips, giving her a softer silhouette. Her blouse would be of a thin, oyster-coloured silk, with a bow at the neckline. As she is travelling, she would wear a felt hat, with a wide brim. At the beginning of the scene, she is wearing glasses, but when she takes these and her hat off, she becomes particularly attractive (at least in Hannay's eyes). ❸ In my interpretation, she has a job with some responsibility, possibly as a high-ranking secretary and her clothes should suggest that she would look appropriately dressed for any professional engagement. ❹ She would be carrying a small, structured handbag and wear little jewellery besides small earrings. She would wear moderately high heels with a practical ankle strap. Her make-up would include red lipstick, pale face powder and she would have neatly waved chin-length hair, all popular make-up and hairstyle choices for this period. ❺

In the rest of the play, her costume will become more dishevelled. ❻ She has become soaked on the moors, and in the hotel scene she will take off her jacket, looking immediately softer and more vulnerable. ❼ She will be wearing stockings, with a seam up the back as was typical of the 1930s, which she will have to remove in that scene. ❽ In contrast to Annabella, her costume will be more practical and less ornamental, but she will look more worldly and sophisticated than Margaret. ❾

Annotations (right and left margins):

- Costume appropriate for character and period of the play
- Discusses fit and effect
- Considers accessories and effect
- Discusses character and effect of costume
- Discusses accessories, make-up and hairstyle
- Discusses how costume may change throughout play
- Relates changes in costumes to plot
- How costume helps to convey action of play
- How costume makes her stand out from other female characters

TASK 16

Draw a sketch showing Richard Hannay at the beginning of the play and then two further sketches showing him disguised in the Milkman's cap and coat (Scene 5) and in the Crofter's overcoat (Scene 15). Label the three sketches with details about the colours, fabric and shape of the costumes.

TASK 17

Write several paragraphs answering the following question as a costume designer:

> Focus on Scene 3, from Annabella's line: 'Annabella Schmidt' to Hannay's 'Frankly, I don't.'
>
> You are a designer working on one aspect of this extract.
>
> Describe how you would use your design skills to create effects that support the action of this extract and explain why your ideas are appropriate both for **this extract** and the **play as a whole**.

After you have completed your work, check to make sure you have:

✓ Referred to fabric, colours, shape/fit, condition.

✓ Included headwear/footwear, if appropriate.

✓ Considered make-up and hairstyle.

✓ Explained how the use of costume helps the action of the extract.

✓ Related your answer to the play as a whole.

 TIP

You might want to consider the following:

▶ how your costumes will establish the characters of Hannay and Annabella

▶ how the costumes will help to establish the romantic action of the scene

▶ how the costumes will reinforce the period of the play.

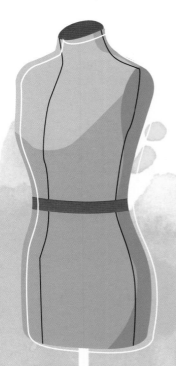

Set design

For the set design, you might consider:

▶ stage configuration
▶ how you suggest the location and atmosphere of the location
▶ the scale (how large) your set will be
▶ if there will be any levels, ramps or stairs
▶ the entrances/exits
▶ if there will be backdrops, flats or projections
▶ the colour palette you will use
▶ how the materials, textures and shapes will help to create a suitable setting
▶ which props are needed.

One of the challenges is to decide how realistic or artificial/stylised you want your set to be.

Below are two incomplete mindmaps of set design ideas: one with many realistic ideas and the other more abstract/stylised. Add more legs to the mindmap to incorporate your set design ideas, including props.

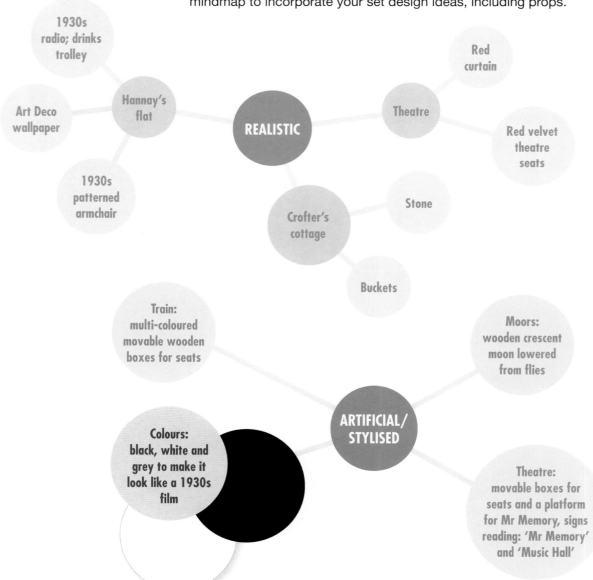

TASK 18

a Create your own mindmap in your notebook, focusing on Alt-na-Shellach and note ideas of how that set could be designed in either a realistic or stylised way.

b Pick out one prop from your realistic ideas and research online how you could make it look authentic for the period. Then draw a detailed sketch in your notebook.

c You have been asked to design the set for Scene 2. You need to create both a stage area and an audience/theatre box area for Hannay and Annabella.

Draw a sketch showing:

▶ the colours and textures (gilt? red? black? smooth? soft? rough?) you will use

▶ the materials for the set (velvet? wood? satin? metal?)

▶ the scale of the set in relation to the size of the actors

▶ any levels (platforms? seats?)

▶ where key events such as entrances/exits will occur.

Below is an excerpt from one sample response.

Sets out design intentions

Throughout my design I want to emphasise that the audience is seeing a play and will add a number of artificial, theatrical touches. ① At the beginning of this scene, I will have a wooden sign lowered from the flies that reads 'Music Hall' and, as I have chosen to stage it for theatre in the round, I will have the Compere enter through the audience bringing a double-sided painted sign that says, 'Mr Memory', show it to all the audience, and then hang it on a stand, which also fits with the Music Hall setting. ② Mr Memory will stand on a small wooden platform that has been brought on specially for him. Hannay and Annabella will sit in red cane chairs, which will be re-used in other scenes. ③ Onstage will be a rack of clothes so that the actors can do all their quick changes onstage later in the play. ④ When Annabella shoots the gun, I will have the Compere appear with a sign that says 'Bang!' to emphasise the comic and artificial nature of the play. The characters will exit through the audience, adding excitement. ⑤

Identifies stage configuration, materials and effect

Considers materials and colours

Suggests design choices for the rest of the play

Identifies how space can be used and effects

TASK 19

a Write your own paragraph based on your ideas for how Scene 2 could be staged, which may be realistic or stylised. It is important that you explain why you are making your choices.

b Now choose one of the following settings and answer the question below:

Hannay's flat, the Crofter's cottage or the Highland train.

> You are a designer working on one aspect of design for this extract.
>
> Describe how you would use your design skills to create effects that support the action of this extract and explain why your ideas are appropriate both for **this extract** and the **play as a whole**.

Lighting design

When creating your lighting design you might consider how to create:

▶ time of day and, possibly, season

▶ atmosphere

▶ focus to highlight particular moments

▶ how to help convey the setting, action and characters of a scene (such as a follow spot to focus the audience on a character's journey or backlighting to make them appear mysterious).

Some of your tools are:

▶ colours

▶ angles and intensity

▶ light from onstage sources (streetlamps, headlights, candles, lamps, torches)

▶ use of shadow and silhouette

▶ special effects

▶ use of blackouts or fades.

TASK 20

Copy and complete the mindmaps below, which have been started for you, to make notes on the different lighting demands of the scenes set in London and those in Scotland.

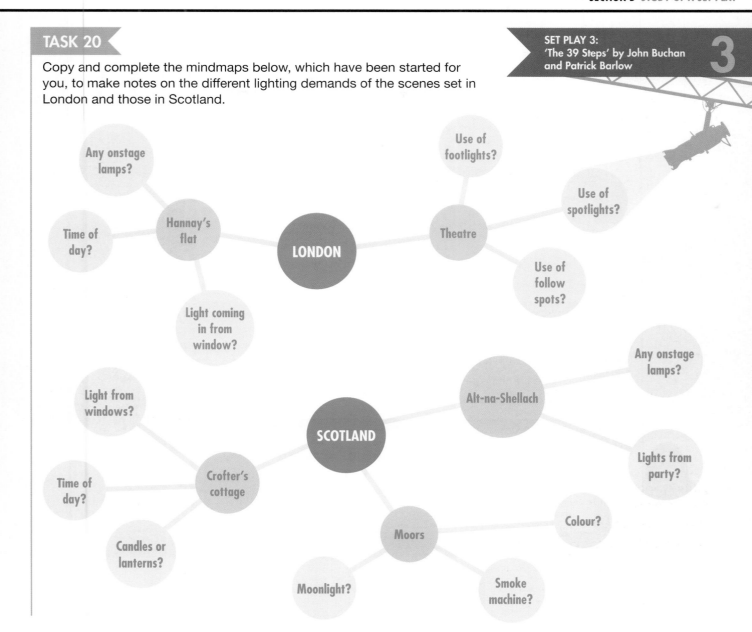

Below are some short excerpts from various responses to the demands of lighting '**The 39 Steps**'.

A

In order to capture the atmosphere of Scene 2, I will use footlights, which were common in Music Halls. **1** They will throw a light up into Mr Memory and the Compere's faces, causing an eerie effect. **2**

Using correct technical term of 'footlights' and explains reason for choice including period and location

Explains effect

B

Hannay is a character who is quickly attracted to women. I will emphasise this with my lighting choices. When he first sees Pamela I will used coloured gel lighting to cast a dreamy, blue light to make her stand out from the others. The blue light will switch back to the normal lighting state, a yellowish wash of colour, the moment the policeman enters the scene.

C I will use blackouts at moments of suspenseful danger. For example, when Hannay disappears off the train, there will be a blackout that will suggest that he might have died. The lights will then fade up to a misty, green-blue light, which will backlight Hannay who is 'hanging periously' from a girder.

D In Scene 16, to highlight the nerve-wracking quality of the party at Alt-na-Shellach, I will use wild, flashing, coloured lights every time the Professor's door is opened, with mysterious shadowy figures suggested by the use of gobos.

E For the scene on the moors (Scene 25) I will cast a greyish light on the high layer of mist created by either dry ice or a smoke machine. Above, there will be a high-angle blueish light suggesting moonlight.

F I want to create a cosy atmosphere at the McGarrigle Hotel. There will be an artificial fire onstage that will cast a warm, orange, low-angled light. There will be small bedside lamps and moonlight entering diagonally from the window.

TASK 21

Read the excerpts above and underline in pencil any references to: colours, angles, special effects, onstage lights, dimming or blackouts.

Sound design

When creating your sound design for '**The 39 Steps**', you will want to consider how to:
- ▶ create atmosphere
- ▶ add to the action and emotion of a scene
- ▶ contribute to the setting and style of the play
- ▶ fulfil practical needs of the script.

Some choices you can make involve:
- ▶ live or recorded sound
- ▶ volume/amplification (use of microphones)
- ▶ naturalistic sound or symbolic sound
- ▶ music.

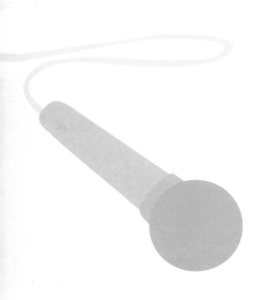

On the right is a sample of possible sound designer notes for Scene 17.

TASK 22

Research different types of music that could be suitable for this play (there are many online resources available). Try to identify suitable music for the following:

a (Scene 2) Music Hall music to introduce Mr Memory.

b (Scene 9) Romantic music when Hannay kisses Pamela.

c (Scene 18) Jitterbug music when Mrs Jordan takes the gun.

d (Scene 21) Patriotic music to underscore Hannay's campaign speech.

TASK 23

Focus on Scene 10 (Forth Bridge) and make detailed notes in your notebook on possible music and sound effects that could be used.

Some choices you could make include:

▶ adding recorded music under the scene

▶ having performers onstage or offstage creating sound effects

▶ adding recorded sound effects such as creaking, wind, water or owls

▶ experimenting with the volume of the sound (suddenly getting louder or softer)

▶ amplifying or distorting voices by using microphones.

Experiment with different versions of this scene and then make notes in your script about which choices you thought were most effective.

Puppet design

There are a few opportunities where puppet design could be useful, such as:

▶ Mr Memory either performed as a large puppet himself or Mr Memory operating a ventriloquist's dummy in Scene 2.

▶ A miniature train with a small puppet of Hannay leaping from carriage to carriage in Scene 9.

▶ The Forth Bridge with a puppet of Richard Hannay dangling from it in Scene 10.

▶ The dogs in Scene 15.

▶ The plane in Scene 15.

▶ The sheep in Scene 24.

If you choose to design a puppet, you must show how your design ideas will add to the development of the action of the play and be consistent with its mood and atmosphere.

When designing your puppet, consider:

▶ type of puppet: glove, hand and rod, marionette, shadow, backpack, etc.

▶ materials: wood, cloth, papier mâché, willow, etc.

▶ how it would be manipulated: onstage puppeteer or from the wings/flown in

▶ size: do you want the puppets to be small (for example, to suggest they are being seen in the distance), life-sized or over-large?

▶ what are the intentions for the extract and play as a whole: would the puppet add to the comedy/action/drama of the piece?

SET PLAY 3:
'The 39 Steps' by John Buchan and Patrick Barlow

3

Alt-na-Shellach. Interior: Recorded eerie music (strings). Low volume.

She opens the door. Wild shadows dance across their faces.

Cocktail party sound effects/ Jitterbug-type music: Recorded: Benny Goodman jitterbug ('Sing, Sing, Sing' or 'Peckin'') Volume loud. Recorded: Sounds of party guests/laughter.

She has second thoughts. Closes the door: Live: Loud door slam.

Music stops: Sudden silence.

▲ Sheep puppets in 'The Shepherd's Life', 2016.

▲ Shadow puppets used in one production of 'The 39 Steps'.

PRACTICE QUESTIONS FOR SET PLAY 3

You will answer the first three questions and then have a choice between question 4 or 5.

Extract from Scene 4:

Focus on the extract from Scene 4, starting with 'ANNABELLA [*even huskier*]: Oh Richard – Richard, – to '[*The phone stops ringing.*]'

1 You are designing a costume for Annabella to wear in a performance of this extract. The costume must reflect the 1930s period setting of '**The 39 Steps**'. Describe your design ideas for the costume. [4 marks]

2 You are performing the role of Annabella.
   Describe how you would use your vocal and physical skills to perform the line below and explain the effects you want to create:

   'There is a man in Scotland … only a matter of days?' [8 marks]

3 You are performing the role of Annabella.
   Focusing on the lines from 'Oh Richard! Richard!' to 'Golly!', explain how you and the actor playing Hannay might use the performance space and interact with each other to create tension and surprise for your audience. [12 marks]

AND EITHER

4 You are performing the role of Hannay.
   Describe how you would use your acting skills to interpret Hannay's character in this extract and explain why your ideas are appropriate both for this extract and the play as a whole. [20 marks]

OR

5 You are a designer working on one aspect of design for this extract.
   Describe how you would use your design skills to create effects that support the action of this extract and explain why your ideas are appropriate both for the extract and the play as a whole. [20 marks]

Extract from Scene 18:

Focus on the extract from Scene 18 from the Professor's 'Unless of course you decide to join us' to Hannay's 'All right Professor. If you think I'm suitable material.'

1 You are designing props or items of furniture for a performance of this extract.
   The props or items of furniture must reflect the 1930s period setting of '**The 39 Steps**'. Describe your design ideas for the props or items of furniture. [4 marks]

2 You are performing the role of Professor Jordan.
   Describe how you would use your vocal and physical skills to perform the line below and explain the effects you want to create:

   'You have no heart, do you Hannay!' [8 marks]

3 You are performing the role of Professor Jordan.
   Focusing on the lines from 'Love!?' to 'Where you really and truly belong', explain how you and the actor playing Hannay might use the performance space and interact with each other to show the tension between you for your audience. [12 marks]

AND EITHER

4 You are performing the role of Hannay.
   Describe how you would use your acting skills to interpret Hannay's character in this extract and explain why your ideas are appropriate both for this extract and the play as a whole. [20 marks]

OR

5 You are a designer working on one aspect of design for this extract.
   Describe how you would use your design skills to create effects that support the action of this extract and explain why your ideas are appropriate both for the extract and the play as a whole. [20 marks]

SET PLAY 4: 'Hansel and Gretel' by Carl Grose

4

Synopsis

The play opens with the **Supernature Chorus** and two rabbits introducing the location and the twins **Hansel** and **Gretel**. Hansel reads his encyclopaedia and Gretel practises her engineering by devising a contraption to get apples from a tree. Their parents arrive and they prepare a happy family meal. The hens, **Diane** and **Maureen**, discuss how happy they are to belong to such a loving family. **Johann** and **Wilhelm**, two musicians, arrive to celebrate the twins' birthday. When the twins blow out their candles, there is a change of atmosphere, signalling a sudden famine.

A year passes: **Mother** and **Father** discuss what a terrible year they have had. For Hansel and Gretel's birthday they are only able to give them a potato. A wind blows down their house. The family sings and dances to try to keep their spirits up. Mother suggests that they take Hansel and Gretel into the forest and let them go. Abandoned in the forest, Hansel and Gretel fall asleep. When they wake, they are frightened and try to find their way back.

Meanwhile, Mother and Father are starving. They do a sad dance and the children return. Mother kills Diane, the hen, for dinner, giving all the food to the children. Gretel creates an elaborate mouse trap, which succeeds in capturing a mouse for the parents to eat. Hansel and Gretel decide to leave, thinking their parents will have a better chance of surviving without them. They head into the forest watched by a **Strange Character**.

KEY TERM:

Supernature: usually means something that is beyond the rules of nature. This may refer to the extraordinary ability of the animals in the play to exhibit many human or extraordinary characteristics, such as the ability to speak.

In **Act 2**, the children wake up in the forest and follow a **Bird** who leads them to a house made of bread. At the Bird's suggestion, they begin eating the house. An **Old Lady** arrives. She tells them they have been eating her house and she invites them in, saying she will cook them something delicious. In the company of the Old Lady and the Bird, they eat their fill and fall asleep. The Old Lady returns and reveals herself to be the Strange Character of the first act. Bird announces that it is the witching hour.

When the children awaken, there are several ominous hints that the Old Lady is not as she first seemed. The children find children's shoes hanging around the cottage. The children want to go home and the Dead Rabbits in the house come to life and advise them to run away. The Old Lady transforms into a **Witch**. She puts Hansel into a cage. While two rabbits sing, Hansel sits in the cage eating. Gretel is ordered to do chores. Bird sings a song in praise of home: Canada. The Witch, who has poor eyesight, wants to know if Hansel has fattened up, but Gretel fools her by offering her a small bone to feel. The Witch still decides to eat him and asks him to season himself.

Meanwhile, Gretel has made a contraption that frees Hansel from the cage. The Witch is knocked into the fire. The children take the food from the Witch's cellar and return to their parents. The band plays.

TASK 1

a With your group, choose ten important plot points from the synopsis and create a still image to capture each moment.

b Discuss the challenges with performing and designing '**Hansel and Gretel**' and write a bullet point list of them. It is important to consider different design elements such as set, costume, music, sound, lighting and puppetry. You might begin by:

▶ creating the animals onstage
▶ making Gretel's contraptions work
▶ emphasising the fairy or folk tale aspects of the story
▶ making the story appealing to a wide audience, including children.

Context

The context of this version of the play is **contemporary storytelling theatre**, which often provides a fresh, comic and fantastical twist on conventional tales. The original fairy tale, 'Hansel and Gretel', has German origins. The most famous early version of it was written by the Brothers Grimm in 1812. It provides an example of clever children facing danger. They outwit the evil witch and save their own family from poverty.

Kneehigh Theatre's '**Hansel and Gretel**' was written by Carl Grose, but involved the collaboration of many people, including musicians, puppeteers and actors. The play reflects the conventions of contemporary storytelling theatre for which Kneehigh, which originally commissioned and produced this play, is famous.

Kneehigh Theatre began as a Cornwall-based theatre with its roots in community theatre. They are now internationally famous for their lively, interactive shows. The **performance style** of the play is **physical comedy**. Some common features of their shows include:

- ▶ striking visual images
- ▶ music
- ▶ use of actors/musicians
- ▶ puppetry or elaborate gadgets
- ▶ physical theatre
- ▶ storytelling/direct address to audience
- ▶ comedy
- ▶ dance
- ▶ **ensemble** work
- ▶ 'talking' animals (actors playing animals).

SET PLAY 4:
'Hansel and Gretel'
by Carl Grose

4

KEY TERM:

Ensemble: an approach to acting involving everyone working together, rather than singling out 'star' performers. It can also refer to a group of actors who play many roles in a play or a chorus. In the case of Kneehigh, there is a number of collaborators, including the musicians and designers.

TIP

Examples of Kneehigh's work are available online, which may help you to imagine what their storytelling style is like.

Kneehigh Theatre productions often tour and are created to appeal to a wide range of audiences. They sometimes utilise some of the features of a **pantomime**, such as using fairy tales, exaggerated characters and speaking directly to the audience. The aim of their performances is not to recreate a realistic world but to offer something more unusual and magical.

Former Artistic Director Emma Rice states that she isn't interested in 'cleverness' but instead celebrates 'foolishness'. She says, 'I love those moments in theatre when it could go either way – the audience could end up laughing or crying' (Lyn Gardner, 'We Like Our Plays to be Foolish', *The Guardian*, 19 July 2004).

TASK 2

a Below are some images from other productions by Kneehigh Theatre. After studying them and using the bullet point list on the previous page, try to locate features or conventions that are common to Kneehigh Productions.

b Write at least six bullet points explaining what typical features of a Kneehigh Theatre production you have noted after reading '**Hansel and Gretel**'. You could begin:

▶ Use of actor/musicians: Johann and Wilhelm.

▶ The Witch is like a pantomime or fairy-tale character.

▲ Three Kneehigh productions: top left 'Midnight's Pumpkin'; top right 'Dead Dog in a Suitcase'; bottom 'The Wild Bride'.

Costume, hair and make-up design inspired by context

TASK 3

Use your understanding of the play's context of contemporary storytelling theatre and the prompts below to design a costume for the **Old Lady** at the beginning of Act 2. She is described in the play as 'A Little Old Lady. She dresses like Fanny Cradock.' Fanny Cradock was a famous television cook in the mid-20th century. Although Fanny Cradock could be a formidable person, the children are not suspicious of the Old Lady at first, so you may want to think about how to make her seem innocent enough to gain their trust, but also believable in her transformation to the Witch. Given the conventions of storytelling theatre, you will want to create a vivid, exaggerated costume.

▲ *Fanny Cradock*

Hair: Wig? Natural? Curled? Straight? Colour?

Headwear: Scarf? Hat? Bow?

make-up: Colours? Highlight certain features? Emphasise age? Add prosthetics?

Justify your ideas. Possible reasons for your choices:

▶ To make her comic.

▶ To make her larger-than-life.

▶ To hint that she is not as she at first seems.

▶ To make her seem other-worldly and strange.

▶ To highlight the fairy-tale aspect of the play.

Dress: fabrics: Dominant colours? Bright colourful prints? Plaids? Stripes? Plain? Lace? Wool? Polyester?

Period: Updated to present day? Vintage – 1950s or 1960s? Victorian?

Shape and fit: Full-length or short? Layers? Tight or billowing?

Accessories: Handbag? Jewellery? Shawl? Sunglasses? (Shape of sunglasses: Round? Oval? Square? Heart-shaped?)

Footwear: Boots? Trainers? High heels? Other?

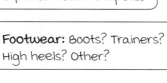

Old lady

TIP

When writing about your costume design ideas, it is important that you not only describe them, but you also justify your choices. How will your choices show that you have understood the character of the Old Lady and the context of contemporary storytelling theatre? You might want to consider how your costume will make the character a 'larger-than-life' creation. You may be influenced by images from classic German fairy tales or you may wish to update your design to the present day by basing them on pantomime characters or contemporary celebrities familiar to the audience. You might include design details that will add to the comedy or the villainy of the character.

TASK 4

Now consider the character of Hansel and draw a sketch of a possible costume for him. It is important to consider: headwear, hair and make-up, shape and fit, colours, materials, footwear.

Download a printable version from Samples & Downloads at www.illuminatepublishing.com.

Set design inspired by context

Contemporary storytelling theatre offers many opportunities for designers to use their imaginations in order to create worlds that are based on fantasy and magical ideas. The main settings are the children's family home, the woods and the Witch's cottage. The expectation of this style of theatre is that your design will be more **stylised** than realistic. It may reflect the magical quality of the script, where animals can talk and witches live nearby. It also needs to incorporate Gretel's elaborate constructions. As a designer, you will need to consider how your design will:

▶ serve the practical needs of the play

▶ show the storytelling setting

▶ suggest the atmosphere and role of the setting.

You may choose to have one basic set to which additional items are added for new locations or you may have a complete set change, for example between Act 1 and Act 2.

After choosing your stage configuration, use the chart below, listing some of the main settings of the play, to begin formulating your ideas for your set design (the requirements have been started for you, but you may discover additional aspects of the set or props that you wish to include).

TIP

Your set may suggest objects or locations without fully creating them in a realistic fashion. You may want to think of recurring colours or materials to make your design consistent. For example, you may choose to give your set a hand-built wooden look or you may prefer to go for metals and scaffolding or emphasise nature and the forest setting through your use of greens and browns. You might also consider an unusual staging configuration, such as an outdoor or promenade performance.

LOCATION: Hansel and Gretel's home

REQUIREMENTS: Objects for apple contraption (plank, pot, bungee cord, rope); stool; apple; wood; axe; chopping block; table; metal chicken feeder contraption; presents (wooden figures of the children); rope and other materials for mousetrap contraption

DESIGN CHOICES:

1 What do you want your basic set to emphasise? The fairy-tale quality of the story? The importance of gadgets and technology? The use of the forest setting and animals? The German origins of the story? The pantomime quality of the play?

2 How will your set add to the comedy of the play?

3 How will your set aid the special effects required by the play (such as contraptions)?

4 What will be your dominant colours?

5 Will you use any levels?

LOCATION: The forest

REQUIREMENTS: Petals and pebbles; dark and scary; shadows; old bicycle; moon; miniature house made of bread

DESIGN CHOICES:

1 How will your set help to create the atmosphere of the forest?

2 How can you show the Witch's house in the distance?

3 How can your set design highlight the Old Lady's first entrance?

4 How could you use colours, textures and levels to increase the sense of isolation and danger in the forest?

LOCATION: The Witch's cottage

REQUIREMENTS: Bread from edible house; door; perch for bird; table; pancakes; blanket; teddy bears; dead rabbits; hanging shoes; large cage; chair; rope; old bicycle; fire; bones; contraption; bucket; axe; **trapdoor**

DESIGN CHOICES:

1 What colours and textures can you use to make the cottage seem inviting and appetising at first?

2 How can you use levels in the set?

3 How will you handle the technical demands of the cage?

4 How can your set design increase the horror of the Witch's activities?

KEY TERM:

Trapdoor: a door in the floor of a stage allowing objects or performers to be dropped, lifted or lowered.

Writing about your design ideas

Question 1 will ask you to consider an aspect of design for the play in relation to its context. Below is a student's plan for the following question:

You are designing a costume for the Bird to wear in a performance of an extract from Act 2 (pages 38–39). The costume must reflect the conventions of contemporary storytelling theatre used in '**Hansel and Gretel**'. Describe your design ideas for the costume.

1 Understanding of the character in the play:

The Bird is a non-naturalistic, fantasy character, who although associated with the Witch, is sympathetic and supportive of Hansel and Gretel.

2 Conventions of storytelling theatre:

Make clear that the Bird is actually an actor. The same actor playing the mother will play the Bird, and she will transform into the Bird by putting on a loose-fitting, knee-length coat made of white, brown and black feathers, which suggest the colouring of a Canada Goose. The coat will be made of feathers, which will look almost glamourous, with a 1920s silhouette (she's a bit of a **flapper**). However, she will wear brown, striped tights and large over-sized boots, which will give her an awkward, comical look. On her head, she will wear a close-fitting aviator-style cap, and goggles, which is a comic way of suggesting that she's ready to take off in flight at any moment. I will apply charcoal grey make-up to her nose, to give it the suggestion of a beak.

3 Relationship to others:

She is described as a 'strange' bird, so should look unconventional and a bit of an outsider, like someone who tries to pull a look together, without really succeeding. She might seem very clumsy and earth-bound. The Bird would like to be braver than she is and is ruled or bullied by the Witch.

4 Character as expressed by costume:

The Bird is proud of being Canadian, so to emphasise this I would have her wearing a scarf with the distinctive red and white Canadian Flag with a maple leaf on it.

TIP

It is important to know that there are many other interpretations of how the Bird might be costumed.

KEY TERMS:

Non-naturalistic: stylised, not realistic.

Flapper: a girl in the 1920s associated with daring behaviour, wearing short skirts and dancing to jazz music.

TIP

It is important that you justify your ideas. Explain why you are making these specific choices, don't just describe what they will look like. How do your choices of fabrics, colours, shape and fit, accessories, make-up and so forth help to convey the character, the play and its conventions?

1 Understanding of the character in the play:

2 Conventions of storytelling theatre:

3 Relationship to others:

4 Character as expressed by costume:

TASK 5

Using the above plan as a guide, create your own plan for the character of the Father in Act 1 (pages 15–16).

You are designing a costume for the **Father** to wear in a performance of an extract from Act 1. The costume must reflect the conventions of contemporary storytelling theatre as used in '**Hansel and Gretel**'. Describe your own design ideas for the costume.

Practical exploration of the play's style and themes

When writing about performing roles in the play, you must demonstrate that you understand the characters and how they interact. You need to use the performance space to show your understanding of the play. Below are some exercises to help you explore practically your understanding of the play, its characters and its style.

Storytelling conventions

In order to feel confident of the exaggerated, comic style required of the play, try Tasks 6 and 7.

TASK 6

For each of the following emotions create two still images. The first should be a naturalistic image and the second a highly exaggerated one:

▶ hunger   ▶ anger

▶ love   ▶ fear.

Make a note of the differences between the two. (How large are the gestures? How do the facial expressions contribute to the exaggerating?) Then locate moments in the play when those exaggerated positions could be used.

TASK 7

Choose a scene, such as one of the children's birthday parties or the Witch preparing to cook Hansel, and play it **as if your audience were all young children**. How could you make the piece interesting and clear to a young audience? How scary should it be to be enjoyable and exciting, yet still appropriate for a very young audience?

Note in pencil on your script or in your accompanying notes any discoveries you make, such as: 'Look at the audience on this line to share the joke' or 'Speak loudly at this point to emphasise the danger.'

Pantomimes are designed to appeal to family audiences, including young children: 'Mother Goose' amateur production, Aberystwyth Arts Centre. ▶

Animals

There are many animals shown in the play, including the Bird, the hens, the rabbits and Graham the ferret. Some of the animals might be depicted by puppets while others might be portrayed by actors. Task 8 helps you to create the animals as actors.

SET PLAY 4:
'Hansel and Gretel'
by Carl Grose

4

▲ *'Under the Rainbow',
Polka Theatre*

TASK 8

a Choose one of the animals or birds mentioned in the play. Think about how they move and any sounds they might make.

b Walk around the room fully human. Be aware of the way you usually walk. What is your posture like? Do you lead with a particular body part? How fast or slow do you move? Is your walk smooth or bouncy? Are your steps large or small?

c When someone calls out 'one' imagine you are 1/10th the animal or bird you have thought about. How does that change the way you are walking? Are your movements quicker or slower? Larger or smaller?

d Now carry on assuming more characteristics of the animal as the numbers called out get higher, until you are fully that animal at 'ten'. If you are a hen, you might be leaning forwards, clucking, pecking at the ground, walking quickly then suddenly stopping, jerking your head forwards, etc.

e Now return to the number 'five', when you are half human and half animal. Which characteristics of the animal or bird have you kept? You might, for example, tuck your arms behind you like wings, but not peck fully to the ground.

f Now imagine that you have to speak as your animal. How can your voice be human, but also convey the animal you are portraying? Does your hen 'cluck' with disapproval or how might the rabbits' teeth affect their voices?

g Note your discoveries in pencil on your script or in your notebook.

h Answer the following question, focusing on the role of Maureen the hen:

> Describe how you would use your vocal and physical skills to perform the line below and explain the effects you want to achieve.
>
> 'Well get busy, Diane. For what good is a chicken who cannot lay?'

It is important to consider:

▶ how Maureen may be performed as half human and half animal (or supernature, so clearly something extraordinary and unexpected)

▶ how you could alter your voice to suggest some hen characteristics

▶ how you could alter your gestures, body language and posture to suggest a hen

▶ how you will note the effects you want to achieve such as the comedy of the scene and Maureen's fearful nature.

i Lastly, consider how you could make costumes for the characters using easily found, everyday objects, such as a rubber glove for the comb of the hens or slippers or wooden spoons for the rabbits' ears. Sketch your ideas, making notes on how this could add to the comedy of your design.

'Well get busy, Diane. for what good is a chicken who cannot Lay?'

Interpretation of character

You will need to show how you can interpret a character. This means that you understand the character's motivations and goals, as well as the obstacles they face. Then you must be able to use your vocal and physical skills to portray the character and create particular effects for the audience such as tension, comedy, romance, surprise, pity or sorrow.

Look below at one interpretation of the character of the **Mother** (your interpretation may differ).

Interpretation:

FACTS:

Background: married to Father, mother to twins. Lives simply off the food they raise or hunt

Job: Mother to Hansel and Gretel. Responsible for the chickens and feeding the family

PHYSICAL APPEARANCE:

I imagine the Mother to be thin (not much to eat). She may even appear rather dainty, which will make it funny when she comes in holding a 'dead rabbit aloft'.

HAIR:

Long yellow plaits (possibly a wig?).

VOICE:

I think to connect to the idea that they work the land, I would have her use a country accent, perhaps Cornish. This might also make her sound warm and motherly. She would have a pleasant, musical voice. This will make it more surprising and comic when she suddenly threatens the chickens with 'chop, chop'.

BODY LANGUAGE:

At first, she will move quickly and with energy, with a mater-of-fact attitude towards her work and putting food on the table, but as the hunger takes hold this will change. She will begin to walk more slowly, with her head lowered and her hands across her empty stomach. She would look with big yearning eyes towards any possibility of food. She will work as part of a team with Father and their actions will complement each other.

COSTUME:

As the original fairy tale was German, my idea is to create a comic, modern interpretation of traditional German folk dress. So I will put her in a green **dirndl** skirt, a green laced bodice with a white lacy under-blouse and a white apron. I will have the apron embroidered with comic scenes from their lives: rabbits being chased by axes; hens laying eggs; the twins as babies, etc. She will wear heavy, clog-like shoes and have a wreath of flowers in her hair, which, as she becomes poorer, will be replaced by a wreath of dead flowers. In the final scene, she is wearing rags of her former outfit.

PROPS:

Basket for collecting eggs.

EFFECT ON AUDIENCE:

The audience should feel sympathy for the Mother who is trying her best to feed her children. Her attempts at making the best of a bad situation may be comic.

TASK 9

Using your own understanding of the characters in the play and how they could be interpreted, create an interpretation on paper of Hansel using the following headings:

Age, Physical appearance, Voice, Body language, Costume, Hair, Make-up, Effect on audience.

In this instance, think about total characterisation, which includes facts about the characters and their appearance as well as how they could be interpreted through acting, costume and make-up choices. This will help you to think about all aspects of interpreting the character, even when writing about acting or design.

KEY TERM:

Dirndl: a dress or skirt, often seen in traditional Austrian or Bavarian outfits, which is gathered at the waist and falls to about knee-length.

Performing choices

In question 2, you will be asked to discuss in detail how you would perform a particular line as a given character.

For example:

You are performing the role of _____.

Describe how you would use your vocal and physical skills to perform the lines below and explain the effects you want to create.

Sample:

> **HANSEL: page 10:** 'It says here the universe is infinite, that is has no end ... Imagine that!'

This is the audience's introduction to Hansel and I would like to create through my vocal and physical choices what a bright but dreamy character he is. **①** As they live in the countryside, I will use a rural accent, perhaps Scottish with a soft burr to it, making my 'r's very distinctive. **②** I will pronounce the words precisely, fascinated by the idea of the universe. There will be a hint of wonder on the words 'no end'. I will exclaim loudly 'Imagine that' hoping to get a reaction from Gretel **③** and, for the first time, making direct eye contact with her. Physically, I will walk, around the stage, taking large confident steps, with my nose stuck in a comically large book. **④** I will handle the book with care, showing how important it is to me. **⑤** My facial expression will be serious and engrossed until I look up at Gretel, smiling and wide-eyed at my discovery. To add to the comedy, I will nearly bump into things onstage, but Gretel, who is following me around, will guide me away from them, without my apparently noticing. This establishes our relationship as team players – while I may think about big ideas, she is the one who gets things done practically. **⑥**

Understanding of character

Vocal skills and explanation

Vocal skills and effect

Physical skills

Physical skills and effect

Physical skills and effect. Understanding of play and characters

Experiment with different ways of using your vocal and physical skills for each of the following lines:

FATHER: page 12: 'Hansel, my boy. Put that damn encyclopedia down. I think it's high time I taught you how to chop wood.'

GRETEL: page 16: 'it's an auto-rotating bucket-winch chicken feeder!'

MAUREEN: page 19: 'Times are rough. You said this would happen, this blight upon the land.'

MOTHER: page 21: 'What are we to do? We have *nothing*.'

WILHELM: page 36: 'Hansel. Gretel. Take the very last of our bread.'

OLD LADY: page 47: 'Go home, dears? Why? Whatever for?'

BIRDY: page 51: 'Oh, those poor children, trapped against their will, longing for home.'

Rehearsing for a physical theatre performance of 'Dixit Dominus'. ▶

TIP

It is important that you write in the first person ('I') so you can fully imagine your own performance of the role. Don't only describe the vocal and physical skills you will use, but also think about how your choices will add to the audience's understanding of the play's comedy, the character and the character's relationships with others.

TASK 11

a Make notes for each of the above lines on the following:
   ▶ Vocal skills: ▶ Physical skills:
   ▶ Effects achieved:

b Then, using the example about Hansel on the previous page as a guide, write an answer to the same question referring to each of the characters and lines.

c Check your work by writing 'V' next to each vocal skill, 'P' next to each physical skill and 'E' next to an effect. Make sure that you have answered the question fully.

TIP

It is important to know that the costumes for the 'birds' don't have to look like animals at all. You may like to base them on famous celebrities or other comic stereotypes who capture the spirit of the birds.

Character revision sheet

Below is an example of a character revision sheet based on the character of **Maureen**, which has been partially completed. Copy the grid and complete it.

Character and importance to the play	maureen Maureen and Diane are the family's hens. They provide a source of food and also represent when the family is having good or bad times.
What do they want?	Wants to be well-fed and comfortable.
What obstacles do they face?	The family becomes poor and can no longer feed them and she is in danger of being eaten.
What are their key scenes?	Act I: Providing eggs and being fed (page 14). Gretel's new hen-feeding invention (pages 16–17). After famine strikes (pages 19–20). Note: Diane sings a song about Maureen's death (page 30).

How might they be costumed?	How might their hair and make-up be done?
Draw a simple sketch or write a description of it. Consider: • colours • fabrics • shape and fit • character's personality and status	Draw a simple sketch or write a description of it. Consider: • style and colour of hair • type of make-up (realistic or fantasy; colours; how it is appropriate for character, setting and period)

How might they use body language?	
• posture • gait (the way they walk) • facial expression	

How might they use their voice?	
Emotional range (angry, sad, happy, irritated, desperate, dominating, etc.) Pitch and volume (how low or high; how loud or soft) Accent or other distinctive vocal features	

Choose one important line and analyse how they might say it.	

TASK 12

Using the above grid for guidance, create similar revision sheets for all major characters including: the Old Lady, Hansel, Gretel, Father, Mother, Birdy and Diane.

Download a printable version from Samples & Downloads at www.illuminatepublishing.com.

Using the performance space and interaction with others

There are opportunities to explore the space and interaction with others in many ways in the play. You might think about how you could include the audience in your performance by **breaking the fourth wall** or how to create particular comic effects through the use of physical comedy. Many of the characters work as part of a pair, such as: **Mother and Father**; **Hansel and Gretel**; **Diane and Maureen**; **the Rabbits**; and the **Bird and the Old Lady**.

Consider how that relationship might affect their movements. Do they mirror each other? Does one control the other? Do they ever move together? Do they provide a contrast to one another? When you are writing about how you will use the performance space and interaction with others, make sure that you focus on the effects you wish to achieve, such as tension, comedy, surprise, humour, pity or sorrow, and how you will use your skills to achieve them.

> **KEY TERM:**
>
> **Breaking the fourth wall:** breaking the imaginary wall between the actors and performers by speaking directly to the audience.

TASK 13

Look closely at Act 2, page 42, when the Old Lady is feeding the twins.

a Read the scene, taking particular note of any stage directions.

b Decide what stage configuration you are going to use: end on, theatre in the round, thrust, promenade, proscenium or traverse. Draw the configuration on a piece of paper and mark where the entrances will be and any pieces of furniture.

c Decide what effects you wish to achieve in this scene. To help you do this, decide how you will handle the following issues:

▶ How and where the Old Lady and Birdy will dance.

▶ How the use of props will add to the comedy of the scene.

▶ If the Old Lady and Birdy will act as a team.

▶ If Hansel and Gretel will act as a team.

d How will you use stage space? Try the following:

'The Old Lady and Birdy dance and make a tower of pancakes.'

▶ The Old Lady and Birdy do a Morris Dance (a type of folk dance), breaking off to throw pancakes one by one onto a plate. At some points they will stand at opposite ends of the stage, so pancakes will have to travel a long distance.

▶ The Old Lady and Birdy do a tango-style dance on the table with the tower of pancakes between them, which they offer temptingly to the twins.

▶ The Old Lady makes bossy, jagged dance moves, while Birdy cowers below her catching the pancakes that are being thrown at them. The Old Lady will throw some pancakes into the audience.

Hansel and Gretel's reaction:

▶ The twins stand up straight, their arms interlocked, staring up in delight at the Old Lady.

▶ The twins chase after the plate of pancakes, each pushing the other out of the way trying to get closer.

▶ The twins do an elaborate 'high fives' with each other in celebration. They then reach for the pancakes, but remember their manners and hit each other's hands away.

e Continue working through the scene, experimenting with different staging configuration ideas. When you have finished, answer the following question:

> You are performing the role of **Hansel**.
>
> Focusing on the lines 'She's the best cook in all the land!' to 'Take your fill, sweethearts!', explain how you and the actors playing Gretel, the Old Lady and Birdy might use the performance space and interact with each other to create a joyful response to the food for the audience.

Answering a question about character interpretation

If you choose to answer question 4, you will need to write about how you would use your acting skills to interpret a character both in the extract provided and in the play as a whole.

An example of this sort of question might be:

> You are performing the role of **Gretel**.
>
> Describe how you would use your **acting skills** to interpret Gretel's character in this extract (Act 2, pages 46–47, from 'GRETEL: And what about all those?' to 'GRETEL: Auntie? I accuse you of being … a witch!') and explain why your ideas are appropriate both for **this extract** and the **play as a whole**.

Below is a sample student plan for this question.

TIP

It is important to include both vocal and physical skills. Highlight key moments when these skills can be discussed.

This extract:

1 Character of Gretel and reasons for acting choices:

Gretel is a resourceful, bright girl who will do anything to protect her brother. In this scene, Gretel's suspicions about the Old Lady are confirmed and she accuses her of being a witch.

2 Acting skills: vocal:

I will play Gretel as having a bright, youthful voice, with a slight rural accent – as she lives in the country. At first, I am trying to be polite and don't want to upset the witch. I will start the scene speaking slowly and clearly on 'And what about all those?' But the pace of the scene will increase and the upwards inflection of my questions will get more persistent until I exclaim 'That's because you're blind!' This outburst is out of character, but I know something is wrong. I will pause before I say 'a witch' for dramatic effect.

3 Acting skills: physical:

At first, I will be smiling, hiding my suspicions. However, as I walk around the room, taking in all the odd things in it, my expression will get more serious. I will stubbornly cross my arms on the line 'Well she is!' I will stand on a bench to gain dominance and point at the Old Lady when I say 'I accuse you of being … a witch!'

Rest of play:

1 Character of Gretel and reasons for acting choices:

Gretel's resourcefulness is important to her whole family. She is always thinking of practical ways to make their lives better. She is bright, yet innocent and doesn't immediately realise her family's problems or the dangers the witch represents.

2 Acting skills: vocal:

Gretel's playfulness, should be shown in her voice. I will use a ready laugh and a cheerful, energetic voice. I work as a partner with Hansel so sometimes we will speak in unison. My optimism will be shown in my singing voice, for example singing brightly 'we are dandy' when clearly the family isn't.

3 Acting skills: physical:

Gretel's confidence will be shown in her lively, energetic movements. I will play her as if she is always busy, confidently putting together her contraptions. She is often protective of Hansel, so I will physically take the lead, grabbing his hand and protecting him. At the end of the play we will both be loaded down with food and our faces will be beaming.

TASK 14

Using the structure of the above plan about Gretel as a guide, create your own plan in answer to the following question:

> You are performing the role of the **Old Lady/Witch**.
>
> Describe how you would use your acting skills to interpret the Old Lady/Witch's character in Act 2, pages 50–51, from '*Enter* WITCH' to 'WITCH *exits*' and explain why your ideas are appropriate both for **this extract** and the **play as a whole**.

TIP

When writing your response as a performer, write in the first person. So 'I would move more quickly' rather than 'The Old Lady would move more quickly.' That will help you to fully imagine yourself playing the role.

Design choices

If you choose to answer question 5, you will be thinking as a designer and commenting on one aspect of design.

For example:

> You are a designer working on one aspect of design for this extract.
>
> Describe how you would use your design skills to create effects that support the action of this extract and explain why your ideas are appropriate for **this extract** and the **play as a whole**.

You may choose to focus on set design, costume design, lighting design, sound design or puppet design. Whichever you choose, you must explain why your ideas are appropriate to the play as a whole. You might refer to:

▶ how your design helps to show the action of the play and the nature of the characters

▶ how your design for the extract is consistent with the design requirements of the rest of the play (for example, don't suddenly change the style of the production)

▶ how you have used design methods that fit in with the mood or atmosphere of the play

▶ props, anything that the actors may carry on stage.

'**Hansel and Gretel**' makes particular demands on the designer because of its non-naturalistic aspects and more fantastical key moments and characters, such as the burning of the witch or the talking animals.

Designers might choose to use levels, trapdoors and 'flying' devices to add to the magical quality, for example by having the Old Lady enter on a suspended bicycle or disappear through a trapdoor. A **revolve** could be utilised to show the journey from the family's home to the witch's.

The costumes might appear to be 'home-made' and thrown together with easily obtained objects or could be elaborate pantomime style outfits.

Music is specified in the script by the many songs and the onstage musicians. Additional music could be added for transitions or to underscore emotional scenes.

Sound effects, such as mechanical noises for Gretel's contraptions or wind and storm noises before the famine, might be added. The lighting could be used to emphasise the unreal fairy-tale nature of the play or to heighten dramatic moments such as the escape from the witch.

A puppet designer might choose to make some of the animals in the piece such as the rabbits or birds as puppets, for example, having hand and rod puppets for smaller animals or a backpack puppet to represent something large such as the Bird.

KEY TERM:

Revolve: a large turntable device that can be turned to reveal a different setting.

Costume design

For the costume design, you might consider:

▶ style, cut and fit of costume

▶ colour, fabric, decorative features

▶ condition (worn or new; neat or wrinkled; clean or stained, etc.)

▶ footwear/headgear

▶ accessories

▶ status or social role of character

▶ make-up and hairstyle.

Below is an extract from a sample response for a design question based on
Act 1, pages 12–13.

Intentions of design

In this scene, I want to establish that the family is a unit together, so the colours are coordinated and they are all dressed in a similar style. ❶ I have decided to update the fairy-tale quality of the story to the 21st century, so while all the characters will be wearing bright colours, the cut of the clothes will be very modern. ❷

Considers colour and shape of outfits

Considers colour and shape of outfits

The recurring fabric will be a red and white gingham. ❸ Father will be dressed in a red and white gingham lumberjack shirt, boots, blue jeans and have a red and white bandana.

Mother will be in a knee-length, red and white gingham, short-sleeved cotton dress with a white apron, and practical flat shoes. Her hair will be up in a neat bun, topped with a red and white bow. ❹

Explains hairstyle

Hansel and Gretel will both be in practical jeans, boots with red and white shirts. Hansel's hair will be tied up in pigtails, using red and white ribbons. Hansel will have round spectacles and always be carrying a book. Gretel will carry a small toolkit with her, showing her early promise as an inventor. ❺

Appropriate use of accessories

At the beginning of the play, they will all look very healthy, and their make-up, with exaggerated rosy cheeks, will emphasise this. ❻

Explains choice of make-up

The completeness of their 'perfect family' look will be a source of comedy and make it more powerful once their situation changes. ❼

Effect of costume choices

Later in the play, their costumes will become more worn. After the famine, Mother will add a drab brown, oversized cardigan full of holes to her outfit and there will be stains on her apron. Father will change into ripped baggy jeans. ❽

How costumes are altered in rest of play, showing understanding

As their parents have sacrificed for them, Hansel and Gretel will manage to look more presentable.

At the end of the play, the parents' costumes will be reduced to rags. Father's jeans will be shredded to knee-length shorts and the mother's dress will be ripped and covered in brown stains. Her apron and cardigan will both be missing and her hair will be loose. Their make-up will emphasise their gaunt, unhealthy appearance with brown circles around their eyes and in the hollows beneath their cheek bones. ⑨

The difference between Hansel and Gretel's relatively healthy appearance and the parents' will add a serious element to the play and emphasise how the children's resourcefulness has saved the day. ⑩

Details of changes in costumes and make-up

Relates to play as a whole

TASK 15

Draw sketches in your notebook showing three stages of the Old Lady's outfit: the Strange Character (page 28); the Little Old Lady (page 39); and the Witch (page 47). Label the three sketches with details about the colours, fabrics and shapes of the costumes and how the costume will demonstrate the change in the effect the character has on the audience.

TASK 16

Write an answer to the following question as a costume designer:

Focus on page 47 from 'BIRDY: Yes! She is a witch …' to '*The* WITCH *exits*.'

You are a designer working on one aspect of this extract.

Describe how you would use your design skills to create effects that support the action of this extract and explain why your ideas are appropriate both for **this extract** and the **play as a whole**.

 TIP

You might want to consider the following:

▶ how your costumes will establish the character of the Witch

▶ how the costumes will add to the element of surprise, danger or comedy

▶ how the costumes will reinforce the style of the play.

After you have completed your work, check to make sure you have:

✓ Referred to fabric, colours, shape/fit, condition.

✓ Included headwear/footwear, if appropriate.

✓ Considered make-up and hairstyle.

✓ Explained how the use of costume helps the action of the extract.

✓ Related your answer to the play as a whole.

Set design

For the set design, you might consider:

▶ stage configuration

▶ how you suggest the location and atmosphere of the location

▶ if there will be any levels, ramps or stairs

▶ the entrances/exits

▶ if there will be backdrops, flats or projections

▶ the colour palette you will use

▶ how the materials, textures and shapes will help to create a suitable setting

▶ which props are needed.

One of the challenges is to decide how realistic or artificial/stylised you want your set to be.

TASK 17

Below are two incomplete mindmaps of set design ideas, one with questions about the setting for the family's home, the other with questions about the Witch's cottage. Copy and complete the mindmaps by answering as many questions as you can.

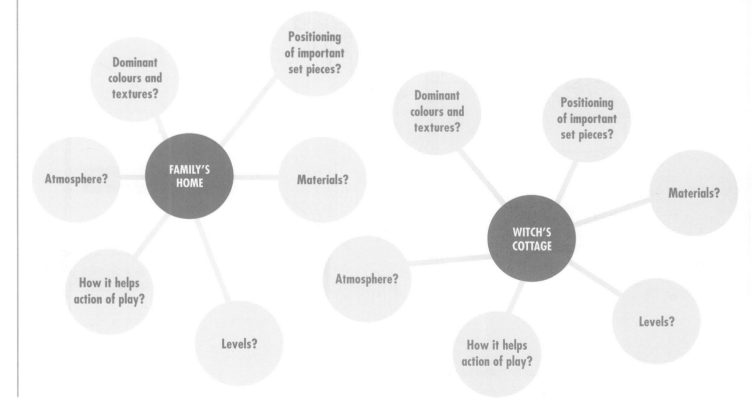

TASK 18

Choose one significant prop or piece of scenery used in Act 1 and one used in Act 2, and sketch several ideas for how each one could be designed. For example, if you chose the cage from Act 2, one version might look like a giant bird cage, with ornate metalwork; another might be a more frightening black iron-steel contraption, while the third might look hand-crafted and wooden. Label each of your designs and decide which you think best meets the needs of your interpretation of the play.

TASK 19

You have been asked to design the set for Act 1, pages 22–23,
when Hansel and Gretel have their second birthday with the potato cake.

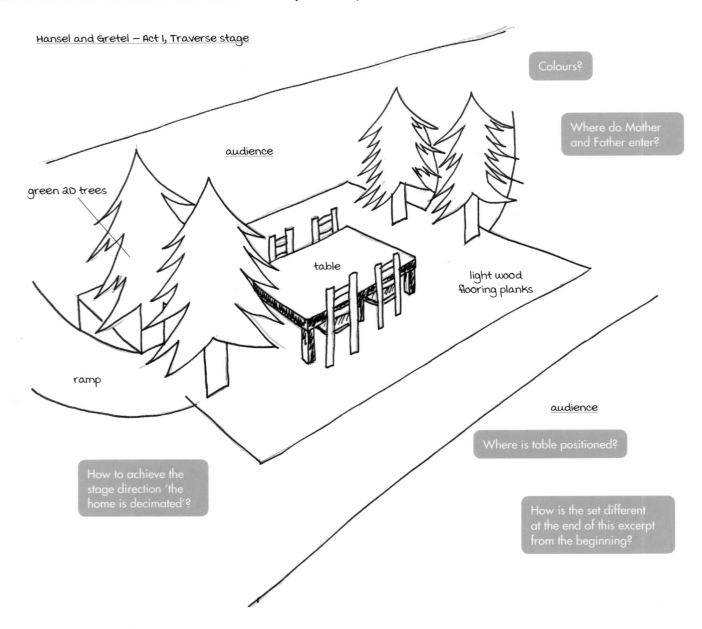

Hansel and Gretel — Act I, Traverse stage

Colours?

Where do Mother and Father enter?

green 2D trees

audience

table

light wood flooring planks

ramp

audience

Where is table positioned?

How to achieve the stage direction 'the home is decimated'?

How is the set different at the end of this excerpt from the beginning?

Choose a staging configuration and then draw a sketch showing:
- the colours and textures you will use (greens? white? browns? rough? smooth? other?)
- the materials for the set (wood? metal? cloth? other?)
- the scale of the set in relation to the size of the actors
- any levels (ramps? scaffolding? trees? benches? stools? table?)
- where key events like entrances/exits will occur.

Then write a paragraph explaining your ideas.

Below is an excerpt from one sample response to Task 19:

Sets out design intentions

In my interpretation of the play, I want to emphasise its storybook quality. ❶ I will have a backdrop of a bright blue sky and evergreen trees showing the woodland setting. There will be holes in the backdrop from which various woodland characters and puppets can appear. For the song, I will have puppets appearing from the holes in the backdrop joining in with the song. ❷ To show that the family live off nature, their table will be a tree which has been split and roughly assembled into a long table with matching benches, which will be positioned downstage centre. ❸ There will be a plaid cotton tablecloth of blue and green on the table.

As I am designing for a thrust stage, I will be able to have tall cut-out trees as well as the backdrop upstage. There will be shorter shrubs and tree stumps downstage and on the sides that won't block the audience's sightlines, but will make the woodland setting noticeable. ❹ When the 'howling famine wind' occurs, I will alter the set by using wires. One wire will yank the tablecloth off the table, while others will pull up the shrubs and raise them up to the flies and out of view. The benches will be knocked over and the puppets will either disappear or be comically dangling from the holes in the backdrop. The family may cower under the table. ❺

Explains how the set can help the action of the scene and considers colours

Considers materials, positioning and desired effect

Considers stage configuration

Identifies how space can be used and effects

TASK 20

Create a design for Act 2, pages 49–50, from Hansel's song to 'WITCH: Now go. Fix the fire' for the theatre configuration of your choice. Sketch and label your ideas. Remember to consider:

▶ entrances/exits and areas for key moments

▶ use of backdrops or projections

▶ the practical demands of the scene

▶ the atmosphere and style of your production.

Then answer the following question:

> You are a designer working on one aspect of design for this extract.
>
> Describe how you would use your design skills to create effects that support the action of this extract and explain why your ideas are appropriate both for **this extract** and the **play as a whole**.

Lighting design

When creating your lighting design you might consider how to create:

- ▶ time of day and, possibly, season
- ▶ atmosphere
- ▶ focus to highlight particular moments
- ▶ how to help convey the setting, action and characters of a scene (such as a follow spot to focus the audience on a character's journey or backlighting to make them appear mysterious).

Some of your tools are:

- ▶ colours
- ▶ angles and intensity
- ▶ light from onstage sources (lanterns, candles, lamps, torches)
- ▶ use of shadow and silhouette
- ▶ special effects
- ▶ use of blackouts or fades.

TASK 21

Below are some short excerpts from various responses to the demands of lighting '**Hansel and Gretel**'. As you read them, highlight in pencil any mentions of: angles, specific types of lanterns/lighting equipment, colours, blackouts/fade, onstage lighting, special effects or shadows.

A

Correct technical term —

When the Strange Character first appears, I will use a follow spot ① with a green gel ② and the rest of the stage will be dim. This will emphasise what an eerie character she is and will also add a 'pantomime' feeling to her entrance. ③

Use of colour

Explains effect

B

To show the deterioration of the family's fortunes, I will have the lighting get duller and dimmer throughout the first act. On page 19, I will have the onstage candle suddenly snuffed out but also dim the other lights as well.

C

In Act 2, I want the Witch's cottage to appear too bright. I will use harsh low-angled footlights, which will throw sharp shadows onto the actors' faces, and use a bright orange gel to make the room appear very warm. Later, when the fire is going out, I will have bright, orange lights projecting from low-angled fresnel lanterns in the wings, casting a light up into the actors' faces.

D

The woodland setting will be created by green lights from textured gobo lights, which will suggest the branches of the forest and mysterious shadows.

KEY TERMS:

Fresnel: a common stage lantern that provides a soft-edged beam of light. It can be used to cover a large area of the stage creating a 'wash of light'. It often has 'barn doors', which are metal flaps at the side to provide some control of the spillage of light. It is usually fitted with a colour slot in which colour **filters** can be inserted.

Filter: also sometimes called 'gels', sheets of plastic used to alter the colour of stage lighting.

TASK 22

One of the most exciting opportunities for a lighting designer occurs on pages 59–60 when the Witch is knocked into the flames and then twice re-emerges.

Sketch three different lighting states you could create in order to emphasise the comic horror of the Witch's death. Think about the angles of your lights, the colours you would use, the intensity and any special effects you could create.

Sound design

When creating your sound design for '**Hansel and Gretel**', you will want to consider how to:

▶ create atmosphere
▶ add to the action and emotion of a scene
▶ contribute to the setting and style of the play
▶ fulfil practical needs of the script.

Some choices you can make involve:

▶ live or recorded sound
▶ volume/amplification (use of microphones)
▶ naturalistic sound or symbolic sound
▶ music.

Below is a sample of possible sound designer notes for Act 1, page 23.

> The woodland: live: offstage, Wilhelm and Johann can be heard playing accordion and a clarinet, perhaps a funny version of a pop 'Happy Birthday' type song.
>
> 'They go to blow': live: the song abruptly stops, possibly followed by the sound of the clarinet shrilly squeaking and the accordion being dropped.
>
> 'But a howling famine wind': live: offstage the actors playing Wilhelm and Johann begin banging pots and howling.
>
> 'FATHER: Oh, damn this famine!': live: offstage, banging and howling stops. Wilhelm and Johann use their voices to make soft wind noises.

TASK 23

Focus on the end of the play, pages 62–63, and make detailed notes on possible music and sound effects that could be used.

Some choices you could make include:

▶ adding recorded music under the scene
▶ having performers onstage or offstage creating sound effects
▶ adding recorded sound effects such as birds singing
▶ experimenting with the volume of the sound (suddenly getting louder or softer)
▶ amplifying or distorting voices by using microphones
▶ if particular music or sound effects should accompany particular characters, such as Graham the ferret
▶ type of music appropriate for any dancing/singing interludes
▶ researching **yodelling** and thinking about the effects you could achieve with this.

Experiment with different versions of this scene and then make notes in pencil in your script about which choices you thought were most effective.

KEY TERM:

Yodelling: a type of singing that involves rapidly alternating between low and high pitches.

Puppet design

Puppets are frequently used in contemporary storytelling. If you choose to design a puppet, you must show how your design ideas will add to the development of the action of the play and be consistent with the mood and atmosphere.

Some opportunities for puppet design in '**Hansel and Gretel**' include:

▶ the rabbits

▶ the hens

▶ the birds that end Act 1 and begin Act 2

▶ Graham the ferret

▶ the miniature house and tiny bird at the end of Act 1.

When designing your puppet, consider:

▶ Type of puppet: for example, you might design shadow puppets, marionettes, hand and rod puppets or giant backpack puppets that are worn by puppeteers.

▶ Materials: wood? Cloth? Bamboo? Willow? Papier mâché? String? Wire?

▶ How it would be manipulated: onstage puppeteer? Held by a performer? Offstage puppeteer?

▶ What are the intentions for the extract and the play as a whole?

TASK 24

Locate every mention of Graham the ferret in the play and make notes on what you think the importance of Graham is. Then draw a sketch of how he could be depicted, labelling your sketch with the following:

▶ Type of materials: fabrics/materials? Fur? Yarn? Wood? Willow? Papier mâché? Cloth?

▶ Manipulation: onstage puppeteer? Offstage puppeteer? Wires? String?

▶ Size: length? Width?

▶ How to create comedy: speed of movement? Comical 'home-made' appearance. Expressions? Amount of movement?

▲ Goose puppet in 'War Horse'.

▲ Little Angel Theatre production of 'Alice in Wonderland'.

▶ For more information on puppet design see 'Texts in Practice', pages 253–256.

PRACTICE QUESTIONS FOR SET PLAY 4

You will answer the first three questions and then have
a choice between question 4 or 5.

SET PLAY 4:
'Hansel and Gretel'
by Carl Grose

4

Extract from Act 1:

Focus on Act 1, pages 31–32, from 'MOTHER *wails to the heavens*' to 'HANSEL *eyes* FATHER *warily.*'

1   You are designing a costume for Father to wear in a performance of this extract. The costume must
    reflect the conventions of contemporary storytelling theatre as used in 'Hansel and Gretel'. Describe your
    design ideas for the costume.   [4 marks]

2   You are performing the role of Father.
    Describe how you would use your vocal and physical skills to perform the line below and explain the
    effects you want to create:

    'Wife? What are you doing?'   [8 marks]

3   You are performing the role of Father.
    Concentrating on the lines from 'I know you do, my dear …' to the end of the song, explain how you and
    the actor playing Mother might use the performance space and interact with each other and Hansel and
    Gretel to show the change from a sorrowful to a joyful response.   [12 marks]

AND EITHER

4   You are performing the role of Mother.
    Describe how you would use your acting skills to interpret Mother's character in this extract and explain
    why your ideas are appropriate both for this extract and the play as a whole.   [20 marks]

OR

5   You are a designer working on one aspect of design for this extract.
    Describe how you would use your design skills to create effects that support the action of this extract
    and explain why your ideas are appropriate both for this extract and the play as a whole.   [20 marks]

Extract from Act 2:

Focus on Act 2, pages 45–46, from *'Enter* OLD LADY' to 'HANSEL & GRETEL *laugh nervously.*'

1   You are designing props or a set for a performance of this extract.
    The props or set must reflect the conventions of the contemporary storytelling theatre used in 'Hansel
    and Gretel'. Describe your design ideas for the props or set.   [4 marks]

2   You are performing the role of Hansel.
    Describe how you would use your vocal and physical skills to perform the line below and explain the
    effects you want to create:

    'Oh. Ha! For a moment there I thought you meant I was on the menu!'   [8 marks]

3   You are performing the role of Hansel.
    Focus on the lines from 'Howboutrabbitrabbitrabbit?' to 'Oh. Why Hansel, *you* are', explain how you and
    the actors playing Gretel and the Old Lady might use the performance space and interact with each other
    to create a sense of comedy for the audience.   [12 marks]

AND EITHER

4   You are performing the role of the Old Lady.
    Describe how you would use your acting skills to interpret the Old Lady's character in this extract and
    explain why your ideas are appropriate both for this extract and the play as a whole.   [20 marks]

OR

5   You are a designer working on one aspect of design for this extract.
    Describe how you would use your design skills to create effects that support the action of this extract
    and explain why your ideas are appropriate both for this extract and the play as a whole.   [20 marks]

5 SET PLAY 5: 'Noughts and Crosses' by Malorie Blackman and Dominic Cooke

Synopsis

Sephy Hadley, a teenage member of the Crosses, the ruling black class, is on her family's private beach. **Callum McGregor**, a member of the Noughts, the white underclass, joins her and asks if he can kiss her.

Callum has passed the test to join Sephy's school, Heathcroft, and Sephy is tutoring him. After she leaves, Callum speaks to the audience about his family: his older brother, **Jude**, and his troubled sister, **Lynette**, who has been changed by a mysterious incident.

His mother **Meggie** is worried about Callum being educated with the Crosses, but his father, **Ryan**, thinks it is the only way he will succeed.

On the first day of school there is a demonstration against the Nought students being taught at Heathcroft. Sephy tries to intervene to protect Callum and the other Noughts, but ends up offending him, by referring to them as 'Blankers'. Later, he asks her never to use that word again.

At dinner, the Hadleys hear Sephy's father, **Kamal**, who is the Deputy Prime Minister, denounce the Liberation Militia, as an 'illegal terrorist group' run by Noughts. Jude supports the group.

At school, Sephy tries to sit with Callum and the other Noughts at lunch. Callum moves away from her. After school, Callum runs into Sephy on the beach. She accuses him of being a snob and they argue. The next day at school a Cross girl gang bullies Sephy. When Callum hears about the fight he tries to see Sephy, but Sephy's mother, **Jasmine**, denies him entry.

At Callum's house, Lynette and Jude are arguing. Lynette believes that she is black and therefore one of the Crosses. Ryan explains that Lynette and her boyfriend, **Jed**, were attacked by Nought men because Lynette was going out with a Cross. Lynette snaps out of her dream-state and realises that she is two years older than she thought and her boyfriend isn't coming back. Later, she tells Callum that she misses living in a fantasy world.

Lynette then goes missing. Police arrive to say that Lynette has died. At Lynette's wake, Sephy arrives and receives a hostile welcome.

Three months later, Callum tells the audience about the changes in the McGregor household. Jude and his father are going to secret political meetings. Callum is the last of the Noughts to remain at Heathcroft.

Two months after this, Callum calls Sephy and they agree to meet at the shopping centre. However, when Callum gets ready to go out, his father forbids him. Callum realises that something is going to happen at the shopping centre and rushes out. Callum pulls Sephy away from the centre as a bomb explodes.

Back home, Callum and his mother watch a report about the bombing, which was carried out by the Liberation Militia. Meggie confronts Ryan and Jude about their involvement in the bombing. Jude says that everyone was meant to be evacuated but Ryan says he planned that people should die, saying he had no choice as he was protecting his family. Meggie says he has been brainwashed and throws him out of the house. Callum accuses Jude of knowing that their father is covering for him and that Jude was responsible.

Act 2, Sephy is at her house telling the audience about Jasmine's drinking. Her father has a girlfriend and is leaving the family after the next election.

A reporter announces that Ryan has been arrested. Callum and his mother discover that someone is paying Ryan's legal fees. Callum is suspended from school. Callum is a witness at his father's trial. Despite the defence, Ryan is found guilty and sentenced to death. Jasmine insists that they go to watch him being hanged.

At the last minute, he receives a reprieve and instead is sentenced to life imprisonment. Sephy and Jasmine argue about 'duty' and Jasmine's drinking.

That night, Callum's house is burnt to the ground. Kamal announces that he is sending Sephy to boarding school.

Callum sneaks into Sephy's bedroom and tells her how angry he is. She responds that really they love each other. They hug and wonder if they should run away together. They fall asleep. They are awoken by Sarah, the Hadley's secretary, and Jasmine at the door. Sarah helps to hide Callum from the suspicious Jasmine. Callum tells Sephy he can contact her at his aunt's address. A reporter announces that Ryan was killed trying to escape from prison.

Now September, Callum is sad because he's heard nothing from Sephy. Jude convinces Callum to take part in something that will 'make a difference'. Sarah arrives with a letter for Callum from Sephy, but she misses him. Sephy leaves for boarding school.

Over two years later, Sephy and Callum exchange letters. She then meets him on the beach. They kiss and a group of Noughts, led by Jude, attack and abduct her. The group demand a ransom for Sephy's release. Callum videos Sephy reading a statement addressed to her father.

When they are left alone, Sephy and Callum make love. When Jude and the others come back, they think Callum has raped Sephy and that she will now have to be killed. Jude and Callum fight and Sephy escapes.

Sometime later, Sephy and Callum arrange to meet on the beach. Sephy reveals that she's pregnant. They are surrounded by police and Callum is arrested. Kamal tells Callum he should convince Sephy to terminate her pregnancy and, if he does, he will commute his death sentence to a prison sentence. Callum refuses. Sephy and Callum declare their love. Callum is hanged.

The play ends with Sephy on the beach holding her baby, Callie Rose.

Context

The content of '**Noughts and Crosses**' is contemporary 'epic' theatre. Epic theatre is a term associated with the German director Bertolt Brecht (1898–1956) to describe a type of political theatre that he promoted. Epic theatre rejects naturalistic dramatic theatre and instead calls attention to the artificial aspects of a play. Some techniques associated with epic theatre include:

- minimal setting
- clear political focus
- **direct address** to the audience
- **episodic** structure
- stylised acting
- use of captions or projections.

The play is set at an unspecified time and place, in what some might think is a **dystopian** world. Although the Noughts and Crosses are inventions of the author, much of the play is recognisable to a contemporary audience, such as the technology, the school and the shopping mall. By introducing the powerful Crosses and victimised Noughts, Blackman wants the audience to examine their own expectations and prejudices. She has said she was inspired to write it based on:

> … a lifetime of experiences. Some of the racist incidents in the book were based on real events from my own childhood. And I also wanted to play with the idea that 'history is luck' to a certain extent. What if Africans had invented trans-oceanic travel and colonised Europe and America?
>
> ('Q&A with Malorie Blackman', www.malorieblackman.co.uk/index. php/qa-with-malorie/)

The playwright and director, Dominic Cooke, specifies in the script that he wants the 'scenes to flow into one another with no gaps' and that there should be 'a minimum of props and clutter'. There should be 'no blackouts except where stated'. This suggests that the play will have to be staged in a fluent and efficient way that avoids the demands of full detailed sets or lengthy scene changes.

However, you may choose to create a design that has more detail and props than the original production, but ensure that you explain your reasons for any choices you make.

KEY TERMS:

Direct address: speaking directly to the audience.

Episodic: a series of loosely connected scenes.

Dystopian: referring to an imagined world where society is presented in a highly negative light. Writers often create dystopian worlds in order to warn people about present dangers.

 CHALLENGE

Brecht famously said that 'Art is not a mirror with which to reflect reality but a hammer with which to shape it.' He didn't want the audience just to be entertained by the play, but wanted them to be educated and encouraged to take action.

Think about the play '**Noughts and Crosses**' and write a bullet point list of what you think the author Malorie Blackman and the playwright adaptor Dominic Cooke want the audience to think about after seeing it.

CHALLENGE

Research production photographs of plays by Brecht or plays with dystopian settings such as '**1984**' by Headlong or '**The Effect**' at the National Theatre. Note any design features that you think could be used in '**Noughts and Crosses**'. Through your design choices, how can you make clear that you are presenting an alternative, negative world, for example by the use of technology or symbols?

► For more about epic theatre see page 200.

Costume, hair and make-up design inspired by context

TASK 3

Using your understanding of the play's context of contemporary 'epic' theatre, create a costume for **Jude McGregor** using the prompts below. You might wish to consider if there are any costume details that will indicate Jude's rebellious nature, his identity as a 'Nought' and his family's lack of money. Will you create costumes that reflect fashions today or create altered 'dystopian' fashions? Will you have all the Nought characters dressed similarly or will their costumes reflect their individual personalities?

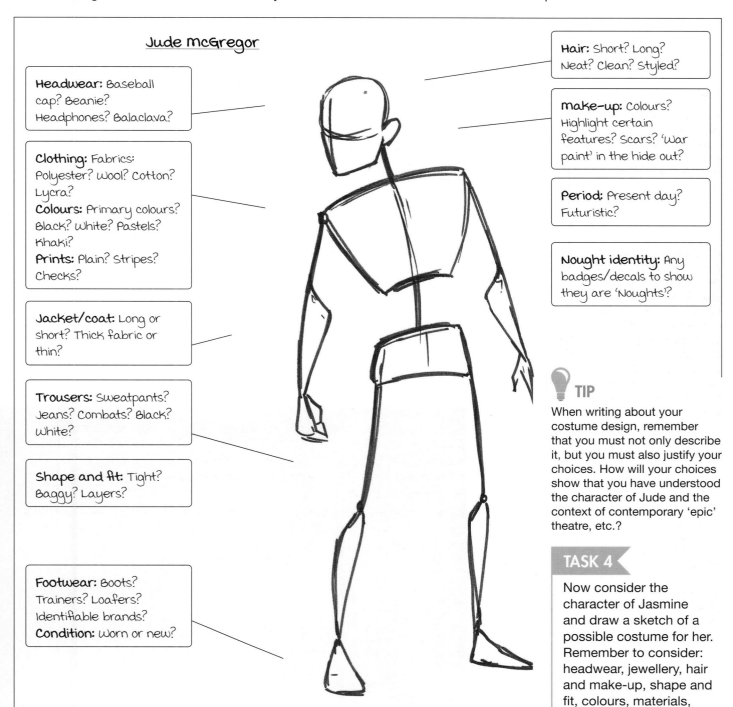

Jude McGregor

Headwear: Baseball cap? Beanie? Headphones? Balaclava?

Clothing: Fabrics: Polyester? Wool? Cotton? Lycra?
Colours: Primary colours? Black? White? Pastels? Khaki?
Prints: Plain? Stripes? Checks?

Jacket/coat: Long or short? Thick fabric or thin?

Trousers: Sweatpants? Jeans? Combats? Black? White?

Shape and fit: Tight? Baggy? Layers?

Footwear: Boots? Trainers? Loafers? Identifiable brands?
Condition: Worn or new?

Hair: Short? Long? Neat? Clean? Styled?

Make-up: Colours? Highlight certain features? Scars? 'War paint' in the hide out?

Period: Present day? Futuristic?

Nought identity: Any badges/decals to show they are 'Noughts'?

TIP

When writing about your costume design, remember that you must not only describe it, but you must also justify your choices. How will your choices show that you have understood the character of Jude and the context of contemporary 'epic' theatre, etc.?

TASK 4

Now consider the character of Jasmine and draw a sketch of a possible costume for her. Remember to consider: headwear, jewellery, hair and make-up, shape and fit, colours, materials, footwear.

Download a printable version from Samples & Downloads at www.illuminatepublishing.com.

Set design inspired by context

Contemporary 'epic' theatre offers many opportunities for designers to use their imaginations and current technology. For example, you could use **projections** to create captions identifying key scenes; video could be utilised to show news reports; a futuristic world could be imagined through choices in colours, materials and architecture. Given the many different locations, you may wish to keep the design simple and flexible. Some scenes occur outside and others inside, so you may consider how your design will reflect this. There may be opportunities for actors to mime objects rather than them being realistically presented. You could think about how the use of levels, steps, ramps or ladders could aid your ability to convey the plot in an epic style.

The chart on the following page lists a few of the key locations of the play with some of the requirements suggested by the script (you may discover others) and some of the design questions to answer.

TASK 5

Answer the questions on each of the settings in the chart on page 127 and add any requirement notes as you discover them.

TASK 6

You are designing props or items of set for Act 2, Scene 21. The props or items of set must reflect the conventions of contemporary 'epic' theatre used in '**Noughts and Crosses**'. Describe your design ideas for the props or items of set.

You should include:

▶ How the props or items of set contribute to the contemporary 'epic' conventions (such as creating non-naturalistic settings, highlighting political message, use of captions, moving fluently from one scene to the next, 'minimum of props and clutter' as specified by playwright/director).

▶ How the objects or items of set contribute to the action of this scene.

KEY TERM:

Projection: projecting a film or still image to form a theatrical backdrop.

TIP

Your set may suggest objects or locations without fully creating them in a realistic fashion. You may want to think of recurring colours or materials to make your design consistent. For example, you may associate a certain colour with all the Noughts' locations and a different colour for the Crosses'. You could suggest that everything owned by the Noughts is old and worn, while everything owned by the Crosses is new and clean. You may have an overall concept of using a restricted palette of colours or materials to create a futuristic feeling to the play or you may look at a particular time period and base your design on that.

TIP

Projections are part of a set and not, as many students think, lighting design.

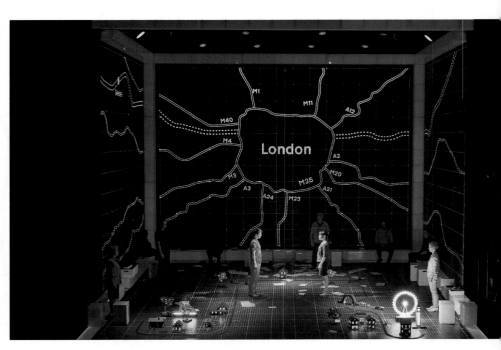

Projections on the walls and floor of the set of 'The Curious Incident of the Dog in the Night-Time' enhance the minimalistic set. ▶

LOCATION: Beach

REQUIREMENTS: Give the impression of being outside by the sea. Isolated/private.

DESIGN CHOICES:

1 Where on the stage configuration of your choice would you place this scene?

2 What are the dominant colours and textures that you would use?

3 Are there any practical items of set, such as a sign, fence or blanket, that you would use to identify it as a beach?

4 Is there any technology that you wish to use such as projections or video?

LOCATION: School dining hall

REQUIREMENTS: Area to collect food. Noughts' table. Seats.

DESIGN CHOICES:

1 This is a complex scene – how will you use the stage space to show: the collection of food; sitting at the Noughts' table; '*the dining hall melts away, leaving CALLUM alone*'?

2 What colours and materials could you use to convey the atmosphere of the school dining hall?

3 How can you indicate if you are setting this in the present day or a future time period?

LOCATION: Sephy's house

REQUIREMENTS: TV room. Empty chair. Suggestion of wealth and space.

DESIGN CHOICES:

1 How will you handle the reporter's speech? Will you use technology to have either a recorded or live version of the projected? Or will they appear on the stage? Or both?

2 How can you suggest the wealth of Sephy's house? How will it differ from Callum's?

LOCATION: The prison

REQUIREMENTS: Execution chamber. Area for Ryan where he could be hanged. Hood. Noughts on one side of the room, Crosses on the other.

DESIGN CHOICES:

1 Where will you place this on the stage configuration of your choice to give this scene maximum dramatic impact?

2 How will you place the Noughts and Crosses groups to highlight the conflict between them?

3 Where will the entrance for the Prison Governor be to give his announcement dramatic impact?

4 What colours will you use in this scene to highlight its frightening nature?

LOCATION: Callum's house

REQUIREMENTS: Table. Chairs. Family home. Not particularly well-off.

DESIGN CHOICES:

1 Where on the stage configuration of your choice would you place this scene?

2 What are the dominant colours and textures that you would use?

3 What style of tables and chairs would you use in order to indicate if you are setting this in the present day or a future time period?

4 Are there any other objects you would use to identify what the McGregors are like?

5 Would you use any captions or projections in this scene?

LOCATION: Café at Dundale Shopping Centre

REQUIREMENTS: Possibly stool for Sephy in café. Large enough stage area to represent explosion at end of scene.

DESIGN CHOICES:

1 Could signs (neon? wooden? illuminated? logos?) be used in this scene?

2 How can you suggest a busy, public space?

3 How can the space be used to show Callum trying to escape? (Levels? Ramps? Running across a wide stage?)

4 Where on the stage will the explosion take place? Would the set alter to show that an explosion has taken place? (Shattered glass? Broken objects?)

LOCATION: The trial

REQUIREMENTS: Areas for the judge, lawyers, accused witnesses and clerk to sit or stand. TV/VCR.

DESIGN CHOICES:

1 How will you create a court-like atmosphere?

2 What objects or set pieces are necessary to convey that this is a trial?

3 Will you show the video on the TV screen or have it projected elsewhere?

4 Are there captions that could make this scene clearer or more powerful?

LOCATION: The Hideaway

REQUIREMENTS: A secret place. Isolated. Video camera. Scissors. Hood. TV.

DESIGN CHOICES:

1 How can you create the sense that this is a hidden space?

2 What colours and textures will you use?

3 How can you create the sense that Sephy is trapped here? For example, if there are windows will they be covered or the doors have large locks?

4 How will this location be different from Sephy and Callum's homes?

Writing about your design ideas

Question 1 will ask you to consider an aspect of design for the play in relation to its context. Below is a student's plan for the following question:

> You are designing a **costume** for **Kamal Hadley** to wear in a performance of an extract from Act 2, Scene 3. The costume must reflect the conventions of 'epic' storytelling theatre used in **'Noughts and Crosses'**. Describe your design ideas for the costume.
>
> 1 Understanding of the character in the play:
> Kamal Hadley is the highest-status character in the play and a powerful member of the Cross community. In this scene he has returned home after a break in order to present himself as the perfect father to the press. His costume is a smart suit, crisp white shirt and tie. Polished shoes. A perfect fit, as if it has been personally tailored for him. Gold cufflinks show his wealth.
>
> 2 Conventions of contemporary 'epic' theatre:
> For my design, I have created a slightly futuristic period, so all the characters' clothes will look very streamlined with slim silhouettes and geometric designs on the fabric. Instead of buttoning down the middle, the jackets will button diagonally across the front. The powerful Cross characters will have prominent collars on their shirts giving them a distinguished look. All the Cross characters are associated with the colour blue – so his suit will be navy blue; his tie is blue with a detail of crosses on it. The details of his outfit in contrast to the simpler Noughts, who will be dressed in drab, brown clothing, highlight the political message of inequality in the play.
>
> 3 Relationship to others:
> When he first enters the scene, Sephy thinks he's come back to stay, he has his jacket off and looks more fatherly, but once Juno, his PR, approaches, he snaps back into Deputy Prime Minister mode and puts his jacket back on and buttons it. His costume asserts his role as a powerful Cross.

TIP

It is important to know that there are many other interpretations of how Kamal Hadley might be costumed.

TIP

You should aim to justify your ideas. Explain why you are making these specific choices, don't just describe what he will look like. How do your choices of fabrics, colours, shape and fit, accessories, etc. help to convey the character, the play and its conventions?

1   Understanding of the character in the play:

2   Conventions of contemporary 'epic' theatre:

3   Relationship to others:

TASK 7

Using the above plan as a guide, create your own plan for the character of Lola in Act 1, Scene 7:

> You are designing a costume for **Lola** to wear in a performance of an extract from Act 1. The costume must reflect the conventions of epic theatre used in **'Noughts and Crosses'**. Describe your own design ideas for the costume.

Practical exploration of the play's style and themes

When writing about performing roles in the play, you must demonstrate that you understand the characters and how they interact. You need to use the performance space to show your understanding of the play. The play's performance style is 'epic'. Below are some exercises to help you explore your understanding of the play, its characters and its style.

'Epic' conventions

Throughout the play Sephy and Callum use direct address to express their thoughts and ideas to the audience. Use the Tasks below to experiment with different ways of directly addressing the audience in the play.

TASK 8

Improvise a short scene in which you describe a recent journey you have taken (to school, to the shops, etc.). Then experiment with the following different ways of telling your story:

▶ Stand in one place and tell your story to your group, making eye contact with them as you speak, as if speaking to your best friend.

▶ Tell your story, but only occasionally look at the audience. The rest of the time you are busy doing another chore (packing a bag or arranging chairs, for example).

▶ Tell your story, but halfway through stop and begin acting out the ending of your journey, miming the actions and speaking the dialogue.

TASK 9

a Many of the scenes in the play begin with Sephy or Callum speaking to the audience and then stepping into the action of the scene. Experiment with the staging configuration of Act 1, Scene 1, when Sephy moves from her direct address to sitting with Callum on the beach and Act 2, Scene 6, when Callum moves from his direct address to testifying at his father's trial. Experiment with how you will use the performance space, eye contact and interaction with others in the transition from direct address to dialogue.

b Act 2, Scene 23 has a more complicated use of direct address when Sephy and Callum speak directly to the audience mid-scene. Experiment with different ways of performing this scene using stylised movement and never touching each other. For example:

▶ Both actors kneel two metres apart and say their lines facing the audience.

▶ Both actors do a series of abstract movements, such as warm-up stretches, while speaking.

▶ Both actors stand facing each other and alternate between looking at each other and the audience.

c Based on your discoveries, make bullet point notes on how you could answer the following question:

> You are performing the role of **Callum**.
>
> Focusing on Act 2, Scene 23 from 'What letter?' to 'Against nature', explain how you and the actor playing Sephy might use the performance space and interact with each other to create a sense of the characters' changing relationship for your audience.

REFLECTION

Discuss the effects the different ways of using direct address had on those watching. Do you think any of these versions of direct address could be used in a production of '**Noughts and Crosses**'? For example, do you think Callum and Sephy should stand still and look at the audience throughout the direct address or try one of the other methods of direct address? (There is no right answer, but it is worth exploring different ways of using direct address.)

Physical theatre

Epic theatre sometimes uses **physical theatre** in order to make its message clearer and more interesting to the audience. For example, you might want to use a stylised movement sequence to show that a group of people are angry or despairing. You might use slow motion to spotlight a moment or to break it down for the audience. There might be recurring movements in order to create a visual **motif**.

TASK 10

a Focusing on Act 1, Scene 20 (the Dundale Shopping Centre), try the following techniques:

> ▶ In a group, create the shopping mall through the use of physical theatre and soundscapes. For example, you could physically create a revolving door; create the sounds of the shopping centre such as the espresso machine or centre announcements; create a synchronised movement sequence showing busy shoppers.
>
> ▶ Use of slow motion: while Callum and Sephy are rushing, everyone else could be moving in slow motion.
>
> ▶ Choreograph a movement sequence showing the power of the explosion using slow motion and sound effects.

b In your script note in pencil any uses of physical skills or the performance space that were particularly effective in showing the tension of this scene.

c Now look at Act 1, Scene 7 and Act 2, Scene 19 and note in your notebooks any opportunities for physical theatre in these scenes.

In physical theatre you may use techniques such as slow motion or still images. From 'On the Waterfront' directed by Steven Berkoff. ▼

Interpretation of character

SET PLAY 5: 'Noughts and Crosses' by Malorie Blackman and Dominic Cooke

5

You will need to show how you can interpret a character. This means that you understand the character's motivations and goals, and the obstacles they face. Then you must be able to use your vocal and physical skills to portray the character and create particular effects for the audience, such as tension, comedy, romance, surprise, pity or sorrow.

Look at one interpretation of the character of **Lynette** (your own interpretation may differ).

FACTS:

Background: *Lynette is Callum's and Jude's 20-year-old sister. Her parents are Meggie and Ryan. She is a Nought. Two years before the beginning of the play, she and her Cross boyfriend were attacked by Noughts. She was in intensive care and has not been the same since*

Job: *none*

Interpretation:

PHYSICAL APPEARANCE:

Lynette is white, like Callum, but believes she is black. As she mainly stays inside, I imagine her to be very pale. She is forgetful and dreamy, possibly doesn't eat regularly, so may be thin.

VOICE:

Her voice is soft and otherworldly. She uses a high-pitched, 'little girl' voice on lines such as 'Don't you think I'm beautiful, Callum?' (Act 1, Scene 2). In Scene 12, when she says she is no longer 'bonkers', her voice is lower and more direct. Although it may seem she is 'better' than in the earlier scenes she is actually less happy.

HAIR:

Blonde, plaited.

COSTUME:

Mismatched, slightly childish outfits. She might wear a child's dressing-up tiara and pyjamas, for example.

BODY LANGUAGE:

She doesn't have much energy and will begin a gesture before it trails off unfinished. In Act 1, Scene 2, she might dance or spin around the room. She frequently looks at her own hands in disbelief. When she sees herself in a mirror she doesn't recognise herself.

TASK 11

Using your own understanding of the characters in the play and how they could be interpreted, create an interpretation of Callum. using the following headings: Age, Physical appearance, Voice, Body language, Costume, Hair, Make-up, Effect on audience.

PROPS:

Mirror? A colouring book?

EFFECT ON AUDIENCE:

From the first introduction, the audience should see that Lynette is 'away with the fairies'. At first she seems 'peaceful' but changes in Act 1, Scene 10 when she realises the truth. She is a tragic figure whose death triggers the actions of others.

Performing choices

In question 2, you will be asked to discuss in detail how you would perform a particular line as a given character.

For example:

TIP

It is important that you write in the first person ('I') so you can fully imagine your own performance of the role. Don't only describe the vocal and physical skills you will use, but also think about how your choices will add to the audience's understanding of the play's meaning, the character and the character's relationships with others.

You are performing the role of _____.

Describe how you would use your vocal and physical skills to perform the lines below and explain the effects you want to create.

Sample:

> **SEPHY: page 14:** '*Us* Noughts and *you* Crosses. It makes it sound like … Like I'm in one world you're in another.'

This is an early sign of the tension between the Noughts and Crosses and the frustration that Sephy feels about these conflicts keeping Callum and her apart. ❶ When playing Sephy speaking these lines, I am repeating what Callum has said but with a stronger emphasis. I will say 'us' and 'you' loudly, with my tone of voice on 'you' making it sound like an accusation. I may mimic his voice in a slightly sarcastic way. My accent is 'posh' or educated upper class, highlighting the difference between Callum and me. ❷ I like Callum, so I'm seated close to him. ❸ I feel a bit bad for teasing him about what he's said, so my voice is softer on 'It makes it sound like …' but I don't finish my sentence, possibly because I think what I'm going to say will only make things worse. Instead I touch his arm when I say 'Like I'm in one world and you're in another.' ❹ I want to show him how ridiculous it is that two people as close as we are should be considered so totally different. I'll smile at him, hoping he'll be more hopeful about the future. ❺ From this, the audience should understand both the problems these two characters face and the attraction they feel for each other. ❻

- ❶ Understanding of character and motivations
- ❷ Vocal skills and explanation
- ❸ Physical skills and effect
- ❹ Physical skills
- ❺ Physical skills, facial expression and effect
- ❻ Understanding of play and characters

TASK 12

Experiment with different ways of using your vocal and physical skills for each of the following lines:

> **RYAN: page 17:** 'We'd appreciate some peace and quiet at the dinner table, please.'
>
> **MEGGIE: page 19:** 'Well, I'm not as naïve as I used to be. Jasmine Hadley opened my eyes.'
>
> **SEPHY: page 22:** 'I never fully realised just how powerful words could be.'
>
> **LOLA: page 30:** 'I bet it was one of her Blanker friends. Blank by name and blank by nature.'
>
> **JASMINE: page 80:** 'Who d'you think paid for all their legal fees, you stupid girl?'
>
> **JUDE: page 101:** 'I didn't think you had it in you, little brother.'

TASK 13

a Make notes on the following:
  - ► Vocal skills: ► Physical skills:
  - ► Effects achieved:

b Then, using the example above as a guide, write an answer to the same question, referring to each of the characters and lines.

c Check your work by writing 'V' next to each vocal skill, 'P' next to each physical skill and 'E' next to an effect. Make sure that you have answered this question fully.

Character revision sheet

Below is an example of a character revision sheet based on the character of
Jasmine, which has been partially completed. Copy the grid and complete

Character and importance to the play	Jasmine She is wife of the Deputy Prime Minister, Kamal, and Sephy's and her sister Minerva's mother. She previously employed Callum's mother, Meggie.
What do they want?	To be admired, part of a powerful, high-status family.
What obstacles do they face?	Her husband no longer loves her. Her daughter disobeys her. Her drinking.
What are their key scenes?	Act 2, Scene 1: After arrest of Ryan. Act 2, Scene 3: Kamal returns for public relations interview. Act 2, Scene 7: Tells Sephy to dress up as they are going out. Act 2, Scene 8: Execution chamber when Ryan is reprieved. Act 2, Scene 9: Argument with Sephy. Act 2, Scene 11: Tells Sephy she is being sent to boarding school. Tries to get Kamal to stay. Act 2, Scene 13: Gets Sephy up after she has overslept. Doesn't notice Callum is hiding in Sephy's bedroom.

How might they be costumed?

Draw a simple sketch or write a description of it. Consider:
- colours
- fabrics
- shape and fit
- character's personality and status

How might their hair and make-up be done?

Draw a simple sketch or write a description of it. Consider:
- style and colour of hair
- type of make-up (realistic or fantasy; colours; how it is appropriate for character, setting and period)

How might they use body language?

- posture
- gait (the way they walk)
- facial expression

How might they use their voice?

Emotional range (angry, sad, happy, irritated, desperate, dominating, etc.)
Pitch and volume (how low or high; how loud or soft)
Accent or other distinctive vocal features

Choose one important line and analyse how they might say it.	Act 2, Scene 12: 'What a lovely family meal! We must do it more often.'

it.

TASK 14

Using the above grid for guidance, create similar revision sheets for all major characters including: Callum, Sephy, Kamal, Lynette, Jude, Minerva, Ryan and Meggie.

 Download a printable version from Samples & Downloads at www.illuminatepublishing.com.

133

Using the performance space and interaction with others

There are opportunities to explore the space and interaction with others in many ways in the play. You might think about how you could include the audience in your performance by **breaking the fourth wall** and how you will move from the **direct address** section of the play to the scenes with other characters. You could consider how the conflict between the Noughts and Crosses is shown in their movements.

When you are writing about how you will use the performance space and interaction with others, make sure that you focus on the effects you wish to achieve, such as tension, surprise, humour, suspense, pity or sorrow, and how you will use your skills to achieve them.

tension   surprise

humour   suspense

pity

sorrow

TASK 15

Look closely at Act 2, Scene 9 (Jasmine/Sephy).

a   Read the scene, taking particular notice of any stage directions.

b   Agree what stage configuration you are going to use: end on, theatre in the round, thrust, promenade, proscenium or traverse. Mark where the entrances will be and any pieces of furniture.

c   Decide what effects you wish to achieve in this scene. To help you do this, answer the following questions on the following issues:

  ▶ What is Sephy's relationship to her mother at this point?

  ▶ Why is Jasmine drinking and how much has she drunk before this scene?

  ▶ Has Jasmine ever hit Sephy before?

  ▶ What are Sephy's motivations in this scene?

  ▶ What are Jasmine's motivations in this scene?

d   How will you use stage space? Looking at the top of page 79, try the following:

'*Sephy takes the bottle.*'

  ▶ Sephy watches her mother pour another glass. Then, without giving a warning or changing expressions, she suddenly snatches the bottle, hiding it behind her back.

  ▶ Sephy explodes in anger when her mother pours another glass and grabs the bottle, holding it up high out of reach from her mother, taunting her.

  ▶ Jasmine reaches for the bottle to avoid Sephy's direct eye contact. Sephy moves closer to Jasmine and stares in her eyes as she grabs the bottle. She steps away when her mother moves closer to her.

Jasmine's reaction

  ▶ Jasmine tries to maintain her dignity and stands very still when she says with authority, 'Give me that bottle.'

  ▶ Jasmine, a bit drunk and woozy, lunges towards Sephy trying to grab the bottle and screams, 'Give me that bottle.'

  ▶ Jasmine, humiliated, sags against the table and, without looking at Sephy, says, 'Give me that bottle.'

e   Continue working through the scene, experimenting with different staging configuration ideas. When you have finished, answer the following question:

> You are performing the role of **Jasmine**.
>
> Focusing on the lines 'You don't know every damn thing, Persephone' to 'And when you realise that, maybe you'll stop judging me', explain how you and the actor playing Sephy might use the performance space and interact with each other to create the sense of the tense mother and daughter relationship for the audience.

Answering a question about character interpretation

If you choose to answer question 4, you will need to write about how you would use acting skills to interpret a character both in the extract provided and in the play as a whole. For example:

 TIP

It is important to include both vocal and physical skills. Highlight key moments when these skills can be discussed.

> You are performing the role of **Sephy**.
>
> Describe how you would use your acting skills to interpret Sephy's character in this extract (Act 2, Scene 13, from 'SEPHY: Just … a minute' to 'SEPHY: Just 'cause I overslept?') and explain why your ideas are appropriate both for **this extract** and the **play as a whole**.

Below is a sample student plan for this question.

This extract:

1 Character of Sephy and reasons for making acting choices:

Sephy loves Callum and they have spent the night together in her room, but she has fallen asleep before making their plans for the future. At the beginning of the scene, she has overslept and Callum is in danger of being discovered in the room by her disapproving mother.

2 Acting skills: vocal:

I would play the opening still sounding sleepy and uncertain. I would pause between 'Just' and 'a minute' to give myself time to decide what to do. Before I open the door, I would use two different tones and volumes, depending on whether I am whispering to Callum or shouting through the door. My voice when speaking to Sarah and Jasmine will sound calmer and less urgent than when I speak to Callum. I will use a sarcastic teenage inflection on lines like 'Big deal' or ''cause I overslept' which will hide my fear that Callum will be discovered.

3 Acting skills: physical:

While keeping my voice calm I will be frantically active during this scene: waking Callum up, getting dressed, helping to hide Callum. One moment of stillness will occur when I say to Callum that we haven't done 'anything wrong'. We will maintain eye contact. It will be clear from his reaction that I am living in a dream world and I quickly change pace, clumsily throwing on my dress. I will take a split second to make sure I look presentable in the mirror. Although this is largely a serious scene, there is an element of comedy when Callum is nearly discovered and I help to hide him.

Rest of play:

1 Character of Sephy and reasons for making acting choices:

Throughout the play, Sephy is bright, passionate and loyal. Caught between her family and her love of Callum. They are like a modern day Romeo and Juliet.

2 Acting skills: vocal:

Anger and sarcasm towards parents, particularly Jasmine. When speaking to audience in direct address I will create an intimacy, explaining my thoughts and feelings. Upper-middle-class accent, confident and articulate at school. Act 2, Scene 21, voice is emotional, frightened. Cries when being filmed for video. Pleading with Callum.

3 Acting skills: physical:

Hunched on the floor in Act 2, Scene 21. In love scene (Act 2, Scene 23) combine direct address to audience (facing them) with stylised miming of undressing and touching, to show love scene with Callum.

TIP

When writing your response as a performer, write in the first person. So 'I would move more quickly here' rather than 'Sephy would move quickly here'. That will help you to fully imagine yourself playing the role.

1 Character of Callum and reasons for making acting choices:

2 Acting skills: vocal:

3 Acting skills: physical:

TASK 16

Using the structure of the plan, on the previous page, for Sephy as a guide, write your own plan for the following question:

> You are performing the role of **Callum**.
>
> Describe how you would use your acting skills to interpret Act 2, Scene 23, from 'CALLUM: You should eat something' to 'Do you?' and explain why your ideas are appropriate both for **this extract** and **the play as a whole**.

Design choices

If you choose to answer question 5, you will be thinking as a designer and commenting on one aspect of design. For example:

> You are a designer working on one aspect of design for this extract.
> Describe how you would use your design skills to create effects that support the action of this extract and explain why your ideas are appropriate for **this extract** and **the play as a whole**.

You may choose to focus on set design, costume design, lighting design, sound design or puppet design. Whichever you choose, you must explain why your ideas are appropriate to the play as a whole. You might refer to:

▶ how your design helps to show the action of the play and the nature of the characters

▶ how your design for the extract is consistent with the design requirements of the rest of the play (for example, don't suddenly change the style of the production)

▶ how you have used design methods that fit in with the mood or atmosphere of the play

▶ props, anything that the actors may carry on stage.

'**Noughts and Crosses**' makes particular demands on the designer because of its short episodic scenes and many different settings. You may choose to have a set upon which specific areas represent certain locations such as a raised area that represents the bedrooms or other intimate scenes and a central area in which all large public scenes, such as the trial or shopping mall, would occur. Another option would be to have a single set upon which simple scene changes could occur by having basic items wheeled onstage or carried on by performers or stage crew. Projections or simple 'flying' of objects such as signs could also aid your design. A revolve could be utilised to reveal new locations.

The costumes might reflect today's society, with recognisable school uniforms for the students and suits for the politicians or you may make a stylised choice. Given the many short scenes, music or sound effects could be vital for creating locations, such as crowd noises to establish the busy shopping mall or the sound of waves to create the beach.

Lighting and sound design could be used to emphasise the horror of certain events such as the near hanging of Ryan or the explosion at the shopping mall.

Costume design

For the costume design, you might consider:

▶ style, cut and fit of costume

▶ colour, fabric, decorative features

- ▶ realistic or stylised
- ▶ condition (worn or new; neat or wrinkled; clean or stained, etc.)
- ▶ footwear/headgear
- ▶ accessories
- ▶ status or social role of character
- ▶ make-up and hairstyle.

Below are extracts from sample responses for a question based on Act 1, Scene 7.

SET PLAY 5: 'Noughts and Crosses' by Malorie Blackman and Dominic Cooke

5

A

In my concept for the play, I want to highlight that this is non-naturalistic production. All the characters will wear jumpsuits, but Nought characters will wear black jumpsuits with white crosses on them while the Cross characters will wear white jumpsuits with black circles on them.

B

I am setting my production in the recognisable present day, as if historic events were different, which caused different people to be in power. Each school girl will wear school uniform typical of a fee-paying school: bright striped woollen blazer with a distinctive badge on it; a pleated grey skirt, a white blouse, knee socks, a tie with a cross design on it. However, Lola is the leader of a gang so will have made adjustments to make her outfit a bit rebellious and different. Her skirt will be shorter than the others and she will be wearing large non-regulation hoop earrings. Before the physical fight, the girls will take off their blazers ready to fight with Sephy, showing that despite their 'posh' uniforms they are willing to get into physical fights.

In my concept, all the characters will wear black trousers and a long-sleeve black t-shirt and simply add one important item of clothing to show the character they are playing. So, in this scene, all the characters will be wearing school blazers with a badge with their character name on it. I feel this fits with the 'epic' nature of the play, as it is non-naturalistic and will help to quickly change from scene to scene.

TASK 17

Read the above responses and write 'D' for any detailed description of their design and 'J' for every time they justify their ideas by explaining why they have made those choices.

TASK 18

Draw sketches showing three different stages of Sephy's costumes focusing on Act 1, Scene 1, Act 2, Scene 12 and Act 2, Scene 21. Label your sketches showing how her costume reflects the changes in her character throughout the play.

 TIP

You might want to consider the following:
- ▶ how your costumes will establish the characters of the Nought gang
- ▶ how the costumes will reinforce the meaning of this scene and the play
- ▶ how the costumes will reinforce the style of the play.

▲ *The choice of fabric, including colour and texture, is important for costume design.*

TASK 19

Write several paragraphs answering the following question as a costume designer:

> Focus on Act 2, Scene 22 from 'The Hideaway' to 'PETE: Good thinking.'
>
> You are a designer working on one aspect of this extract.
>
> Describe how you would use your design skills to create effects which support the action of this extract and explain why your ideas are appropriate both for **this extract** and **the play as a whole**.

After you have completed your work, check to make sure you have:

✓ Referred to fabric, colours, shape/fit, condition.

✓ Included headwear/footwear, if appropriate.

✓ Considered make-up and hairstyle.

✓ Explained how the use of costume helps the action of the extract.

✓ Related your answer to the play as a whole.

Set design

For the set design, you might consider:

▶ stage configuration

▶ how you suggest the location and atmosphere of the location

▶ if there will be any levels, ramps or stairs

▶ the entrances/exits

▶ if there will be backdrops, flats or projections

▶ the colour palette you will use

▶ how the materials, textures and shapes will help to create a suitable setting

▶ which props are needed.

One of the challenges is to decide how realistic or artificial/stylised you want your set to be and how you will incorporate the many settings of the play.

THEATRE MAKER ADVICE

Alice Smith, costume and set designer

I was particularly pleased with how the bomb scene [in '**Noughts and Crosses** '] all came together. At that point we had the first layer of paper ripped off the scaffolding and little bits of paper dropped from the ceiling like debris. It made for a real shock to our audience and then a beautiful moving moment as some music played in the background. Along with the lighting, it made for a really atmospheric end to the first half.

TASK 20

Use the mindmaps below to begin working on your ideas for the following two settings: the shopping mall and the Hideaway. Add more legs to the mindmap to incorporate your ideas.

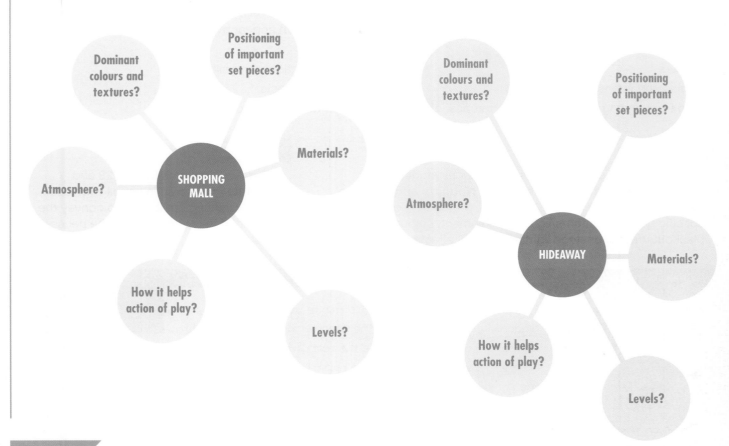

TASK 21

a Choose one significant prop or piece of scenery used in Act 1 and another used in Act 2, and sketch several ideas for how they could be designed. For example, you might choose the school lunch table from Act 1 and Sephy's bed in Act 2. Consider how each item could be used practically and how the design will fit with your other design ideas for the play.

b Create a design for Act 2, Scene 6 from 'THE TRIAL' to 'CALLUM: She's … friend' for the stage configuration of your choice. Sketch and label your ideas. Remember to consider:

▶ entrances/exits and areas for key moments

▶ use of backdrops or projections, if appropriate

▶ the practical demands of the scene

▶ the atmosphere and style of your production.

Then answer this question:

> You are a designer working on one aspect of design for this extract.
>
> Describe how you would use your design skills to create effects that support the action of this extract and explain why your ideas are appropriate both for **this extract** and the **play as a whole**.

Lighting design

When creating your lighting design you might consider how to create:

▶ time of day and, possibly, season

▶ atmosphere

▶ focus to highlight particular moments

▶ how to help convey the setting, action and characters of a scene (such as a follow spot to focus the audience on a character's journey or backlighting to make them appear mysterious).

Some of your tools are:

▶ colours

▶ angles and intensity

▶ light from onstage sources (lamps, torches, etc.)

▶ use of shadow and silhouette

▶ special effects

▶ use of blackouts or fades.

TASK 22

Below are some short excerpts from various student responses to the demands of lighting '**Noughts and Crosses**'. As you read them, highlight in pencil any mentions of: angles, specific types of lanterns/lighting equipment, colours, blackouts/fades, onstage lighting, special effects or shadows.

TASK 23

Read Act 2, Scenes 27 and 28 and annotate your script in pencil with ideas on how lighting could help to convey the actions of these scenes and the necessary tension.

Describes colour and angle of lights

Explains effect

A

In Act 2, Scene 1, I will use a harsh white light, angled sharply diagonally downwards ❶ on the Reporter downstage right to replicate filming lights, ❷ while the rest of the stage is lit with warmer yellow tinted lights. The harsh lights will flick off at the end of the Reporter's section to show the report is over and the 'TV' has been turned off. ❸

Explains transition and effect

B

The lighting in the Hideaway scenes will be dark. I imagine that the windows would be covered, so I will create the effect that all the lighting is coming from artificial onstage lights such as torches or a small table lamp, which will be used during the videoing section. The torches will cast shadows in the room and, when shone on the characters' faces, make them look frightening.

C

For Act 2, Scene 8, I would stress the difference between the crowds watching the impending execution by using a red filter to light the Crosses and a blue one for the Noughts. The red will make the Crosses seem a more violent, blood-thirsty group. When the hood is placed over Ryan's head there will be a spotlight on him, highlighting this moment. At the end of the scene, the lights will slowly fade during Callum's speech, while the crowd disappears.

Sound design

When creating your sound design for '**Noughts and Crosses**', you will want to consider how to:

▶ create atmosphere

▶ add to the action and emotion of a scene

▶ contribute to the setting and style of the play

▶ fulfil practical needs of the script.

Some choices you can make involve:

▶ live or recorded sound

▶ volume/amplification (use of microphones)

▶ naturalistic sound or symbolic sound

▶ music.

SET PLAY 5: 'Noughts and Crosses' by Malorie Blackman and Dominic Cooke

5

TASK 24

With your group, using your voices and any objects you can find, create sound effects for Act 1, Scene 3 (the school gates).

Some effects you could make include:

▶ the sound of the school bell

▶ crowd noises/shouting

▶ police car arriving/police siren

▶ cheers.

Then perform the scene with one person 'controlling' the volume by indicating when noises should get louder and when softer.

Then focus on the next scene, Act 1, Scene 4 (the beach), and discuss how the demands of this scene are different. Make notes on the various ways you could use sound to help this scene.

Some choices you could make include:

▶ adding recorded music in the transition to or under the scene

▶ having performers onstage or offstage creating sound effects

▶ adding recorded sound effects such as ocean waves or seagulls

▶ experimenting with the volume of the sound (suddenly getting louder or softer)

▶ amplifying or distorting voices, by using microphones.

Experiment with different versions of this scene and then make notes in pencil on your script about which choices you thought were most effective.

REFLECTION

Discuss the effect of the sudden silence at the end of the scene.

Note any discoveries you have made in pencil in your script.

PRACTICE QUESTIONS FOR SET PLAY 5

You will answer the first three questions and then have a choice between question 4 or 5.

Extract from Act 1, Scene 21:

Focus on Act 1, Scene 21 from 'RYAN: What's for supper?' to 'CALLUM: It was on the news.'

1   You are designing a costume for Ryan to wear for a performance of this extract. The costume must reflect the conventions of contemporary 'epic' theatre used in 'Noughts and Crosses'. Describe your design ideas for the costume.   **[4 marks]**

2   You are performing the role of Ryan.
     Describe how you would use your vocal and physical skills to perform the line below and explain the effects you want to create:

     'What I did or didn't do is none of your business.'   **[8 marks]**

3   You are performing the role of Ryan.
     Focusing on the section from 'Jude, keep your mouth shut, d'you hear?' to 'It was on the news', explain how you and the actors playing Jude, Callum and Meggie might use the performance space and interact with each other to create the sense of conflict in the family for your audience.   **[12 marks]**

AND EITHER

4   You are performing the role of Callum.
     Describe how you would use your acting skills to interpret Callum's character in this extract and explain why your ideas are appropriate both for this extract and the play as a whole.   **[20 marks]**

OR

5   You are a designer working on one aspect of design for this extract.
     Describe how you would use your design skills to create effects that support the action of this extract and explain why your ideas are appropriate both for this extract and the play as a whole.   **[20 marks]**

Extract from Act 2, Scene 8:

Focus on Act 2, Scene 8 from 'SEPHY: How to make my desperate thoughts reach him?' to 'RYAN: Long live the ...'

1   You are designing a setting for a performance of this extract.
     The setting must reflect the conventions of contemporary 'epic' theatre used in 'Noughts and Crosses'. Describe your design ideas for the setting.   **[4 marks]**

2   You are performing the role of Jasmine.
     Describe how you would use your vocal and physical skills to perform the line below and explain the effects you want to create:

     'Sit down, Persephone and stop making an exhibition of yourself.'   **[8 marks]**

3   You are performing the role of Jasmine.
     Focusing on the lines from 'Not now, Sephy' to 'Long live the Liberation Militia', explain how you and the actor playing Sephy might use the performance space and interact with each other to create a sense of tension for your audience.   **[12 marks]**

AND EITHER

4   You are performing the role of Sephy.
     Describe how you would use your acting skills to interpret Sephy's character in this extract and explain why your ideas are appropriate both for this extract and the play as a whole.   **[20 marks]**

OR

5   You are a designer working on one aspect of design for this extract.
     Describe how you would use your design skills to create effects that support the action of this extract and explain why your ideas are appropriate both for this extract and the play as a whole.   **[20 marks]**

SET PLAY 6: 'A Midsummer Night's Dream' by William Shakespeare

Synopsis

Set in **ancient Greece**, 'A Midsummer Night's Dream' opens in the court of **Theseus** (the Duke of Athens) who is planning his wedding to **Hippolyta**, the Queen of the Amazons. **Egeus** arrives in the court to complain about the love his daughter, **Hermia**, feels for **Lysander** and her refusal to marry **Demetrius**. Ordered to obey her father, Hermia and Lysander reveal their plans to run away to Hermia's best friend, **Helena**. Helena, who is in love with Demetrius, tells him of their plans and all the lovers escape to the Woods. The audience is also introduced to the 'Mechanicals', a group of workmen, including their lead actor, **Bottom**, a weaver. Their 'director', **Quince**, assigns them parts in a play they hope to perform at the royal wedding. They agree to rehearse in the Woods.

The scene changes to the Woods where the warring King and Queen of the fairies, **Oberon** and **Titania**, argue over who should have custody of a changeling boy. In order to get revenge on Titania, Oberon orders his sidekick, **Puck**, to use a special flower to make her fall in love with something horrible. Puck transforms Bottom with an 'ass's head' and Titania falls in love with the donkey-like Bottom. Puck also causes both Lysander and Demetrius to fall in love with Helena and abandon Hermia.

When the spell wears off, Titania is horrified to see Bottom and returns to Oberon. Bottom believes that everything that has happened was a dream. The lovers fall asleep and the spell on them is removed. Theseus arrives, with others from the court, and orders his huntsmen to waken the lovers. Lysander and Hermia are united again and Demetrius declares his love for Helena.

In the final act, the lovers, Hermia, Lysander, Helena and Demetrius, join Theseus and Hippolyta to watch a play about the doomed lovers Pyramus and Thisbe, performed by the Mechanicals in honour of Theseus's and Hippolyta's wedding. The play ends with the fairies blessing the house and Puck invites the audience to applaud.

TASK 1

a Working with your group, create ten still images that capture the main plot points of the play.

b From your understanding of the plot, make a short bullet point list of what you think will be the biggest challenges for performers and designers of this play. In addition to the acting challenges, try to think of challenges for the following design elements: costume, set, sound and lighting.

For example:

▶ ancient Greek setting

▶ transformation of Bottom

▶ creation of mythical/fairy worlds.

▲ *Examples of ancient Greek women's clothing.*

▲ *Examples of ancient Greek men's clothing.*

Examples of ancient Greek architecture. ▼

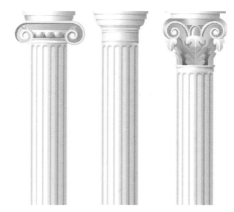

Context

Although the play was written in the Elizabethan times, Shakespeare chose to set it in **ancient Athens** in **Greece**, and this is the original setting you will write about. The play opens in Athens in the palace of Theseus. In Greek mythology, Theseus was greatly respected for his ability to overcome obstacles and win battles. Among his many successful battles was one against the Amazons, a group of warrior women, and he conquered Hippolyta, their Queen. At the opening of the play, he and Hippolyta are discussing their upcoming marriage, which will occur in four days' time. A wedding like this would be an important event as it would represent the uniting of rival groups and also serve as an occasion for a large celebration.

Ancient Athens was a large and important city. It was a centre of power known for its beautiful buildings, such as temples, courts and theatres.

The Greeks believed in a set of gods and goddesses, including Diana, who was the goddess of the moon and hunt. When Hermia is threatened either with death or to go to 'Diana's altar', this means that she would live a 'single life' as a nun in Diana's temple. At this time, a daughter was expected to obey her father's wishes, so her refusal would have been shocking. Her father, Egeus, has brought his complaint to the most important person in Athens and his word would be law.

In term of clothing, **chitons** were flowing tunics worn primarily by men, but also by some women. They could be long or short and were often belted at the waist. Women typically wore a long, draped garment called a **peplos**, which often had a decorative clasp at the shoulder.

Ancient Greek clothing required little sewing, but was generally draped and pinned or held in place with a belt or girdle. The fabric was often plain linen or wool, although more expensive clothing might have some design or embroidery on the borders. Characters such as the workmen might have clothing made of coarser homespun fabric and their clothing often gave indications of their occupations. **Starveling** is a tailor, so his costume might be neatly sewn and precisely fitted. Bottom is a weaver, so he may have woven the fabrics he wears. In cold weather, the ancient Greeks would wear a heavy, wool cloak called a **himation**, which could also serve as a blanket.

When considering your design ideas, think how you may use aspects of ancient Greek architecture and art to influence your sketches in order to show that you have understood the ancient Athens setting.

TASK 2 ◄

On the left and below are some images from ancient Greece. Write a paragraph or create some sketches explaining how these images could influence a designer's concept of '**A Midsummer Night's Dream**' for the first scene of the play. For example, what colours, shapes and decorative features do you notice and which ones could be borrowed to create your designs?

Costume, hair and make-up design inspired by context

Hippolyta was queen of the Amazons. The Amazons were a powerful group of women who were said to 'fight like men'. Although Theseus has defeated Hippolyta and she has agreed to be his bride, you may want to keep some of the warrior aspects of her character in your design. Use the figure below to begin making choices on how you would dress **Hippolyta** in order to portray her character and the setting of the play.

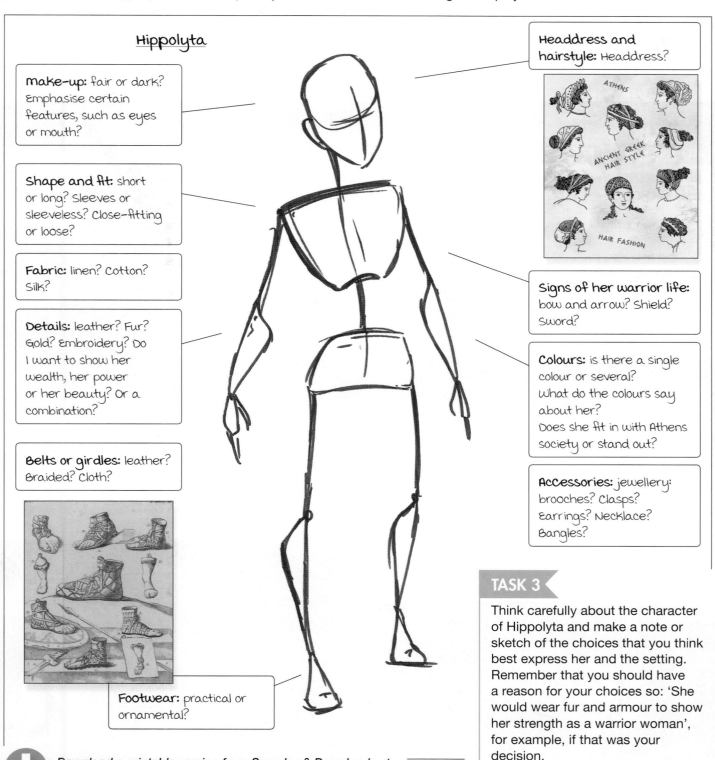

Hippolyta

make-up: fair or dark? Emphasise certain features, such as eyes or mouth?

Shape and fit: short or long? Sleeves or sleeveless? Close-fitting or loose?

Fabric: linen? Cotton? Silk?

Details: leather? Fur? Gold? Embroidery? Do I want to show her wealth, her power or her beauty? Or a combination?

Belts or girdles: leather? Braided? Cloth?

Footwear: practical or ornamental?

Headdress and hairstyle: Headdress?

ATHENS
ANCIENT GREEK HAIR STYLE
HAIR FASHION

Signs of her warrior life: bow and arrow? Shield? Sword?

Colours: is there a single colour or several? What do the colours say about her? Does she fit in with Athens society or stand out?

Accessories: jewellery: brooches? Clasps? Earrings? Necklace? Bangles?

TASK 3

Think carefully about the character of Hippolyta and make a note or sketch of the choices that you think best express her and the setting. Remember that you should have a reason for your choices so: 'She would wear fur and armour to show her strength as a warrior woman', for example, if that was your decision.

⬇ *Download a printable version from Samples & Downloads at www.illuminatepublishing.com.*

Set design inspired by context

Although designs for '**A Midsummer Night's Dream**' often use other contexts, for the purpose of question 1, you are required to base your design on the ancient Athens setting. This provides the opportunity for you to research and be inspired by images from Greek architecture and art.

Below are some of the key locations of the play with some of the requirements suggested by the play (you may discover others) and some design questions you should answer.

TASK 4

As a set designer, you want to show that Theseus's palace is a place of power and order. Here are some Greek architectural and artistic features that you could use: columns, statues, vases, masks, fountains, marble and stone.

Choose the features that you think would help your design and then copy and complete the following sentences:

In order to show the importance of Theseus's palace I would use _____ because

_____

These show choices show the setting of ancient Athens by

_____

LOCATION: THESEUS'S PALACE – ACT 1, SCENE 1

REQUIREMENTS: A palace

DESIGN CHOICES:

1 What choices of materials could you use to suggest the ancient Greek setting?

2 What colour palette would you use to suggest the setting?

3 How might you use common Greek architectural features such as columns or fountains in your design?

4 How could your design show the power that Theseus has in Athens?

LOCATION: ATHENS – ACT 1, SCENE 2

REQUIREMENTS: Place suitable for the Mechanicals to rehearse

DESIGN CHOICES:

1 How will this location differ from that of the Palace?

2 What props could you add to this scene to suggest the ancient Athens setting or the Mechanical's professions? For example, if you set this scene in the Greek equivalent of a pub, what props might be there? If the Mechanicals have arrived straight from work, will they bring any tools with them or carry on working during the rehearsal?

LOCATION: THE WOODS – ACTS 2, 3, 4

REQUIREMENTS: Fairy kingdom, Titania's bower. Location for the Mechanicals to rehearse. Area for the lovers to fight. Area where the lovers are discovered sleeping

DESIGN CHOICES:

1 How will the Woods be different from the formality of Theseus's court?

2 What materials and colour palette will you use?

3 How could your design for Titania's bower be influenced by Greek clothing, such as draping fabrics?

4 Could there be any remnants of Athens' life in the Woods, such as broken statues or columns, or do you want it to be totally different from the Palace?

LOCATION: THESEUS' PALACE – ACT 5 (INCLUDING THE MECHANICALS' PERFORMANCE)

REQUIREMENTS: Palace arranged for wedding celebrations, Area for the Mechanicals to perform their play

DESIGN CHOICES:

1 How would the palace of the first act be transformed for the wedding? What decorations might there be?

2 Where would the stage for the actors be positioned and where would the audience sit?

Writing about your design ideas

Question 1 will ask you to consider an aspect of design for the play in relation to its context. Below is a student's plan for the following question:

You are designing a costume for **Hippolyta** to wear in a performance of this extract from the first scene of the play. The costume must reflect '**A Midsummer Night's Dream's**' original setting in ancient Athens. Describe your design ideas for the costume.

1 Hippolyta's character:

Queen of the Amazons, battled Theseus.

2 Ancient Athens setting:

Chiton, item of dress worn by both men and women, linen fabric, girdle at waist. However, it would be a shorter chiton, showing her strong legs. Laced sandals. Gives a sense that she could run away.

3 Reflecting her character:

Use of leather in belt, arm bands and headdress to show her toughness of spirit and her warrior past.

4 Use of accessories in this extract:

Wears a gold necklace — a gift from Theseus. Shows that he has conquered her and now owns her. Her hair will be up with sharp, spiky pins keeping it in place, but also making her look dangerous. Make-up will be used to darken her skin to a deep olive colour, fitting with the setting and her athletic, outdoor life. Although wearing a white chiton, her other accessories make her stand out from the others in the court.

TIP

It is important to know there are other interpretations of how Hippolyta might be costumed.

It is also important that you discuss make-up and hair design as part of the costume design.

TIP

It is important to explain why you have made your design choices. For example, why you have made them and how they are appropriate for the context, character and scene. You might use phrases such as 'This reflects the ancient Athens setting by …' or 'This is appropriate for a powerful character in this society because …'.

CHALLENGE

In Act 5, Scene 1, we see Hippolyta and Theseus again, after they have been married. What changes do you think might have occurred in the way they dress in this scene compared with the first scene? Will their costumes seem more festive or elaborate? Will there be something that shows they are now a married couple, such as a matching piece of jewellery, a headdress or colour-coordinated clothing? If you were answering a question about costume design, how would you explain your decisions for the different costumes for this scene?

TASK 5

Now answer the same question for Act 1, Scene 1, but focus on Theseus instead.

How will you make choices in his costume that will show:

▶ his status

▶ the ancient Athens context

▶ his character in the first scene?

1 Theseus' character:

2 Ancient Athens setting:

3 Reflecting his character:

4 Use of accessories in this extract:

Practical explorations of the play's characters and themes

Parents and children

Improvise a scene, set in the modern day, in which a teenager does something that makes a parent angry, for example coming in late at night.

The parent's motivation is to make the teenager apologise and promise never to do it again.

The teenager's motivation is to avoid punishment and to convince the parent to allow them more freedom.

Look at lines 22–82 of Act 1, Scene 1 and make notes about how you could use your discoveries. For example:

REFLECTION

a   What types of arguments does each use to get their way?

b   How do they use physical expressions to show their feelings?

c   How could these ideas and actions be applied to Egeus and Hermia in **'A Midsummer Night's Dream'**?

So angry with Hermia I can barely look at her. Stand very upright to show I'm powerful.

EGEUS: ❶ Full of vexation come I, with complaint Against my child, ❷ my daughter ❸ Hermia.

Point at Hermia, emphasise word 'child' – she doesn't know what she's doing.

Spit out the word 'daughter' – she's only a girl, she must obey me.

Love

TASK 6

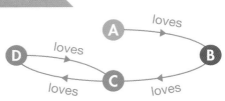

Using the above diagram for reference, create a silent, mimed scene in the setting of your choice (for example, a party, classroom, workplace) where each character tries to get the attention of the person they love.

a   How do the characters show love through eye contact, proximity and gestures?

b   How could this be applied to the lovers in **'A Midsummer Night's Dream'**?

c   Now apply the way characters express their affection to Act 3, Scene 2, lines 43–64, when Hermia is trying to find Lysander while Demetrius is chasing her, proclaiming his love.

d   Make notes on your discoveries in pencil on your script. For example:

DEMETRIUS: ❶ O, why rebuke you him that loves ❷ you so? Lay breath ❸ so bitter on your bitter foe?

HERMIA: Now I but chide; ❹ but I should use thee worse, ❺ For thou, I fear, hast given me cause to curse. ❻

1   What is Demetrius' stance and body language like here?

2   What tone of voice might he use to say 'loves'?

3   How close is he to her here?

4   What might Hermia's tone of voice be like here?

5   What actions might Hermia make here?

6   Where is Hermia looking on this line? Is she making eye contact or looking for Lysander?

Transformations

TASK 7

Working in small groups, choose an animal or bird that you will all become. For example, one group may transform into eagles, while another become mice or panthers. At first you will move around the room fully human. However, when someone calls out 'one' you will assume some characteristics of your chosen animal. As the numbers called out get higher, you will more completely inhabit your animal, so by the time you hear 'ten' you are fully that animal, both physically and vocally. Then practise going straight from one to ten and back.

REFLECTION

a   How did you alter your voice and movement when moving from human to animal? Did you use a different **register** of voice (higher or lower)? What part of your body did you lead from (head, shoulders, hips, feet)? How did the speed of your movement change?

b   How can you connect this transformation to Bottom? Look at Bottom's lines (77–80) in Act 3, Scene 1 as Pyramus. Then look at the lines after he is transformed with the ass's head, from line 97. How can Bottom change his stance and voice to show that he is different? Try a few ideas both physically and vocally. You might consider:

▶ volume, pitch and tone of voice

▶ body language, gait and gesture

▶ how he becomes more 'ass-like' both vocally and physically.

KEY TERM:

Register: the vocal range of the voice (upper, middle or lower registers); the variety of tones of voice.

TASK 8

Imagine you have been asked to answer the following question:

You are performing the role of **Bottom**.

Describe how you would use your vocal and physical skills to perform the lines below and explain the effect you want to create:

'What do you see? You see an ass head of your own, do you?'

Interpretation of character

The vivid and amusing characters in '**A Midsummer Night's Dream**' have contributed to its lasting popularity. A successful production must discover ways of interpreting the characters and bringing them to life for a modern audience. Characters such as Bottom and Puck should make a very strong first impression. Use the mindmaps below to explore how Bottom and Puck could be interpreted. Add more legs to the mindmaps to incorporate your ideas.

THEATRE MAKER ADVICE

Peter Forbes, actor, playing Bottom in the Regent's Park production of 'A Midsummer Night's Dream', 2003.

I think Bottom is written as a larger than life character. He is very forceful in the scene where Quince is handing out parts for the Mechanicals to play. He could appear very selfish, trying to steal everyone else's thunder. I think what lies behind that is a huge enthusiasm for doing the play, and making it as good as it can be. The challenge is to find the right balance between his selfish desire to play every part, and his genuine love of acting and being part of the group. The same applies to the play within a play, 'Pyramus and Thisbe' in Act 5. It would be very easy to send up the acting of the amateur theatricals, but I think the challenge is to play the truth that they are trying their best to be convincing in their roles and to act well. The trick is not to comment on the performance style but to play the Mechanicals playing their roles as well as they are able.

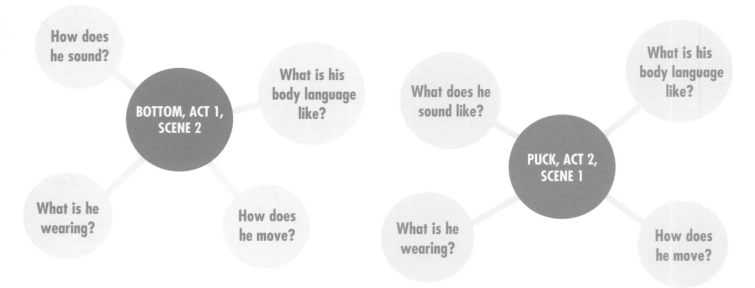

How does he sound?

BOTTOM, ACT 1, SCENE 2

What is his body language like?

What is he wearing?

How does he move?

What does he sound like?

What is his body language like?

PUCK, ACT 2, SCENE 1

What is he wearing?

How does he move?

TASK 9

Draw a sketch or write a paragraph of your first impression of Bottom, including how he would stand and what he would be wearing at this point. Consider what colours and types of fabrics might be in his costume. He works as a weaver. Do you think that would influence his costume?

TASK 10

Draw a sketch or write a paragraph of your first impression of Puck, including how he would stand and what he would be wearing at this point. Consider what colours and types of fabrics might be in his costume. He is part of the fairy kingdom. Do you think that would influence his costume?

Performing choices

In question 2, you will be asked to discuss in detail how you would perform a particular line as a given character.

For example:

TIP

It is important that you write in the first person ('I') so you can fully imagine your own performance of the role. Don't only describe the vocal and physical skills you will use, but also think about how your choices will add to the audience's understanding of the play's meaning, the character and the character's relationship with others.

TIP

Possible desirable effects include:

▶ to show the character's love, shock, anger, reluctance or excitement

▶ to make the audience feel sympathy, amusement, surprise or the seriousness of the situation

▶ to have an impact on another character such as dominating, seducing, teasing or manipulating.

You are performing the role of _____.

Describe how you would use your vocal and physical skills to perform the lines below and explain the effects you want to create.

Example:

> **OBERON: Act 11, Scene 1:** 'Tarry, rash wanton! Am not I thy lord?'

I would speak these lines quickly and sharply, **①** using the lower register **②** of my voice, implying that I am a powerful and important character. **③** my sharp, cutting voice would aim to stop Titania in her tracks when she tries to leave. **④** There would be a slight pause **⑤** before I ask the question 'Am not I thy lord?' I would emphasise **⑥** the word 'lord' in order to establish my status and that I expect Titania to obey me. There could be a seductive tone **⑦** to the question and I would grab her wrist on the final word, pulling her closely to me to demonstrate my physical dominance over her.

- Use of pace
- Use of pitch

- Desired effects
- Desired effects
- Use of pause
- Use of inflection

- Use of intonation

TASK 11

Experiment with different ways of using your vocal and physical skills for each of the following lines:

HELENA: Act 2, Scene 1: 'I am your spaniel; and, Demetrius, The more you beat me I will fawn on you.'

DEMETRIUS: Act 3, Scene 2: 'O Helen, goddess, nymph, perfect, divine – To what, my love, shall I compare thine eyne?'

HERMIA: Act 3, Scene 2: 'O me, you juggler, you canker-blossom, You thief of love!'

TITANIA: Act 4, Scene 1: 'O, how I love thee! How I dote on thee!'

BOTTOM: Act 4, Scene 1: 'It shall be called "Bottom's Dream", because it hath no bottom; and I will sing it in the latter end of a play before the Duke.'

PUCK: Act 5, Scene 1: 'Give me your hands if we be friends, And Robin shall restore amends.'

TASK 12

a Make notes on the following:
   ▶ Vocal skills: ▶ Physical skills:
   ▶ Effects achieved:

b Then, using the example above as a guide, write an answer to the same question referring to each of the characters and lines above.

c Check your work by writing 'V' next to each vocal skill, 'P' next to each physical skill and 'E' next to any mention of effects. Check your work ensuring that you have answered this question fully.

Character revision sheet

Below is an example of a character revision sheet based on the character of **Oberon**, which has been partially completed. Copy the grid and complete it.

Character and importance to the play	Oberon Oberon is King of the fairies. His war with Titania causes conflict in the woods. His plot to get revenge on her causes the misunderstandings between the lovers.
What do they want?	To get revenge on Titania for not giving him the changeling boy.
What obstacles do they face?	Titania is fighting with him and Puck puts the secret spell on the wrong lover.
What are their key scenes?	Act 2, Scene 1: argument with Titania Act 3, Scene 2: scene with Puck when he discovers Puck has put the spell on the wrong lover. Act 4, Scene 1: wakes Titania and they are reunited. Act 5, Scene 1: blessing the house.

How might they be costumed?	How might their hair and make-up be done?
Draw a simple sketch or write a description of it. Consider: • colours • fabrics • shape and fit • character's personality and status	Draw a simple sketch or write a description of it. Consider: • style and colour of hair • type of make-up (realistic or fantasy; colours; how it is appropriate for character, setting and period)

How might they use body language?	
• posture • gait (the way they walk) • facial expression	

How might they use their voice?	
Emotional range (angry, sad, happy, irritated, desperate, dominating, etc.) Pitch and volume (how low or high; how loud or soft) Accent or other distinctive vocal features	

Choose one important line and analyse how they might say it.	Act 2, Scene 2 'Ill met by moonlight, proud Titania.'

TASK 13

Copy a blank version of the above grid into your exercise book and then complete a similar sheet for each of the major characters in the play, including: Helena, Hermia, Lysander, Demetrius, Titania, Oberon, Puck and Bottom.

 Download a printable version from Samples & Downloads at www.illuminatepublishing.com.

Using the performance space and interaction with others

There are many exciting opportunities to use the performance space in a creative and exciting way in '**A Midsummer Night's Dream**'.

For example, in Act 3, Scene 2 there is an argument between the lovers, when Lysander and Demetrius pursue Helena and reject Hermia. The staging configuration needs to reflect the changing emotions and affections of the characters. For example, think about when a character:

▶ may be isolated or excluded by other characters

▶ may seek affection or protection from another character

▶ might try to separate other characters from each other.

TASK 14

Read the scene from Hermia's line 'Why are you grown so rude?' (line 262) to Hermia's line 'Why, get you gone! who is't that hinders you?' (line 317) and answer the following questions:

a   Pick a stage configuration (theatre in the round, thrust, end on, traverse, proscenium) and explain how you will use it to best serve the scene. For example, have you chosen a stage configuration that will encourage entrances through the audience or one that allows for large pieces of scenery the characters might use?

b   In the beginning of this scene, Hermia believes that Lysander still loves her. How would you, as an actor playing Hermia, use the following techniques in order to pursue Lysander and get his attention? Consider:

   ▶ eye contact   ▶ proximity

   ▶ gesture   ▶ touch

   ▶ movement towards him or away from him.

c   Looking closely at Lysander's lines that begin 'Ay, by my life' (line 277), explore how you as the actor playing Lysander can convey his rejection of Hermia and love for Helena using the following:

   ▶ eye contact (or avoidance of eye contact)

   ▶ proximity

   ▶ gesture

   ▶ movement towards or away from other characters.

d   Helena and Hermia turn against each other in this scene. Create a still image to convey their relationship on the following lines:

> **HERMIA:** But that my nails can reach unto thine eyes.
>
> **HELENA:** I pray you, though you mock me, gentlemen
> Let her not hurt me.

Once you've completed the still image, either have someone take a photograph of it or quickly sketch the positions you have assumed. Then annotate it with notes about how you have used gesture and body language to express their relationship at this point. This may be useful for describing how you could use physical skills on a particular line.

▲ Hermia turns against Helena in Act 3 of 'A Midsummer Night's Dream'.

 TIP

Look for turning points in scenes when emotions or relationships change. Make sure that in the movements it is clear when Hermia decides that they have joined forces against her or when she decides to blame Helena.

Sample response based on Act 2, Scene 1, from 'And even for that do I love you the more' to 'Unworthy as I am, to follow you.'

Q3. You are performing the role of **Helena**. Focusing on this extract, explain how <u>you</u> and the <u>actor playing Demetrius</u> might use the <u>performance space</u> and <u>interact</u> with each other as you perform this speech to <u>amuse</u> and <u>surprise</u> the audience. ❶

> Underlining key words like this helps to make sure you are covering all aspects of the question

We will be performing this scene in the round ❷ on a stage that will have several fallen trees on it, which will cause obstacles for us when I, as Helena, am chasing Demetrius, and allow us to use levels to establish our relationship. ❸

> Starts immediately with correct terminology, but could explain why that is helpful for this scene (i.e. constant movement, proximity of audience)

I love Demetrius and refuse to accept his rejection, ❹ so I will try to maintain eye contact with him and establish as close a proximity as possible. This will be amusing to the audience because the boundaries and behaviour that were observed in Court have clearly broken down. For example, I will pursue Demetrius and then trip over one of the tree branches, so that I am actually on the ground when I say the line 'I am your spaniel'. ❺ The audience will be shocked and amused because my position will suggest how far I am willing to lower myself, but also that I literally will be on the ground like a dog. Demetrius will show his dominance by standing on one of the fallen trees, making him even higher over me, and will kick out at me and turn his back when I say 'strike me'. ❻ This will be surprising to the audience because this is not how we expect men to behave towards women.

> Shows an understanding of the purpose of the scene and how setting can enhance it
> Understanding of character's motivations

> Provides detailed example of staging configurations relating to dialogue

> Shows how levels can enhance interaction

On the lines, 'neglect me, lose me' I will crawl towards him and reach for his ankles, causing him to jump away from me. My posture at the end of this speech will be slumped and defeated. I will hold my hands before me in a pleading gestures and look at him sadly, willing him to change his mind. ❼

> Suggests appropriate use of gesture

Answering a question about character interpretation

If you choose to answer question 4, you will be writing about your interpretation of a character. For example:

Focusing on Act 1, Scene 1 from Lysander's line 'How now my love' (line 128) to his line 'So quick bright things come to confusion' (line 149) answer the following question:

> You are performing the role of **Hermia**. Describe how you would use your acting skills to interpret her character in **this extract** and in the **play as a whole**.

Below is a sample plan in response to this question.

Planning

Intro about Hermia:

Type of character she is and her motivations: relationship with father, threat of death or a single life; love for Lysander.

Extract

1 Use of facial expressions and voice: thinks she is going to cry: 'tempest of my eyes'.

2 Relationship/interaction with Lysander: they work as a team, but she is angrier than he is.

3 In love: close proximity to Lysander, use of eye contact.

Rest of play

1 Rest of play: defiant in first scene, proud posture, firm tone of voice.

2 Rest of play: change in Act 3, Scene 2, confused and hurt, then angry with Helena.

3 Rest of play: comic fight, jump on Lysander's back, chase Helena as if to scratch out her eyes.

4 Rest of play: Act 5: return to loving character.

Conclusion:

How your acting choices will show how Hermia changes and develops in the play.

> **KEY TERM:**
> **Proximity:** the distance between people or objects; how near or far.

TASK 15

Using the above plan as a guide, create your own plan in answer to the following question:

> Focusing on Act 3, Scene 1 from Bottom's line 'Are we all met' (line 1) to Snout's line 'Will not the ladies be afeard of the lion?' (line 25), answer the following question:
>
> You are performing the role of **Bottom**. Describe how you will use your acting skills to interpret Bottom's character in **this extract** and the **rest of the play.**

1 Use of facial expressions and voice:

2 Relationship/interaction with Lysander:

3 In love:

TASK 16 CONTINUED ON PAGE 156

Focus on Act 5, Scene 1 from '*Enter* FLUTE *as* THISBE' to '*Exeunt* BOTTOM *and* FLUTE'.

Consider voice and physical skills: how will the actor playing Flute change his voice and movements in order to create the character of Thisbe? Vocally, remember to consider: tone, pitch, pace, volume, emphasis and accent. For movement, think about: gestures, eye contact, posture and use of space.

Comic effects: how can the actors use the performance space and their interactions with each other to create comic effects?

Consider: the timing of the approaches to the wall; if anything goes wrong when they are speaking through the wall; any exaggerated romantic positions they might assume; how each of the characters exits.

'How now my love.'

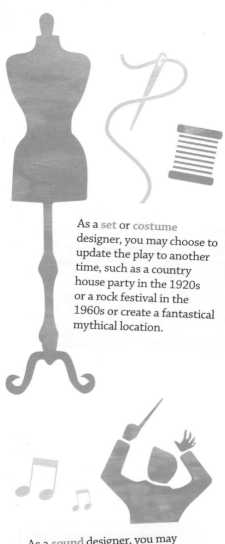

As a set or costume designer, you may choose to update the play to another time, such as a country house party in the 1920s or a rock festival in the 1960s or create a fantastical mythical location.

As a sound designer, you may choose to find music that reflects a certain time period or you could consider having onstage musicians. Sound effects or use of microphones could help to create magical effects in the Woods.

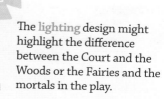

The lighting design might highlight the difference between the Court and the Woods or the Fairies and the mortals in the play.

TASK 16 CONTINUED

The rest of the play: in Act 1, Scene 2 how can you portray Flute's attitude about playing a female character in the play? How might he react when Bottom is transformed in Act 3, Scene 1? How could comedy be created in his final speech as Thisbe?

Then answer the following question:

> You are performing the role of **Flute**.
>
> Describe how you would use your acting skills to interpret Flute's character in this extract and explain why your ideas are appropriate both for **this extract** and the **play as a whole**.

Design choices

If you choose to answer question 5, you will be thinking as a designer and commenting on one aspect of design.

For example:

> You are a designer working on one aspect of design for this extract.
>
> Describe how you would use your design skills to create effects that support the action of this extract and explain why your ideas are appropriate for **this extract** and the **play as a whole**.

You may choose to focus on set design, costume design, lighting design, sound design or puppet design. Whichever you choose, you must explain why your ideas are appropriate to the play as a whole. You might refer to:

▶ how your design helps to show the action of the play and the nature of the characters

▶ how your design for the extract is consistent with the design requirements of the rest of the play (for example, don't suddenly change the style of the production)

▶ how you have used design methods that fit in with the mood or atmosphere of the play

▶ how your understanding of the technical aspects of your chosen design specialism will support your design ideas

▶ props, anything that the actors may carry on stage.

'A Midsummer Night's Dream' offers many opportunities for a designer to show their imagination and design flair. Question 1 of the examination focuses on the ancient Athens setting of the play and for question 5, you may wish to continue looking at this context or you may choose another setting that you believe would demonstrate your understanding of the play and its design possibilities. Whichever design specialism you choose you will want to consider how you can show the three worlds of the play:

▶ the **Court** (including Theseus, Hippolyta, Egeus and the lovers)

▶ the **Fairies** (including Titania, Oberon and Puck)

▶ the **Mechanicals** (including Bottom, Quince and Flute).

Costume design

For the costume design, you might consider:

▶ style, cut and fit of costume

▶ colour, fabric, decorative features

▶ realistic or stylised

▶ condition (worn or new; neat or wrinkled; clean or stained, etc.)

▶ footwear/headgear

▶ accessories

▶ status or social role of character

▶ make-up and hairstyle.

As a costume designer you will be responsible for designing costumes, including practical choices about the fabrics and fit, for the play's characters. You may wish to:

▶ establish the differences or similarities between the three worlds of the play

▶ show aspects of each character's personality and their role in the world

▶ show if the characters change in the course of the play.

Unlike question 1, for this question you do not have to follow the ancient Athenian setting. However, if you plan to retain it, your court characters might wear light, flowing clothes. Men would wear short tunics, belted at the waist and sandals. The women would wear long linen dresses. However, by Act 3, they have been fighting and tramping through the Woods, so their clothes might be muddy.

In contrast, at the end of the play, they might be dressed in their finest clothes to celebrate the Court wedding. You might want to colour-coordinate outfits to indicate that they have ended up with the correct person.

On the other hand, you may choose to update your setting, and the fabrics and silhouette of the costumes will reflect your choices, but make sure you still consider how the characters, their roles and status in this world created by your production are shown by their costumes.

The Mechanicals need to be shown to be of a different class from the Court characters. Designers may establish this by a choice of rough fabrics to create practical work clothes for them. Some designers seek to differentiate each of the workmen by showing some aspects of their professions, so Starveling, who is a tailor, might wear glasses because his work requires close attention to detail, and his clothes are neat and well-sewn. Tinkers, like Snout, hammer metal objects in hot forges, so he might have a costume that is more soiled from work and allows freedom of movement.

Bottom undergoes an important transformation when Puck puts an ass's head on him and it is up to the designer how realistic or fantastical this will be. Additionally, all of the Mechanicals will wear different outfits in Act 5 when they perform their play for the Court.

TASK 17

Create three images for Bottom showing how he will be costumed:

a when he is rehearsing

b when he is transformed

c in the final act, when he is playing Pyramus.

Consider: fabrics, shape and fit, colours, character, status and setting.

SET PLAY 6: 'A Midsummer Night's Dream' by William Shakespeare **6**

TIP

If it is helpful to you, you may support your answer with sketches or diagrams.

▲ *The lovers fight in Act 3 of 'A Midsummer Night's Dream' Young Vic, 2017.*

▲ *The lovers fight in Act 3 of 'A Midsummer Night's Dream', National Theatre, 1992.*

TIP

If you are going to have an artificial ass's head for Bottom – what materials might you use? Papier mâché? Fabric? Canvas over a wooden or willow frame? Will it fully cover his face or only part of it? Will it have any special features such as a moving mouth or ears? Are there any ways this costume will add to the comedy of the scene?

The fairies offer a particularly creative opportunity for designers. Some are inspired by traditional images from fairy tales, choosing pastel colours and shimmering wings, while others seek their inspiration in nature, using feathers, animal or reptile-style skin and earthen colours. Others alter more modern clothing to create an effect that is magical and playful, such as the 1989 Royal Shakespeare Company punk-inspired production, which dressed the fairies in tutus and Doc Marten's boots. A 2016 Shakespeare's Globe production was influenced by Bollywood, yet retained features of Elizabethan dress, such as ruffs and farthingales (a hooped skirt).

There are many opportunities for using make-up to create the fairy-tale world, such as: body paint; coloured foundations; strong eye make-up; animal- or floral-inspired designs.

TASK 18

In the final act of the play, the Mechanicals perform for Theseus, his bride Hippolyta and their wedding guests. Read Act 5, Scene 1 from Flute's line 'My love! Thou art my love, I think?' (line 191) to Snout's line 'And being done, thus Wall away doth go' (line 202) and then complete the following:

a   Draw a sketch of a design for the Wall costume for Snout in order to create a comic effect that fits with his character.

b   Design: draw a sketch of the wig, make-up and costume that will transform Flute into the Greek tragic heroine, Thisbe.

c   Then answer the following question as a costume designer:

> Describe how you would use your design skills that support the action of this extract and explain why your ideas are appropriate both for **this extract** and the **play as a whole**.

After you have completed your work, check to make sure you have:

✓ Referred to fabric, colours, shape/fit, condition.

✓ Included headwear/footwear, if appropriate.

✓ Considered make-up and hairstyle.

✓ Explained how the use of costume helps the action of the extract.

✓ Related your answer to the play as a whole.

Set design

For the set design, you might consider:

▶ stage configuration

▶ how you suggest the location and atmosphere of the location

▶ if there will be any levels, ramps or stairs

▶ the entrances/exits

▶ if there will be backdrops, flats or projections

▶ the colour palette you will use

▶ how the materials, textures and shapes will help to create a suitable setting

▶ which props are needed.

One of the challenges is to decide how realistic or artificial/stylised you want your set to be and how you will incorporate the different settings of the play.

There are two main settings for the play: the **Court** and the **Woods**. Most modern productions differentiate between these settings through specific design choices. When developing your set design you should consider the:

▶ atmosphere and mood

▶ practical requirements of the set and how the performers can use the space

▶ location and how it helps to tell the story.

You will wish to establish a very different atmosphere in the Court from the Woods. Below are two sample mindmaps with early ideas for contrasting the two locations (your ideas may be different). Copy the mindmaps below and add more legs to incorporate your ideas.

Authority · Sharp lines · Marble · Clean · **COURT** · White · Smooth · Draping fabrics · Day

Disorder · Dirt · Shadows · Dark · **WOODS** · Mysterious · Green · Night · Rough textures

For the Court, you may want a set that suggests Theseus's power and importance. You could emphasise the classical setting of the opening by researching Greek architecture and its use of columns and sculptures. If updating your setting, you will want to find another location that will show Theseus' authority and provide a contrast to the Woods, whether it is the 1920s drawing room of a local aristocrat or the palatial offices of a film producer.

In contrast, the Woods may be freer and wilder. You may wish to explore how nature can be presented onstage. In the Woods, there are a number of instances when characters overhear others, so you may want to establish where the characters can hide. Some productions use levels to good advantage, having sections of the set constructed on higher planes upon which the characters, such as an acrobatic Puck, can climb or Titania can use as a magical sleeping **bower**.

KEY TERM:

Bower: an enclosed, shady place under branches of trees.

TASK 19

Focus on Act 2, Scene 1, the scene between Puck and the Fairy, draw a sketch of the Woods for the stage configuration of your choice that highlights:

▶ the period and atmosphere of the setting you have chosen

▶ the colours and textures of your design (consider, for example, if the flooring will be smooth or covered with dirt, straw, mud or leaves)

▶ how the actors could use the space (for example, climbing a tree, running down a ramp, hiding behind a shrub)

▶ if your Woods will be realistic or more fantastical.

Now is the mural down between the two neighbours.

TASK 20

Create a design for Act 5, Scene 1 from 'QUINCE: Gentles, perchance …' to 'THESEUS: Now is the mural down between the two neighbours' for the theatre configuration of your choice. Sketch and label your ideas. Remember to consider:

▶ entrances/exits and areas for key moments

▶ use of backdrops, curtains or projections, if appropriate

▶ the practical demands of the scene (where will the Mechanicals enter and perform? Where will the Court audience sit?)

▶ the atmosphere and style of your production (for example, if there are any opportunities for your design to highlight the comedy of this scene).

Here is one option of a theatre in the round setting (yours may be different):

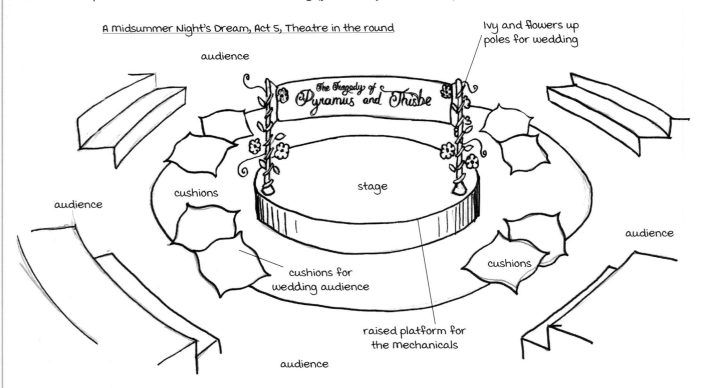

A Midsummer Night's Dream, Act 5, Theatre in the round

Then answer this question:

> You are a designer working on one aspect of design for this extract.
>
> Describe how you would use your design skills to create effects that support the action of this extract and explain why your ideas are appropriate both for **this extract** and the **play as a whole**.

Lighting design

When creating your lighting design you might consider how to create:

▶ time of day and, possibly, season

▶ atmosphere

▶ focus to highlight particular moments

▶ an impression of the setting, action and characters of a scene (such as a follow spot to focus the audience on a character's journey or backlighting to make them appear mysterious).

Some of your tools are:

▶ colours

▶ angles and intensity

▶ light from onstage sources (lanterns, candles, lamps, torches)

▶ use of shadow and silhouette

▶ special effects

▶ use of blackouts or fades.

SET PLAY 6:
'A Midsummer Night's Dream'
by William Shakespeare

6

TASK 21

Below are some short excerpts from various responses to the demands of lighting '**A Midsummer Night's Dream**'. As you read them, highlight any mentions of: angles, specific types of lanterns/lighting equipment, colours, blackouts/fade, onstage lighting, special effects or shadows.

A

For Act 2, Scene 1, I will have Titania and Oberon backlit by a large shining moon, so that they are seen in silhouette on the line 'Ill met by moonlight'. ❶ Then I will use profile spots to highlight their faces ❷ in the scene in order that their expressions can be read more clearly by the audience.

> Uses correct technical term and explains effect

> Uses correct technical term and explains effect

B

For Act 1, Scene 1, the Court will be lit with a bright rosy wash of front lighting, which will highlight the rich fabrics used in the palace. As my production is set on a Greek island, I will also use yellow filtered side lighting to represent the light entering the palace windows showing the sunny weather.

C

I will use dim lighting to create the mystery of the Woods. At the beginning of Act 2, Scene 1, the fairy will enter carrying a lantern that will bob about as she converses with Puck, adding to the humour of the scene. The trees in the Woods will be illuminated by multi-coloured fairy lights.

D

In Act 3, Scene 2, I will use a smoke machine or dry ice to create a mist that the lovers must travel through. The stage lighting will be textured with gobos, which will cast shadows, making it easier for Puck to appear and disappear.

KEY TERM:

Gobos: metal cut-outs that are used to project patterns, such as leaves, stars, swirls or waves.

E

As I want the scenes to flow into each other, I won't use any blackouts, but, in the transition from Act 1 to Act 2, the lights will dim and the filtered lights will change from yellows and oranges to silvery blue colours. In Act 4, Scene 1, there will be low-angled, rose-tinted lighting to suggest sunrise.

'This is the *Woman* but not this the *Man'*

TASK 22

Read Act 3, Scene 2 from the opening to 'PUCK: This is the woman, but not this the man.' Make notes in your script, in pencil, on how you could use lighting to do the following:

- ▶ create the location of the Woods and the darkness of the night-time setting
- ▶ create shadows and mystery
- ▶ highlight the entrance of Demetrius and Hermia.

Sound design

When creating your sound design for '**A Midsummer Night's Dream**', you will want to consider how to:

- ▶ create atmosphere
- ▶ add to the action and emotion of a scene
- ▶ contribute to the setting and style of the play
- ▶ fulfil practical needs of the script.

Some choices you can make involve:

- ▶ live or recorded sound
- ▶ volume/amplification (use of microphones)
- ▶ naturalistic sound or symbolic sound
- ▶ music.

TASK 23

With your group, using your voices and any objects you can find, create sound effects to show the transition from Act 1, Scene 2 to Act 2, Scene 1.

Some effects you could make for Act 1, Scene 2:

- ▶ the sounds appropriate for where the Mechanicals are meeting (a pub? a village hall? a school?)
- ▶ sounds of weather (is it raining? windy?)
- ▶ music (what might the Mechanicals sing as they exit or is there music playing where they are?).

Some effects for Act 2, Scene 1:

- ▶ The sounds of the Woods: owls, wind, crackling twigs.
- ▶ The sounds of the fairy world: giggles, snatches of songs, sighs.
- ▶ Music (what might the Fairies be singing before the 1st Fairy entrance?).

Then perform the transition from the last lines of Act 1, Scene 2, to the first lines of Act 2, Scene 1, with one person 'controlling' the volume by indicating when noises should get louder and when softer, while everyone else creates the soundscape.

 REFLECTION

How could sound be used to make the Woods seem a more magical location?

Note any discoveries you have made in your script in pencil.

TASK 24

Now focus on the next scene, Act 2, Scene 2, from Titania's entrance with her train to Oberon's entrance, and discuss the demands of this scene. Make notes in your notebook on the various ways you could use sound to help this scene.

Some choices you could make include:

▶ adding recorded music in the transition to or under the scene

▶ having performers onstage or offstage creating music and sound effects

▶ adding recorded sound effects such as owls or bird song

▶ experimenting with the volume of the sound (suddenly getting louder or softer)

▶ amplifying or distorting voices, by using microphones.

Here are some sample notes of one interpretation of the scene:

Recorded sounds of the woods: owls, running water, rustling of leaves. I want the woods to sound alive.

Recorded animal noises throughout this section: hooting, soft cries, rustling. This reflects Titania's lines.

The Fairies have instruments: recorders, simple xylophone, tambourine. They play softly and rhythmically. The Fairies sing. The sound should be comforting and show the Fairies working as a team to serve Titania.

Use reverb on microphones, overlapping sound of 'lulla' continues throughout rest of song. This should sound other-worldly.

Much quieter. End reverb. Silence instruments.

No sound effects. Silence except for Fairy's voice. Possible amplified sound of breathing?

Drumbeat, live but offstage – signals Oberon's entrance. Contrast to Titania, harsher, louder. This signals a mood change.

> **KEY TERM:**
> Reverb: an echoing effect.

Puppet design

You may wish to consider designing puppets to add to the magical, fantastical quality of the play. For example, some possible opportunities for puppetry include:

▶ Act 2, Scene 1: shadow puppets to accompany Titania's tale of the Changeling boy.

▶ Act 2, Scene 2: marionettes flown in to create the singing Fairies.

▶ Act 3, Scene 1: hand and rod puppets to portray Peaseblossom and the other Fairies.

▶ Act 5, Scene 1: hand/glove or Punch and Judy style puppets to accompany Quince's prologue.

If you choose to design puppets, remember to write about how they will function within the scene and how they will add to the action and atmosphere of the play.

▲ *Consider the colours and fabrics you will use to create your puppet.*

PRACTICE QUESTIONS FOR SET PLAY 6

You will answer the first three questions and then have a choice between question 4 or 5.

Extract from Act 1, Scene 4:

Focusing on Act 1, Scene 1, from Lysander's line 'How now my love' (line 128) to his line 'So quick bright things come to confusion' (line 149).

1   You are designing a setting for a performance of this extract. The setting must reflect 'A Midsummer Night's Dream's' original setting in ancient Athens. Describe your design ideas for the setting.   [4 marks]

2   You are performing the role of Hermia.
    Describe how you would use your vocal and physical skills to perform the line below and explain the effects you want to create:

    'Belike for want of rain, which I could well

    Beteem them from the tempest of my eyes.'   [8 marks]

3   You are performing the role of Hermia.
    Focusing on the lines from 'How now my love?' to 'O cross!', explain how you and the actor playing Lysander might use the performance space and interact with each other to show the your relationship and the despair at your situation for the audience.   [12 marks]

AND EITHER

4   You are performing the role of Lysander.
    Describe how you would use your acting skills to interpret Lysander's character in this extract and explain why your ideas are appropriate both for this extract and the play as a whole.   [20 marks]

OR

5   You are a designer working on one aspect of design for this extract.
    Describe how you would use your design skills to create effects that support the action of this extract and explain why your ideas are appropriate both for this extract and the play as a whole.   [20 marks]

Extract from Act 3, Scene 1:

Focusing on Act 3, Scene 1 from Bottom's line 'Are we all met' (line 1) to Snout's line 'Will not the ladies be afeard of the lion?' (line 25).

1   You are designing a costume for Quince to wear in a performance of this extract.
    The costume reflects 'A Midsummer Night's Dream's' original setting in ancient Athens. Describe your design ideas for the costume.   [4 marks]

2   You are performing the role of Quince.
    Describe how you would use your vocal and physical skills to perform the line below and explain the effects you want to create:

    'Well, we will have such a prologue; and it shall be written in eight and six.'   [8 marks]

3   You are performing the role of Quince.
    Focusing on the lines from 'Are we all met' to 'How answer you that?', explain how you and the actor playing Bottom might use the performance space and interact with each other in order to create the comedy of this scene for the audience.   [12 marks]

AND EITHER

4   You are performing the role of Bottom. Describe how you will use your acting skills to interpret his character in this extract and the play as a whole.   [20 marks]

OR

5   You are responsible for one design element of the play. Describe how you use design skills that will support the action of this extract and the play as a whole.   [20 marks]

WHAT HAVE I LEARNED?

CHOICE OF SIX PLAYS

CONTEXT: COSTUME
- Make-up and hair
- Condition
- Fabrics
- Shape
- Colours

CONTEXT: SET
- Furniture
- Props
- Materials
- Colours
- Texture
- Scale

VOCAL SKILLS
- Pace
- Accent
- Inflection
- Intonation
- Pitch
- Pause
- Emotional range

PHYSICAL SKILLS
- Body language
- Movement
- Posture
- Eye contact
- Gesture
- Facial expression

DESIGN
- Location
- Mood
- Atmosphere
- Period
- Time

USE OF PERFORMANCE SPACE
- Interaction with others
- Creating effects for audience
- Interpreting character

EXAM
- Everyone answers questions 1, 2 and 3
- THEN Choose question 4 (Performance) OR question 5 (Design)

CHECK YOUR LEARNING

If you are uncertain of the meaning of any of the terms above, go back and revise.

 Why not use the downloadable version of this summary as a basis for your own checklist of what you have learned from Samples & Downloads at www.illuminatepublishing.com.

SECTION C
LIVE THEATRE PRODUCTION

THE SPECIFICATION SAYS...

▶ Students must learn how to analyse and evaluate the work of live theatre makers (performers and/or designers).

  ▶ How the play has been interpreted in the production seen and what messages the company might be trying to communicate.

  ▶ The skills demonstrated by the performers and how successfully meaning was communicated to the audience by the performer.

  ▶ The design skills demonstrated in the production and how successfully meaning was communicated to the audience through design.

ASSESSMENT FOCUS

Assessment objective: AO3: Demonstrate knowledge and understanding of how drama and theatre is developed and performed.

Assessment objective: AO4: Analyse and evaluate the work of others.

TIP

The play for Section C MUST NOT be the same play as the one you studied for Section B.

TIP

Your area of focus may either be on performance or design (you will be given a choice of two design focuses).

TIP

You will never be asked to retell the plot of the play you see. You will need to analyse the production, NOT the story.

For Section C of your examination, you will be asked to answer one of three questions based on a live or digital theatre production you have seen.

To prepare for this question you will:

▶ view a production of live or digital theatre

▶ make notes on different performance and design elements

▶ analyse how the performers' acting skills or designer's choices helped to communicate the characters, action and style of the play to the audience.

What to look for in a live theatre production

Usually, when people go to the theatre they go for one reason: to be entertained. They may not break down the different elements of the play that made them laugh, cry or gasp in surprise. They simply know if they were interested in what they saw and if, in their opinion, it 'worked'. As a student of drama, you must learn to separate the different elements of the production and then evaluate to what extent they contributed to the success of the performance.

One of the exciting aspects of going to the theatre is that, although the audience is experiencing the event together, everyone's reaction to it will be slightly different. You only need to read theatre reviews to realise that even professional theatre-goers disagree on the quality of what they saw. Many things can influence your perception of a play, including:

▶ how familiar you are with the play

▶ if the content of the play is relevant or of interest to you

▶ if you know about the actors in the play

▶ how much people around you are enjoying the play.

For Section C, regardless of how much you enjoyed the play, you must be able to show that you have understood the contribution of the actors or designers, and that you can analyse and evaluate their work.

Audiences are influenced by a variety of production elements, including the actors and design. ▶

Production elements

This mindmap gives you an idea of the different elements you should be analysing. You can use it for the basis of your notes for any show you see. Add more legs to the mindmap to incorporate your ideas.

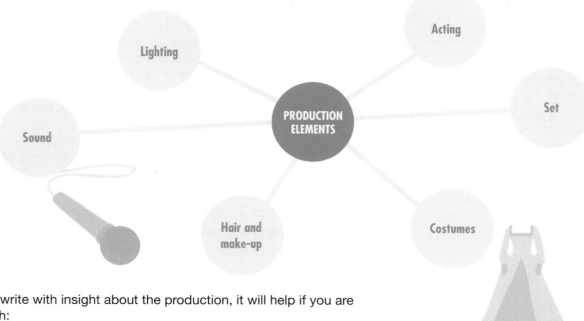

In order to write with insight about the production, it will help if you are familiar with:

▶ the plot and characters

▶ the features of the style/genre of the production

▶ the context of the play/production.

The best responses will come from students who have developed an understanding of the play and production. Some ways of doing this include:

▶ reading reviews (some people prefer to read these after seeing the play, so that their own opinions are not influenced in advance, while others prefer to read them beforehand so that they can look out for particular moments when watching the performance)

▶ reading interviews with the performers or creative team, such as the director or designers

▶ finding and studying production photographs.

All of these activities will help you to be a more critically aware audience member.

Writing about performers

Typically, you will be asked to evaluate one or more actors' use of voice and physical skills, use of space and if they created convincing characters. Depending on the style of the play, you may observe different **performance conventions**, such as: direct address, when they speak directly to the audience; audience interaction, when they involve the audience in the production; or choral speech, when the performers speak together as a group. Different periods and types of plays use different conventions. For example, in Shakespearean plays, you may notice conventions such as **soliloquies**, when a character speaks alone onstage, or **asides**, when they address a remark to the audience before returning to the scene.

> **KEY TERMS:**
>
> **Performance conventions:** techniques used in a particular type of performance, such as soliloquies in Shakespeare or direct address in an epic play.
>
> **Soliloquy:** a speech when a character is alone onstage.
>
> **Asides:** when a character breaks out of a scene to speak briefly to the audience.

Performers' vocal interpretations

Performers' vocal interpretation of character, such as:

- accent
- intonation
- pitch

- volume
- timing
- pace

- delivery of lines
- phrasing
- emotional range.

Actors are trained to use their voices. On a very basic level, an actor must have the skill to project their voice at an appropriate volume and to **enunciate** clearly enough so that they can be heard and understood by all the audience, no matter how large the theatre is. But, beyond that, their voices are essential for expressing the play's characters and actions.

Accents

The use of **accents** conveys many aspects of their character's background, such as:

- education
- where they were brought up

- social class
- occupation.

When an actor is using an accent, consider why this choice was made:

- Does the accent say something about where the character is from?
- Does it suggest something about the period or setting of the play?
- Does it give an indication of the character's education or attitudes?

But accents are only one small part of an actor's job. They must also use their voice to show feelings and to create effects such as tension or comedy. Actors achieve effects through many different uses of their voices and there is no easy formula where you can simply say, 'He spoke loudly, so he was powerful' or 'She spoke quickly so she was funny.' However, it is worth beginning to break down the ways the actors you hear use their voices.

> ### KEY TERMS:
>
> **Enunciate:** to pronounce or articulate words.
>
> **Accent:** a way of pronouncing words that is associated with a particular country, region or social class. This includes foreign accents, such as an American or German accent.

THEATRE MAKER ADVICE

Alex Harland, performer

I recently saw Glenda Jackson playing King Lear at the Old Vic. It's a tricky part for any actor to play, and I have often seen actors resort to shouting a lot as they attempt to portray Lear's frustration and descent into madness. In Glenda Jackson's performance, she managed to avoid this whilst encapsulating Lear's growing impotence. So good was her performance that the fact she was playing what is traditionally a male role ceased to be important or relevant.

Examples and effects of vocal skills

TASK 1

Use the chart opposite to identify and analyse the vocal skills you observe, although there are, of course, many other possible variations. Obviously, you will not hear all these examples, but these are prompts to help you consider vocal skills in detail. After noting your observations, think about the effects achieved. For example, if someone shouts, the effect might be that they are showing their authority or their anger. If someone speaks with a high-pitched voice, the effect might be that they are conveying their youthfulness or their fear. If someone speaks slowly, they might be uncertain or creating tension.

VOCAL SKILLS	EXAMPLES		POSSIBLE EFFECTS
Volume	1	Speaks loudly/shouts	
	2	Speaks softly/whispers	
	3	Voice suddenly gets louder or softer	
Pitch	1	Uses higher vocal register	
	2	Uses lower vocal register	
	3	Changes pitch – such as suddenly going up or down at the end of a line	
	4	Changes pitch to imitate another character	
Timing/pace	1	Speaks slowly	
	2	Speaks quickly	
	3	Pauses at a particular moment	
	4	Speaks at a different or the same tempo as another character	
Intonation	1	Speaks warmly or tenderly	
	2	Speaks sharply or aggressively	
	3	Emphasises certain words	
Phrasing	1	Hesitates at the beginning of a line or mid-line	
	2	Emphasises the verse of a line	
	3	Makes the poetry of a line clear and attractive	
	4	Speaks informally/casually 'throwing lines away'	
Emotional range	1	Voice breaks/sobs	
	2	Giggles or laughs while speaking	
	3	Speaks with control (such as attempting to control anger or sorrow)	
	4	Speaks romantically	
	5	Screams	

 Download a printable version from Samples & Downloads at www.illuminatepublishing.com.

TASK 2

Read the responses to actors' performances below and decide if the actors, through their use of vocal skills, have created a serious or a comic effect.

The actor's voice suddenly broke and there was a long pause as if he was unable to continue. After a second, he softly said, 'She was my daughter.' He emphasised the words 'was' showing that was in the past and said 'daughter' tenderly making it clear that his daughter was no longer alive. Behind him, the chorus of women began a gentle wailing sound that gradually increased in volume until it was over-powering.

The two actors worked in a tight partnership. Their dialogue consisted of a series of rapid-fire exchanges. The actor playing Rob used his lower register and had a booming voice, while Jenny's voice was higher pitched and more cutting. Their use of their voices in the trial scene was very confident and the characters acted as if they were experienced court officials, but when they suddenly paused and looked blankly at each other and then at the audience, it was clear that they were talking nonsense. Together they asked persistent, forceful questions of the defendant, but their mispronunciation of longer words showed how silly they were. Their pompous attitude was punctured by the witness's simple answer, 'I don't know.'

TIP

When writing about physical actions, don't just note what the actions are, but consider how they help to tell the story. For example, instead of just writing 'He has his arm around her waist' you could write, 'He tries to restrain her by protectively putting his arm around her waist.'

▲ *'People, Places, Things',*
National Theatre, 2016.

▲ *'Curious Incident of the Dog in the*
Night-Time', 2016.

TASK 3

Reading the responses on the previous page, note examples of actors using pitch, volume, timing, pace, pause and emotional phrasing to achieve either a comic effect or a dramatic effect.

Delivery of lines

Delivery of lines simply means how an actor says their lines and conveys their meaning. One way of writing about vocal skills is to discuss how certain lines were said (or delivered) by the actors and the effect on the audience. If you have the opportunity to read the play beforehand, you may want to note a few lines that you want to listen out for in particular, in order to note how they are delivered. On the other hand, while you are watching the play certain lines may stand out. Try to note your impressions of these as soon as you can as it is easy to forget after even a very short passage of time.

Performers' physical interpretation

Performers' physical interpretation of character, such as:

build   age   height   facial features

movement   postures   facial expression

gesture

The type of physical skills you see will depend in part on the style of play you are viewing. You may be seeing a stylised piece that makes demands on the actor's physical skills. They may be required to mime, create physical theatre or differentiate between a range of characters when multi-roling. On the other hand, a more naturalistic production may offer more subtle physical opportunities, where actors can express emotions by something as small as a shrug, a change in posture or a raised eyebrow.

Many directors feel that, before an actor speaks, a large part of their job is done simply by how they look and their stage presence.

TASK 4

Think of a line you have seen delivered memorably from a play or film and write in as much detail as you can about how it was delivered and what the effect was.

TASK 5

Look at the photographs on the left and on the following page and try to describe the characters' physical stage presence and the physical interaction between them. Think of as many descriptive words as you can for each example.

▲ 'Zastrozzi', Williamstown Theatre Festival

▲ 'The Chronicles of Kalki', Company One, 2015

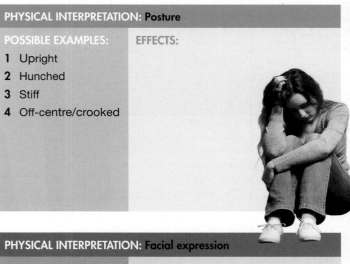

▲ 'Song for a Future Generation', Williamstown Theatre Festival, 2015

TASK 6

Copy and complete the chart below to suggest some possible effects of performers' physical interpretation of characters in the performance you see (there are, of course, many others you might see, so this list can be extended and altered to suit the production you view).

PHYSICAL INTERPRETATION: Movement

POSSIBLE EXAMPLES:	EFFECTS:
Gait/way of walking:	
1 Graceful	
2 Limp/stagger	
3 Awkward	
4 Hurried	
5 Slow/shuffling	

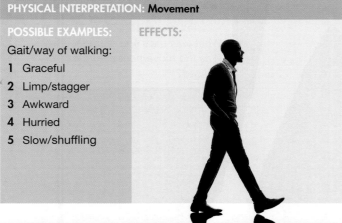

PHYSICAL INTERPRETATION: Posture

POSSIBLE EXAMPLES:	EFFECTS:
1 Upright	
2 Hunched	
3 Stiff	
4 Off-centre/crooked	

PHYSICAL INTERPRETATION: Gestures

POSSIBLE EXAMPLES:	EFFECTS:
1 Pointing	
2 Outstretched arms	
3 Wringing hands	
4 Fist	

PHYSICAL INTERPRETATION: Facial expression

POSSIBLE EXAMPLES:	EFFECTS:
1 Smiling	
2 Pleading	
3 Sad	
4 Tense	
5 Shocked	

Download a printable version from Samples & Downloads at www.illuminatepublishing.com.

Evaluating an actor's performance

Use the figure and questions below to note details of an actor's performance you are evaluating.

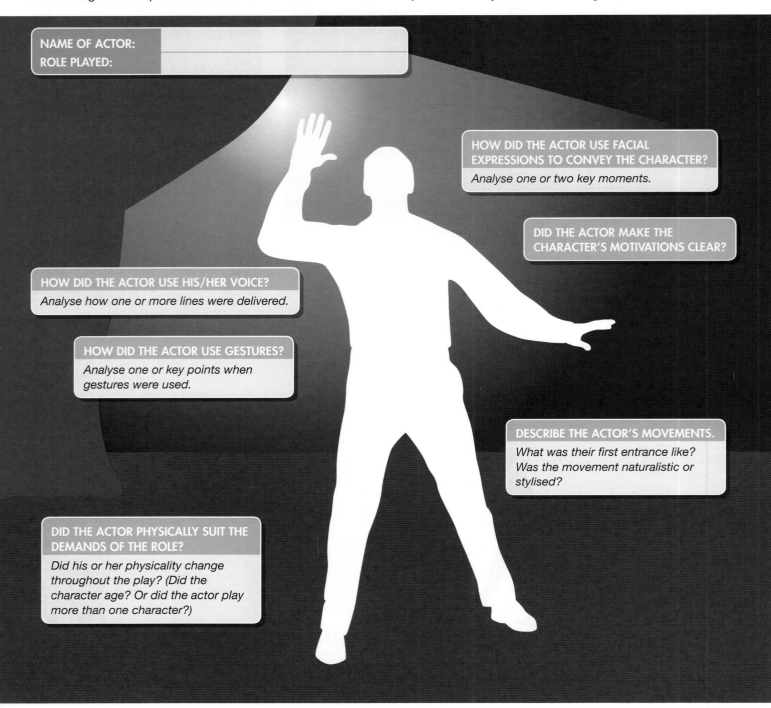

NAME OF ACTOR:

ROLE PLAYED:

HOW DID THE ACTOR USE FACIAL EXPRESSIONS TO CONVEY THE CHARACTER?

Analyse one or two key moments.

DID THE ACTOR MAKE THE CHARACTER'S MOTIVATIONS CLEAR?

HOW DID THE ACTOR USE HIS/HER VOICE?

Analyse how one or more lines were delivered.

HOW DID THE ACTOR USE GESTURES?

Analyse one or key points when gestures were used.

DESCRIBE THE ACTOR'S MOVEMENTS.

What was their first entrance like? Was the movement naturalistic or stylised?

DID THE ACTOR PHYSICALLY SUIT THE DEMANDS OF THE ROLE?

Did his or her physicality change throughout the play? (Did the character age? Or did the actor play more than one character?)

Write at least three sentences summing up your impression of how effective this actor was in meeting the demands of portraying a character in this production.

 TIP

It is important that you write about the acting as someone who is knowledgeable about theatre and not as a fan.
You need to weigh up how successful specific elements of the actor's performance were, using the correct terminology.

 Download a printable version from Samples & Downloads at www.illuminatepublishing.com.

Evaluating an actor's performance in a production

In this question, you aren't being asked to simply **describe** what you see, you must also **analyse** and **evaluate** it. Many students find it difficult to tell the difference between these three skills.

> Example:
>
> In Act 1, the actor playing Chris was **tall and thin**, and walked in a **hesitant, stooping** way. ❶ **Whenever a new character appeared onstage**, his **gestures** would become more jagged and **vocally** he showed his uncertainty by **stuttering**, **particularly when Sally appeared**, which **emphasised** how tongue-tied he was in her presence. ❷ This **worked well** as it showed his transformation in Act 2, when he threw off his previous shyness and **convincingly** became the dashing hero of Sally's fantasies. ❸

Evaluating theatre is something that professional theatre critics do every day. Their responses are not exactly like those you will be writing for your examination, as they will be writing about many different elements of a production and they often aim to entertain as well as to evaluate, but reading their work can provide an inspiration for your own writing.

KEY TERMS:

Describe: to write what you saw, heard or experienced.

Analyse: to examine something, perhaps by looking at the different elements of it, and to explain it.

Evaluate: to judge or form an opinion of something, such as explaining what effect was created and how successful it was.

❶ Description

❷ Analysis

❸ Evaluation

TASK 7

Read the excerpts of actors' performances below and then answer the questions in the margins.

Still, it is Gough who is the major pull. She comes on – snorting, smoking, eyes so screwed up they barely function – ❶ looking as if she has been badly assembled from an Ikea kit. Caught between wrath and terror, she seems to rear away even as she stoops forward. ❷ ('Review of Denise Gough in People, Places & Things' by Susannah Clapp, 6 September 2015, *The Observer*)

Delivering the verse with a warm expressiveness, Ejiofor's magnificent, exotic-accented Othello ❸ exudes a calm charisma and has the kind of spiritual presence that would make you dread doing anything shabby in his presence. Never has an Othello been less quick to jealousy, nor has more movingly revealed the agony as well as the anger in his mistaken sense of betrayal. ❹ ('Review of Chiwetel Ejiofor in First Night: Othello, Donmar Warehouse, London' by Paul Taylor, 4 December 2007, *The Independent*)

It helps of course that at 17, Radcliffe is exactly the same age as the character he is playing, and he superbly lays bare the sheer rawness of youth, the sudden mood swings of adolescence, and that intense unforgettable feeling that you are in a hostile world all on your own ❺ ... The actor keeps turning the emotion on a sixpence, switching from sullen anger to raw vulnerability, or from terrible pain to a sudden childlike innocence and charm. ❻ ('Review of Daniel Radcliffe in Equus' by Charles Spencer, 28 February 2007, *The Telegraph*)

TASK 8

Choose an actor whose work you have enjoyed and write a paragraph evaluating how they used their acting skills to convincingly create a character.

What does this tell us about Gough's use of facial expression, gestures and props?

What does this tell us about her use of physical actions and performance space?

What does this tell us about Ejiofor's speaking voice and use of accent?

What do you learn about Ejiofor's characterisation and portrayal of emotions from this?

What does this tell us about Radcliffe's believability in playing this role in terms of conveying the character's youth?

From this description how effective do you think Radcliffe's performance was? Pick out key words and explain whether this gives you a positive or negative impression of the performance.

A critical evaluation of an actor's performance

The examples on the previous page were all of reviewers giving a positive evaluation of a performance they have seen. However, you may see a performance in which an actor gives, in your opinion, a disappointing performance. You may wish to write about this, but make sure that you support your opinion with evidence from the performance you saw. Here are two critical evaluations of actors' performances.

Very informal

Moves away from discussing acting and instead criticises costumes

> From the moment the actress playing Juliet walked onstage I knew she wouldn't be up to the job. ① First off, she didn't look like a Juliet to me – she was far too old. ② The costumes were very old-fashioned and made her look lumpy and unattractive. ③ She could have been Romeo's mother! Also she was really boring in all of her long speeches. ④ I don't think I was the only one in the audience who was happy rather than sad when she killed herself. ⑤

Could make a more informed statement by explaining how old Juliet should appear to be

Beware of saying something is 'boring' – this may suggest more a lack of effort from you in trying to engage and understand the play. If it is boring explain why. Her voice? Actions?

Makes a general point without any supporting evidence

Mentions interaction and gives an example, although this could be more detailed

Evaluates a vocal skill (verse-speaking)

Provides examples, locating a particular scene and notes gestures and facial expressions, although these could be more detailed

> Unlike Romeo, the actress playing Juliet was less successful in convincing the audience that she was a young person in love. ① Although there was some believable interaction between her and Romeo in the scene where they meet at the party, especially in the playful way they kept catching each other's attention, ② elsewhere she seemed to struggle with the verse-speaking. ③ This was particularly clear in the balcony scene, where her voice was shrill and breathy, at times making it hard to understand or sympathise with her. ④ Similarly, in the scenes with her Nurse, the attempts at humour seemed forced, including some exaggerated use of gestures and facial expressions. ⑤ However, in her final scene, she seemed to find the depth of emotion that had previously evaded her and the entire audience froze when she raised the dagger in her trembling hand before killing herself. ⑥

Compares her performance to another actor's in the play, which suggests evaluation and questions the believability of an aspect of the performance

Chooses a particular scene and gives detailed comments on vocal skills and effect

Chooses a clear example and explains effect achieved

TIP

It is important to focus your evaluation on the actors' performance skills. In most cases, they are not responsible for the costume they are wearing or the script they are speaking.

TASK 9

Write a short paragraph evaluating a performance that you thought could have been improved and remember to give clear examples from the performance and focus on the acting skills.

Evaluating design

Analysing the performance space

As soon as you take your seat in the auditorium, you will begin forming impressions of the play you are about to see. For example, you might note the following:

▶ What the relationship is between the audience and the stage.
Is the audience close to the stage or far away?

▶ Is it an end on or proscenium stage where everyone looks at the stage from the same direction, or is it a traverse, thrust or in the round stage where views may differ, or is it a promenade production where the audience may stand and follow the performers?

▶ What is the shape and size of the stage and how might that influence the type of performance you are going to see?

▶ Is there a stage curtain hiding the set or is the set on view before the play begins?

▶ If you can see the set, where are the entrances and exits? What else do you notice about it?

▶ Can you tell if the actors enter from a backstage doorway or will they enter through the audience?

From the opening moments of the production you will be influenced by elements of the design.
From the design you may learn the:

▶ period (present-day? a period from the past? the future?)

▶ style (naturalistic? stylised? abstract? comic? epic? storytelling?)

▶ mood/atmosphere (mysterious? humorous? tense? playful?)

▶ staging configuration possibilities (levels? entrances? large acting space?)

▶ background or occupations of the characters (a working-class household? a city office? a police station?).

▲ 'Dracula'

▲ 'What It's Like When Two Geeks Love Each Other'

TASK 10

Look at the images above and then write a few sentences explaining what you learn about the play and its design from each production photograph.

You might begin:

From the first image, I can tell that this play is ...

Remember to note what you notice about:

▶ the possible period of the play

▶ the type of costumes

▶ the set

▶ the lighting

▶ the possible style of performance.

 TIP

Notice the different stage configurations used in these two designs. One is an end on stage in an outdoor space, while the other is a traverse stage in a small indoor space. How might the type of theatre where the play is being put on affect the design?

Live theatre performance design evaluation sheet

Use the grid below to make notes on the design of the live production theatre you see.

Title of play	
Where you saw it	
Performance space	
Staging configuration	
Relationship to audience	
How these factors influence design	
SET:	
Type of set (one set or many)	
Naturalistic or non-naturalistic	
Colours and textures	
Size and shape	
Entrances and exits	
Period	
Materials used	
Use of levels/ramps/revolves	
Drapes/curtains/flats/backdrops	
Projections/multimedia	
COSTUMES:	
Colours	
Fabrics	
Shape and fit	
Period	
Changes	
Accessories	
Hair/make-up	
LIGHTING:	
Types of lighting	
Colours	
Angles/positioning	
Special effects	
Blackouts/fades	
SOUND:	
Types of sound	
Use of music	
Volume, amplification, direction	
Live or recorded	
Use of mics/position of speakers	
Sound effects	

TIP

If possible, obtain production photographs from the show you have seen to help you analyse the design features. These are often available online, in programmes or in reviews.

Download a printable version from Samples & Downloads at www.illuminatepublishing.com.

Analysing and evaluating costumes, hair and make-up

The use of costumes, hair and make-up can transform an actor. When analysing and evaluating these elements of a production consider:

▶ if the use of costume is to establish period or setting

▶ if there are costume changes, especially if this suggests a transformation of a character, for example from poor to rich or young to old

▶ if the choices are naturalistic or stylised

▶ how the choice of colours, fabrics and textures create effects

▶ if hairstyles suggest a period, style or character

▶ if make-up is naturalistic or stylised

▶ if the make-up is subtle or has special effects, such as the use of **prosthetics**.

Use the figure on this page to note the costume, hair and make-up of the characters in the play you see.

> Is hair worn up or down? Is it long or short? Does it change at any point? What does it suggest about the character?

> Is the make-up distinctive in any way? Is it used to show age? To show character or style? Is it natural or exaggerated/fantastical?

> What is the **silhouette** of the costume? Is anything distinctive about the length or fit of the costume? What colours and fabrics are used?

> Are there any notable accessories such as hats, shawls, canes or handbags?

> What footwear is worn? Does this suggest an occupation, period or character trait?

KEY TERMS:

Prosthetics: make-up that uses moulds and sculptural techniques to create special effects, such as scars or a false nose.

Silhouette: the outline or shape created by a costume on a figure.

Download a printable version from Samples & Downloads at www.illuminatepublishing.com.

▶ See pages 251–252 in 'Texts in practice' for more information.

Sample student responses writing about costumes

TASK 11

Read the student responses to the following question about the costumes in the production they saw. Rate them 1 to 3 (1 being the best) and then explain why.

> Describe how costumes were used to help create the style of the production. Analyse and evaluate how successful the costumes were in helping to communicate the style of the production to the audience.

Which response was the best at:

▶ describing details of the costumes

▶ analysing how the costumes helped to establish the style and period of the play

▶ evaluating how effective they were?

TIP

If the production takes place in a certain period, you might research that period to make sure you get the terminology correct, such as 'singlets' or 'drop-waist' in the examples on this page.

CHALLENGE

Research the costume and set designers of the production you saw (some designers do both, while others specialise in one or the other). Often designers have websites or other online sources you can access, which will have examples of their work. Some contemporary theatre designers to explore include Tim Shortall (whose advice is found in this book), Alison Chitty, Nick Omerod, Miriam Buether, Tom Scutt, Rob Howell and Es Devlin.

A

The designer of the costumes for 'Chariots of Fire' at the Hampstead Theatre, Michael Howells, created the 1920s period in a naturalistic style through his clever use of fabric and colours. The runners wore outfits very different from contemporary exercise gear. Instead of lycra, they wore simple cotton off-white shorts and singlets. I felt this made them look very vulnerable, almost as if their differences were stripped away when they ran, while also establishing the period setting. When they weren't running, the differences between the characters were highlighted: the formal black dinner jacket that Harold Abrahams wore in the dining scenes contrasted with the rough woven brown country jacket and trousers of Eric Liddell. The fit and styling of Abraham's dinner jacket, in particular, gave him a long silhouette and emphasised his status.

B

One of the themes of the play is social class and the contrasting personalities of the two main runners. One, Harold Abrahams, came from a wealthy, ambitious background and was often shown wearing dinner jackets, a white silk scarf casually hanging around the neck. The other, Eric Liddell, was the very religious son of a Scottish missionary. He was shown in rougher brown clothes. However, both men were dressed similarly when they ran. Liddell's sister wore a simple drop-waist dress.

C

The runners' clothes looked almost comic to me. There was one scene where Abrahams was stripped down to just a pair of shorts and a sleeveless t-shirt while his trainer and a man who seemed to be a butler in a waistcoat looked on. There was also his girlfriend who wore a 1920s style hat and a long dress. Her prettiest dress was the one she wore in the dining scene.

Analysing and evaluating sets

There are many different sorts of sets
that designers might be hired to design.
The production might be a small, touring
production of a naturalistic play or a large
West End musical with many special effects.
Whatever the production, there are some
very basic common elements, such as:

▶ entrances/exits

▶ acting areas

▶ colours/textures to suggest a mood/location.

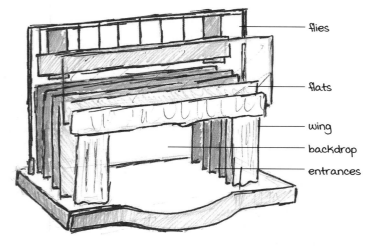

Writing about sets

Naturalistic

You watch a performance that is highly naturalistic.
Some sets have so much believable detail that it is
as if you have walked into someone's front room. These sets are sometimes
in the style of 'box' sets where you have three walls with doors and
windows realistically presented.

Stylised

Stylised sets may have as much detail as a naturalistic set, but their goal
is not to replicate a believable place, but to suggest a setting without
representing it exactly. For example, the set may not have walls or may be
angled or proportioned in an unusual way. It may have symbolic features,
where the set represents an idea from the play.

Minimalistic

Minimalistic sets are simple, basic sets with little stage furniture and only
basic backgrounds. They may be as simple as a black stage with a single
light overhead.

Sets may also combine naturalistic, stylised and minimalistic elements.

▲ A naturalistic box set with period
furniture in 'June Moon'.

Set design terminology

Some of the technical elements you may look for in a set design include:

Cyclorama: a large piece of stretched fabric upon which lights or images
can be projected.

Scrim: a piece of gauze that is used as a screen. Depending on how it is lit,
it can either be transparent or opaque.

Floor covering: what is placed on the floor of the stage. This could range
from linoleum to sand; carpet to wood chips. There may be a design
painted on the floor or images projected onto it.

In addition to the set itself, consider how it is used. For example:

▶ Are there set changes? If so, how are they handled? Do trucks bring on
new scenery? Is there a revolve? Or does one set represent many things?

▶ Are there different levels to the set?

▶ How do the actors enter and exit the stage?

▲ A stylised set with exaggerated use of
colour in 'Shockheaded'.

▲ A minimalistic set with a black
background and simple painted
stage in 'Take the Car'.

▶ For more information about sets go to pages 244–248 in 'Texts in practice'.

Useful terms

Following are some useful terms to use when analysing sets:

Backdrop: a large painted cloth hung as part of the scenery.

Drapes: curtains or other hanging fabric.

Flat: a piece of scenery mounted on a frame.

Furnishings: furniture on the set, such as chairs, cushions, tables.

Multimedia: Using film or other media in a live theatre production.

Projection: Projecting a film or still image to form a theatrical backdrop.

Set dressings: items on the set not actually used as props, but that create detail and interest in it, such as vases or framed paintings on a wall.

Analysing sets checklist

Ask yourself the following questions when analysing sets:

✓ Is there one set that incorporates all the action or several?

✓ Are there a few complete set changes, many minimal set changes or no set changes at all? Do the actors complete the set changes or backstage crew?

✓ Does the action take place on one level or several levels?

✓ What are the main colours used in the set? Do they suggest a certain mood or theme (for example, red for danger or passion; white for purity or innocence)?

✓ Does the set help to establish the location and period?

✓ Does the set tell the audience something about the theme of the play or the lives of the characters?

Evaluating sets checklist

Ask yourself the following questions when evaluating sets:

✓ If the set was naturalistic, how believable did you find it? Were there any details that were particularly effective?

✓ If the set was stylised, how positively did it show the style and action of the play?

✓ If the play was minimalistic, did it help to focus the audience on the characters and plot of the play?

✓ Can you pick out any moments when the set was used effectively?

✓ How well did the set contribute to the mood/atmosphere of the production?

Sample student response writing about the set

Describe how the set was used to support the action in the production. **Analyse** and **evaluate** how successful the set was in helping to communicate the action of the production to the audience.

It was a bold, large-scale set on two levels. ❶ most of the acting took place on the lower level, which served as the living room for the main characters. However, with a few additions of furnishings, such as a bed in the second act, brought on by trucks, that level also served as a park, a phone box and a living room. The set was only minimally dressed, with two modern, low-slung, brown leather chairs and a round, white fur rug. The upstage platform was accessed by two curving ramps and was used for the monologues addressed to the audience. ❷ Above it, a large abstract painting slowly turned, symbolically emphasising the wealth of the two main characters and their preoccupation with art. ❸ The modern architecture, furniture and art used in the set added powerfully to the production, helping to locate it in the rich Manhattan neighbourhood of the play and reinforcing the theme of art. ❹

Description

Description

Evaluation

Analysis

Analysing and evaluating sound

Sound design is an important aspect of theatre. From the moment you walk into the auditorium there may be music playing. Throughout the play there are likely to be sound cues. These may be practical, realistic sounds, such as doorbells, ringing phones or gunshots. They may be more suggestive, such as the amplified sound of water dripping or a ticking clock to show the passing of time. Microphones in musicals are common, but increasingly they are being used in non-musicals as well, sometimes simply to amplify voices, but at other times to create special effects such as capturing the actors' breathing or heighten the importance of between-scene narrations.

Look at the mindmap below to note the types of sound you might notice in a production. Add more legs to the mindmap to incorporate your ideas.

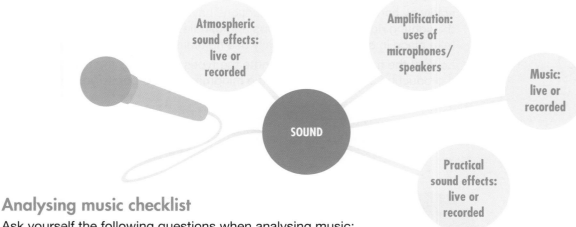

Analysing music checklist

Ask yourself the following questions when analysing music:

✓ Does it help to establish the period or setting of the play?

✓ Does it help to establish the mood of the play?

✓ Is it recorded or performed live?

✓ Does the sound of the music surround the audience or come from a single or several sources?

✓ Does it affect the action onstage (for example, do the characters move in time with it or refer to it in any way)?

✓ Does the volume increase or decrease at certain points?

Analysing sound effects checklist

Ask yourself the following questions when analysing sound effects:

✓ Do they help to establish the time of day, period or location of the play?

✓ Are they important to the plot (such as gunshots or phone calls)?

✓ Are they natural sounding or have they been distorted (such as use of reverb or other special effects)?

✓ Do they come from one direction or many directions?

✓ Does the volume of the sound affect the audience's experience of it?

Evaluating music and sound effects checklist

Ask yourself the following questions when evaluating music and sound effects:

✓ In a naturalistic production, did the music seem appropriate for the time and location or how believable were the sounds?

✓ In a stylised production, did they add to the style of the production? Did they make it more comic? Frightening? Tense?

✓ Were there choices made by the sound designer that actively enhanced the audience's experience of the play?

✓ How well were the sound effects achieved – were the timing, volume and quality correct for the play?

▶ For more information about sound go to pages 240–243 in 'Texts in practice'.

Analysing and evaluating lighting

The type of lighting you see in your live production may depend on the equipment available at the theatre and the requirements of the play. In most indoor theatres, the audience enters with the **house lights** on. When the play begins, these are turned off, so that the audience is in the dark and the stage is lit. Some theatres have advanced state-of-the-art equipment with computerised systems using **LED lights**. Smaller, more basic theatres will operate a basic **lighting rig** in which a limited number of lights are used. In advanced systems, each light can produce many different colours or effects; whereas, in a basic rig, lanterns have coloured **gels** placed in front of them and can only be used for that colour. Some theatres, such as the Sam Wanamaker Theatre at the Globe in London, which is a re-creation of an early 17th-century theatre, are experimenting with productions that are lit solely by candlelight. Some productions have a combination of lights from the lighting rig and onstage lamps and candles. Outdoor productions, which take place in daylight, traditionally use no or limited lighting effects.

Look at the mindmap below to note the types of lighting you might notice in a production. Add more legs to the mindmap to incorporate your ideas.

KEY TERMS:

House lights: lighting that makes the audience visible.

LED lights: light-emitting diodes (LEDs) are light sources that have a high light output but use relatively little power.

Lighting rig: the structure that holds the lighting equipment in the theatre.

Gels: coloured transparencies used to create different-coloured lighting.

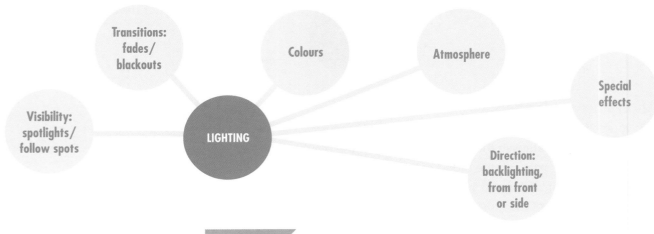

TASK 12

Look at the short excerpts from the sample responses below and decide if the student is commenting on: direction, transitions, visibility, special effects, atmosphere or colours (it may be more than one of these).

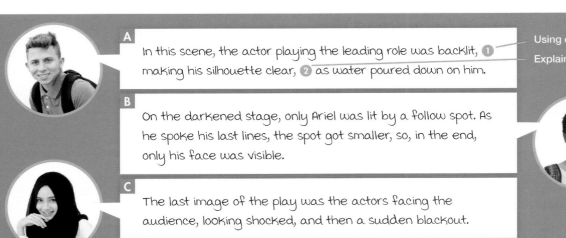

A In this scene, the actor playing the leading role was backlit, ❶ making his silhouette clear, ❷ as water poured down on him.

Using correct terminology

Explains effect

B On the darkened stage, only Ariel was lit by a follow spot. As he spoke his last lines, the spot got smaller, so, in the end, only his face was visible.

C The last image of the play was the actors facing the audience, looking shocked, and then a sudden blackout.

D

After the previous harshly lit scenes, the rosy gentle sidelighting of the breakfast scene, produced by a lighting rig in the wings, established the calm family life in this country kitchen.

E

During the fight scene, strobe lighting was used, which made the violence look particularly shocking.

Analysing lighting checklist

Ask yourself the following questions when analysing lighting design:

✓ How did the lighting designer create certain effects (types of equipment, transitions, etc.)?

✓ How did the lighting designer use colour?

✓ What directions/angles were used in the lighting?

✓ Were any special effects created?

✓ Was lighting used to suggest time of day, location. character, period?

Evaluating lighting checklist

Ask yourself the following questions when evaluating lighting design:

✓ Did any choices made by the lighting design enhance the audience's experience of the performance?

✓ Did the lighting help to focus the audience on certain elements of the performance?

✓ Did the lighting enhance the mood or atmosphere of the performance?

✓ Did the lighting help to convey the action of the performance?

Applying your learning

You will need to be able to use correct terminology in your response. The examiner wants to see if you can describe, analyse and evaluate what you have seen.

TIP

Using the correct terminology, such as the key terms shown on page 182, will help to demonstrate your ability to analyse lighting with insight.

TASK 13

Read the following excerpt for this student's response and, using a pencil, write:

▶ 'D' next to any description   ▶ 'E' next to any evaluation.

▶ 'A' next to any analysis

> The lighting designer created an image of a phone box simply by having a sharp-edged box of light. This was created by a profile spot, which made the light harsh and clearly focused. It was a simple but powerful effect, as the actors could step into the square of light and the audience immediately believed that they were in a separate contained space. The scene ended with a sudden blackout. This made the last image the audience saw the actor's happy expression, which I think was more surprising and appropriate than a slow fade.

▶ **For more information about lighting look at pages 236–239 in 'Texts in practice'.**

PRACTICE QUESTIONS FOR SECTION C: LIVE THEATRE PRODUCTION

Answer one question from this section.

State the title of the live/digital theatre production you saw.

You must answer on a different play to the play you answered on in Section B.

1   Describe how one or more actors used their vocal and physical acting skills to create effective characters.
    Analyse and evaluate how successful they were in communicating their character to the audience.
    You should make reference to:
    *   the use of voice
    *   physical skills
    *   the actors' use of space.   [32 marks]

OR

2   Describe how lighting was used to support the action in the production. Analyse and evaluate how
    successful the lighting was in helping to communicate the action of the production to the audience.
    =You should make reference to:
    *   the types of lighting
    *   the colour and intensity of the lighting
    *   any special effects.   [32 marks]

OR

3   Describe how the set was used to help create the style of the production. Analyse and evaluate how
    successful the set was in helping to communicate the style of the production to the audience.
    You should make reference to:
    *   the appearance of the set
    *   any changes in the set
    *   how it was used by the actors.   [32 marks]

TASK 14

Write an answer to one of the questions above. Then either mark
your own work or swap papers with someone else and mark their
work. Read through it and write:

▶ 'D' next to any description

▶ 'A' next to any analysis

▶ 'E' next to any evaluation.

At the end, write at least one thing that you or they did well and
one thing that could be improved.

 TIP

It is easy just to describe what you have
seen. Remember to analyse and evaluate it.
Some words to use when evaluating might
include:

believable, powerful, disappointing,
convincing, portrays well, conveys,
surprises, moving, atmospheric,
appropriate, adequate, impressive.

Improving your written work

Whatever aspect of the production you are writing about make sure that you:

▶ Give **specific examples and details** from the production.

▶ Use relevant **technical terminology**.

▶ Explain how the performance or design choices helped to **communicate meaning** to the audience.

▶ Explain whether or not the choices were **successful and why**.

Planning your response

A common feature of successful responses is that there is evidence of at least some planning in order to organise ideas and make sure the question is fully answered. There is no one set way of planning your answer to the following question but below are some approaches that work for other students.

Annotate the question:

Use the actual question and make notes around it.

For example:

Assessment objectives:

In your response you must demonstrate that:

▶ You understand how theatre is developed and performed **(AO3)**.

▶ You can analyse and evaluate the work of others **(AO4)**.

▶ When there are bullet points in the question, you must respond to each of them.

③ Large scale; use of blue; sheets create waves; projections for storm

① 'Twelfth Night', Shakespearean production, 17th-century costumes, stylised

② Romantic and comic. Created a beautiful setting, emphasis on nature. Comic potential in Malvolio/ Olivia scenes

> Describe how the set was used to help create the style of the production. ①
> Analyse and evaluate how successful the set was in helping to communicate ② the style of the production to the audience.
>
> You should make reference to:
> ▶ the appearance of the set ③
> ▶ any changes in the set ④
> ▶ how it was used by the actors. ⑤

④ Revolve used for change to second setting. After the excitement of the opening, scene is calmer

⑤ Comedy created in overhearing scene. Use of sundial. Hedges where actors could suddenly appear

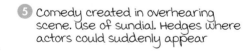
TIP

To **analyse** something you are breaking it down and looking at it closely. To **evaluate** something is to write about the effects that were achieved and if they were successful. You must do both of these.

◀ *An updated production by Emma Rice of 'Twelfth Night', Globe Theatre, 2017.*

Making a mindmap

Another way of planning your response is to create a mindmap.

Planning paragraphs

You could write a quick paragraph plan (below is just one example, the requirements of the question you have or the production you saw may vary):

Introduction: Style of production

Paragraph 1: Appearance

Paragraph 2: Changes

Paragraph 3: Use by actors

Paragraph 4: Analyse what was communicated and evaluate how successful.

Avoiding common errors

Check the list below to see if you have made one or more the following common errors:

✓ No (or incorrect) technical language (for example, referring generally to lighting without anything more specific).

✓ General comments without giving examples from the production.

✓ Saying something is good without explaining why.

✓ Only writing about one or two moments from the play.

✓ Only descriptive with no analysis or evaluation.

✓ No discussion of effect on audience.

✓ Little understanding of the requirements of the play.

✓ One or two points repeated with no development of ideas.

WHAT HAVE I LEARNED?

LIVE THEATRE PRODUCTION

ANALYSING PERFORMANCE

- Vocal skills
- Physical actions
- Performance conventions
- Audience interaction
- Use of stage space

WRITING

- Describe
- Evaluate
- Analyse

ANALYSING DESIGN

- Set
- Sound
- Lighting
- Costume

EVALUATION

- What was being attempted?
- What skills were used?
- What was the effect?
- How successful was it?

TIP

Learn the correct terminology. Your writing will be far more precise, for example, if you can write: 'A profile spot with a green filter was used to single out the main character in the forest' rather than 'the lighting was green'.

CHECK YOUR LEARNING

If you are uncertain of the meaning of any of the terms above, go back and revise.

Why not use the downloadable version of this summary as a basis for your own checklist of what you have learned from Samples & Downloads at www.illuminatepublishing.com.

THE SPECIFICATION SAYS...

Students must learn how to create and develop ideas to communicate meaning in a devised theatrical performance.

Students must learn how to contribute to a devised drama in a live theatre context for an audience. They must contribute as either a performer or designer.

ASSESSMENT FOCUS

Assessment objectives: This is a practical component in which students are assessed on their ability to create and develop ideas to:

▶ Communicate meaning for theatrical performance **(AO1)**.

▶ Apply theatrical skills to realise artistic intentions in live performance **(AO2)**.

▶ Analyse and evaluate their own work **(AO4)**.

What this means is that you will be working in a group, either as a performer or a designer, to create an original devised piece that will then be performed and evaluated. You will perform your piece in front of an audience and write a production log.

KEY TERMS:

Devising: a way of creating drama that begins not with writers or a script but is based on the collaborative efforts of a group of people.

Improvise: to act without a script.

Stimulus: a resource in drama used to start a creative process by providing context, inspiration or focus.

What is devising?

THEATRE MAKER ADVICE

Kerry Frampton, director/performer/ designer, Splendid Productions

Devising is problem solving in the most beautiful and practical way – the pursuit of the clearest way to communicate an idea.

Devising is a way of creating drama without starting with a script. Instead, usually beginning with an idea and a stimulus, actors and designers research, **improvise**, develop and shape scenes until they have a complete piece of drama ready for an audience.

How do we begin?

You will be presented with a range of stimuli. A **stimulus** is something that will spark ideas, discussion and creativity. For example, it could be:

▶ a photograph, painting or sculpture

▶ a poem, news article or short story

▶ a song or piece of instrumental music

▶ a recent or current event

▶ a theme, such as 'Time' or 'War'

▶ a myth or fairy tale

▶ a cultural event such as a festival, carnival or ceremony.

How will we be assessed?

You will be marked on your Devising log, which is divided into three sections:

▶ Section 1: Response to stimulus: (20 marks) (AO1)

▶ Section 2: Development and collaboration (20 marks) (AO1)

▶ Section 3: Analysis and evaluation (20 marks) (AO4)

You are also marked on your contribution to the Devised performance (either as a performer or designer) (20 marks) (AO2)

Total marks = 80

Collaboration and group work

What type of group member are you?

Group work is an essential element in devising (as well as other aspects of drama). Use the exercise below to consider what type of group member you are and how you can improve.

> **TASK 1**
>
> In a small group, you have to agree a topic for a short scene to be performed at an event, such as an assembly. You have five minutes to agree the topic of the scene, assign parts and write the first few lines.

When identifying your strengths and weaknesses in group work, it is good to reflect on your natural attitudes towards group work. Below are descriptions of typical group members:

LEADER: you have ideas and are happy to express them. You enjoy being in charge. You may sometimes be frustrated if others aren't following you or disagree with you.

HELPER: you don't usually lead a group, but you are happy to put forward ideas and work with others. You may assist Leaders to see their ideas through or you may encourage others to take part.

PASSENGER: you don't want to lead and you aren't confident about putting your ideas forward. However, you will go along with what the group wants to do.

BLOCKER: you find group work frustrating and you don't positively help the group. You might tend to argue with others, refuse to cooperate or become distracted.

Moving forwards

If you are a Leader, make sure you:
- listen to others
- check that everyone feels included
- are flexible about adjusting your ideas or compromising when necessary.

If you are a Passenger, make sure you:
- contribute ideas
- are active and not passive
- complete work that is challenging for you.

If you are a Helper, make sure you:
- have your ideas heard
- think about leading part of a task
- are challenged by the work.

If you are a Blocker:
-

Blockers frustrate others because they keep them from fulfilling their potential, but most of all they hurt themselves. Some people are Blockers because it is the only way they feel they can get attention or perhaps they lack confidence in their own work. However, you will receive much more positive attention and learn so much more if you can work productively with others.

 **REFLECTION**

How easy did you find that task? Did your group manage to meet the deadline? What helped or hindered you?

REFLECTION

Thinking back to your actions in Task 1, which description best fits you?

 TIP

Keep reflecting on how you work in groups. Groups need Leaders but they should aim to ensure that everyone is included in the process. Passengers can't just coast – drama is active!

Staying positive

'Yes, and ...'

Being positive is a vital part of successful group work. No one wants to work with someone who is blocking their ideas or making them feel foolish. The game below, 'Yes, and ...' is great for encouraging creativity and cooperation. Remember you can't say 'no'!

Working with a partner, you will start with one of these scenarios (there are many others you can use):

1   You are in a car that has broken down in the middle of nowhere.
2   You have locked yourself out of your house.

Whatever is said, the other person must say, 'Yes, and ...' and add a point.

Example:

The car has broken down.

Yes, and I think I know how to fix cars.

Yes, and I have a car manual somewhere.

Yes, and it says we need a spanner.

And so on …

Deciding if you wish to perform or design

If there are only two students in a group, then both must be performers, as the minimum performance size for a group is two. In any larger group, you have a choice to be a designer instead of performer.

Potential designers should consider:

▶ Will you have access to the equipment you need to create a lighting design, assemble a costume or construct a puppet, etc.?
▶ Do you have an idea for a design that will have a positive impact on a performance?
▶ Are you willing to develop your practical skills in order to realise a completed design?
▶ Will you contribute fully to the devising of the piece?

Potential performers should consider:

▶ Are you happy to develop your theatrical skills in order to perform in front of an audience?
▶ Are you able to learn lines and do you have a positive attitude about rehearsals?
▶ Will you try to provide a performance that will have a positive impact on the live performance?
▶ Will you contribute fully to the devising of the piece?

REFLECTION

Were you positive and did you keep the ideas flowing?

At any point did you block your partner?

What would you improve for the future?

TIP

If you are undecided about whether to choose a performance or design specialism for this component, discuss this with your teacher who can advise you what choice might lead to the most successful outcome for you.

Typical plan for devising

There is no one way to organise a devised piece. Below is just one way that you may approach developing your piece. You might find once you are working that you would like to go back to an earlier stage, such as research or devising, in order to improve a section of your work.

INTRODUCTION TO STIMULI

You will become familiar and work with a range of stimuli such as photographs, articles or music.

CHOOSE STIMULUS

You will decide which stimulus will be the basis of your piece. You will write about this in your Devising log.

RESEARCH STIMULUS

You will work in your group to research different aspects of your stimulus, such as its context, theme, visual images. You will note your research in your Devising log.

DEVISING

Your group will begin devising scenes for your piece. Designers will begin researching and developing their designs. You will improve the structure of the piece. You will agree how your stage will be configured. You will chronicle your discoveries in your Devising log.

REHEARSAL

Your group will agree and set the stage movement and learn lines. Designers will contribute their ideas and skills. You will receive and respond to feedback. You will continue making improvements in the piece. You will note your changes and developments in your Devising log.

TECHNICAL REHEARSAL

You will have a rehearsal to test and adjust any technical elements such as lighting and sound. Design candidates will take a lead role to ensure that all technical/design elements work correctly.

DRESS REHEARSAL

You will have a full rehearsal in costume and with all technical elements in place. Some groups choose to have a small invited audience for this in order to receive last-minute feedback and make final adjustments.

PERFORMANCE

You will perform the piece in front of an audience and the assessor.

REFLECTING/EVALUATING

Review and evaluate your work.

 TIP

Throughout the process you will be making notes, diagrams or recording comments for your Devising log. The final section of your Devising log is an analysis and evaluation of your work.

Getting started with devising

Kerry Frampton,
director/performer/
designer, Splendid
Productions

We specialise in creative adaptations of existing plays or novels, they must have a strong spine of politics or a question about society that we want to explore. Our current production is centred around Leadership, which is pertinent to our current political situation. Normally, we read lots of options and then one will stand out above the others.

Our structure is quite tight, so there are some logistical elements to consider in our choice of material:

- Could this be done with a cast of three?
- What would we like an audience to consider/ponder/question and feel like?
- What is the problem we are trying to solve?

KEY TERM:

Hot seat: one performer sits in a chair and, in character, answers questions.

You will be exposed to one potential starting point, sometimes more than one, for your devised piece. Your exploration of the stimulus should be active and creative. There is no one best way of devising but below are some examples to get you started:

▶ Create a series of still images based on the stimulus and discuss any storylines that may result from those images.

▶ Choose one character inspired by the stimulus and **hot seat** that character to establish a back story.

▶ Create a location inspired by the stimulus, exploring the sounds and sights in the space.

▶ Research the context of the stimulus (when it occurred, why it was important) and create a scene based on that context.

▶ Create a series of quick-fire scenes based on the theme or title of your stimulus.

▶ Choose several characters from the stimulus and write a monologue for each.

▶ Introduce a prop or piece of costume to an improvised scene based on the stimulus.

▲ The blinded cyclops in Splendid Productions' 'The Odyssey'.

Response to a stimulus

Kerry Frampton,
director/performer/
designer, Splendid
Productions

Normally I'm drawn to something that I can see. As a visual learner, if I can see it I can make it, so there has to be a strong image in there somewhere.

For 'The Odyssey' [an ancient Greek tale] I had an idea about how we might blind a Cyclops – which ended up not being in the final piece – I also wondered if we could tell this HUGE fable without the central figure being present. 'Odyssey', with no Odysseus. How do we tell that story? Whose stories are ignored in the original? Where are the women? What about the villains? It then becomes a vehicle of telling everyone else's version of events.

In your Devising log you will be asked to write about the stimuli that your teacher presented to you and the stimulus you chose. You will need to then explain:

▶ Your first response to the stimuli.

▶ The different ideas, themes and setting you considered and how and why you reached your final decision.

▶ What you discovered from your research.

▶ What your own dramatic aims and intentions are (for example, if you are a performer, what you want to achieve in your portrayal of a character).

▶ What the dramatic aims and intentions of the piece were (for example, what theme might your piece explore or what message would it deliver?).

Example

Read the following poem by the acclaimed poet Lemn Sissay twice. The first time, read it aloud so you experience the sound and rhythm of the words and any ideas that stand out. The second time, try to locate the poet's message to the listener.

What if? by Lemn Sissay

A lost number in the equation
A simple, understandable miscalculation
And what if on the basis of that
The world as we know it changed its matter of fact
Let me get it right. What if we got it wrong?

What if we weakened ourselves getting strong?
What if we found in the ground a file of proof?
What if the foundations missed a vital truth?
What if the industrial dream sold us out from within?
What if our unpunishable defense sealed us in?
What if our wanted more was making less?
And what if all of this wasn't progress?

Let me get it right. What if we got it wrong?
What if we weakened ourselves getting strong?
What if our wanting more was making less?
And what if all of this wasn't progress?
What if the disappearing rivers of Eritrea,
the rising tides and encroaching fear
What if the tear inside the protective skin
of Earth was trying to tell us something?
Let me get it right. What if we got it wrong?
What if we weakened ourselves getting strong?
What if the message carried in the wind was saying something?

From butterfly wings to the hurricane
It's the small things that make great change
In the question towards the end of the leases
no longer the origin but the end of species

Let me get it right. What if we got it wrong?
What if the message carried in the wind was saying something?

CHALLENGE

The poet Lemn Sissay (pictured above) has spoken extensively about his interesting life and appeared on the radio show 'Desert Island Discs'. Research his life to see if that could enrich your devised piece.

TASK 2

a   In your group discuss what you think the poet is saying about the world and the dangers that we face.

b   Read through the poem again and underline in pencil any words or phrases that seem important to you.

c   Choose five phrases from the poem and, as a group, create still images for them (such as 'message carried in the wind' or 'industrial dream'). Discuss the images and if any of them suggest a way you could use this stimulus in a dramatic way.

d   Write a list of questions you have for the speaker, such as 'Who are you speaking to?' 'What made you so worried about the world?' 'What do you think we can do?'

e   As a group, hot seat one member who will imagine they are the speaker. That person will think about the speaker's background and experiences. The rest of the group will ask questions. What can you discover about the speaker? Why are they choosing to speak out?

f   The poet seems concerned about changes in the environment. Go online and try to discover what he means by 'disappearing rivers of Eritrea', 'rising tides' and 'end of species'. Research climate change and note any ideas that you think might inspire or contribute to a devised piece.

g   Discuss where you could set a piece based on this poem. Would it be in the present day, the past or the future? Would it be in an existing country or an imagined one?

h   What would you like to achieve in a piece based on this poem? For example, would you like to design a set that would show how the world's environment is changing or would you like to play one of several characters in conflict about climate change?

i   What would you like a devised piece based on this poem to achieve? Would it have a political message about the environment or leaders? Or would it be a personal piece about a character making a discovery or finding a reason to be hopeful? Do you want the audience to have a greater understanding of the issues suggested by the poem or do you want them to be more interested in the emotional journey of the characters?

j   If there are designers in your group, do they have ideas about how design could contribute to an exploration of this stimulus, such as a sound design or type of costume that they would like to explore or are there effects they could create with lighting or puppetry?

k   Make notes for your Devising log explaining your ideas from your initial response to the stimulus.

TIP

Make notes about your work from the beginning. It will make it much easier to explain the process if you have detailed notes that you can shape into your Devising log responses.

CHALLENGE

Try to extend your research beyond the most obvious internet pages. Visit a library, interview people, listen to music and discover images.

THEATRE MAKER ADVICE

Kerry Frampton, director/performer/ designer, Splendid Productions

Sometimes I have a niggle of a thought, an idea that to me is exciting and it'll just be sat in my brain and as I'm going about my daily business I'll have other ideas, or something I'm doing will feed into that. The idea grows and changes and expands. The seeds of each piece are planted and I see what grows and what doesn't.

Examples of stimuli and themes

Below are examples of stimuli and related themes that you could use for a devised piece.

Photography

The photo on the right shows British athlete Dame Kelly Holmes winning Olympic Gold. Use that as a starting point for your devising.

POSSIBLE THEMES: competition, women in sports, strength, overcoming hardship, images of women, triumph and defeat.

Poetry

A Poison Tree by William Blake

I was angry with my friend;
I told my wrath, my wrath did end.
I was angry with my foe:
I told it not, my wrath did grow.

And I waterd it in fears,
Night & morning with my tears:
And I sunned it with smiles,
And with soft deceitful wiles.

And it grew both day and night.
Till it bore an apple bright.
And my foe beheld it shine,
And he knew that it was mine.

And into my garden stole,
When the night had veild the pole;
In the morning glad I see;
My foe outstretched beneath the tree.

POSSIBLE THEMES: friendship, conflict, anger, hypocrisy, consequences.

▲ *Dame Kelly Holmes winning gold in the 2004 Olympics.*

KEY TERM:

Conflict: when two or more characters' desires are in opposition (external conflict) or when a character experiences opposing emotions (internal conflict).

Music

'The March of the Knights' from *Romeo and Juliet*, the ballet music by the Russian composer Sergei Prokofiev.

POSSIBLE THEMES: power, conflict, tribes, families.

Myths

The Greek myth of Eurydice and Orpheus. Orpheus was the son of the god Apollo and a highly gifted musician. He loved Eurydice. One day, Eurydice was bitten by a serpent and died. She descended to Hades in the Underworld. Orpheus was so sad that he begged Hades to let him have his loved one back. He played such sweet music that Hades gave permission to Orpheus to bring Eurydice back to Earth. But there was one condition: he was not allowed to look back at her as they rose from Hades. When they were almost back on Earth, Orpheus looked back to see if Eurydice was still there. Hades snatched her back to the Underworld. Orpheus spent the rest of his days playing sad music and was said to be the inspiration guiding those who wrote mournful tunes.

POSSIBLE THEMES: love, death, trust, journeys, danger.

Art

Yinka Shonibare is a Nigerian-British artist who lives in London. His work explores ideas about cultural identity, often by reimagining situations in a surprising way.

POSSIBLE THEMES: Victorian age, society, fashion, culture, contrasts.

▲ *'Diary of a Victorian Dandy'* by Yinka Shonibare, © Yinka Shonibare MBE. All Rights Reserved, DACS 2017. Image courtesy Stephen Friedman Gallery, London.

Film

Slumdog Millionaire is a 2008 British film directed by Danny Boyle and starring Dev Patel as Jamal Malik, a young man who grew up in an Indian slum who appears on the gameshow *Who Wants to be a Millionaire?* Despite his humble beginnings, Jamal has an amazing ability to answer the difficult quiz questions. He is accused of cheating, but through a series of flashbacks the reason for his knowledge is revealed.

POSSIBLE THEMES: luck, prejudice, intelligence, gameshows, overcoming obstacles.

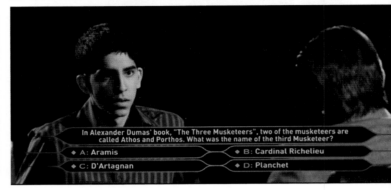

▲ *Slumdog Millionaire*

Novels

Face by Benjamin Zephaniah explores the life of Martin Turner, a popular teenager whose life is transformed after a car accident leaves his face disfigured. He discovers that the change in his appearance affects how even his closest friends treat him. The novel traces the obstacles Martin faces in hospital and when he returns to school.

POSSIBLE THEMES: physical appearance, friendship, overcoming obstacles.

News

Stephen Sutton was diagnosed with terminal cancer at the age of 15. In response, he decided to do two things: compile a 'bucket list' – all the things he wanted to do before he died – and to raise money for charity. In the last years of his life, supported by his family, he: skydived, got a tattoo, became a Guinness World Records holder, hugged an elephant, and played the drums in front of a huge crowd at Wembley. As his popularity grew through social media and celebrity attention, the donations flooded in. By the time he died in 2014, at the age of 19, he had raised more than £3.2 million for charity.

POSSIBLE THEMES: overcoming obstacles, goals, health, social media, families.

History

Suffragettes

In the late 19th century and early 20th century, suffragettes fought for the right for women to vote in elections. Two famous British suffragettes were the sisters Emmeline and Christabel Pankhurst. They believed in 'deeds, not words', and held rallies and protests. In 1909, their group used tactics such as hunger strikes, and some had to endure force-feeding. In 1918, women in Britain over the age of 30, with a few restrictions, were given the right to vote. In 1928 this was extended to women over the age of 21.

POSSIBLE THEMES: **women's rights, protests, politics.**

Musical

The musical 'Hamilton' takes a modern approach to the life of one of America's founding fathers, Alexander Hamilton. It traces his life from his humble origins as an orphan in the Caribbean to his death in a duel. You could research different figures from history and create a short musical based on their lives. But remember, it took Lin-Manuel Miranda, the creator of *Hamilton*, seven years to write the musical, so be realistic about what you can accomplish in the time available.

POSSIBLE THEMES: **ambition, politics, overcoming obstacles.**

Cultural

Weddings

Different cultures celebrate weddings with different wedding customs, superstitions and rules. For example, a Pakistani wedding typically takes several days, as there are four different ceremonies. A traditional Chinese wedding is arranged between families and may include a 'bride price' – money or gifts given to the family of the bride. In some regions of Sweden, the bridesmaids carry bouquets of weeds to ward off trolls. There are many television programmes devoted to the experiences of those hoping to find love, preparing for marriage or competing for a prize of a wedding or honeymoon. You could use the backdrop of a wedding or series of weddings to shape your piece.

POSSIBLE THEMES: **love, money, tradition, family.**

 REFLECTION

What makes a stimulus interesting to explore? How can you ensure that an idea has enough substance to serve as the basis for your piece?

 CHALLENGE

There are some excellent resources available to stretch your ability to devise. One helpful book is *Drama Games for Devising* by Jessica Swale, which provides lots of interesting exercises and games for the various stages of devising. Alternatively, visit the websites of companies that specialise in devising, such as Complicite and Splendid Productions (whose artistic director offers advice in this chapter), that provide useful online resources and DVDs.

TASK 3

a   Read the above possible stimuli and in your group discuss which ones appeal to you most and why.

b   Choose one of the stimuli and create a mindmap diagram of ideas based on it. At this stage be very free with ideas, but think about characters, locations, themes and plots that appeal to you.

Research

Once you have decided on your stimulus and topic you will want to research it in order to develop your ideas. There are many ways of researching a topic. These include:

newspaper articles

online articles

books

documentaries

videos

music

interviews

museums

photographs

For example, if you are devising a piece set during World War II, you could research this by:

- ▶ visiting or looking at the online resources of a museum, such as the Imperial War Museum
- ▶ watching a documentary about World War II
- ▶ reading history books or magazines about the period
- ▶ finding images of World War II fashions
- ▶ listening to popular songs from the period
- ▶ watching a film either set in the period or made during that time
- ▶ locating images of advertising from the period
- ▶ interviewing relatives or someone in your community who remembers it.

How to use your research

Some groups find it best to assign different research responsibilities: one person may be researching music, while another could be reading articles or finding visual images. If you are a designer you should take an active role in helping research areas that will influence the design of the piece. Everyone should contribute to the research process, as you need to show how you have assisted the development of the piece in your Devising log.

Once you have gathered some research, you should share it with the group. then choose the aspects that you think are most useful.

For example, in order to improvise a scene in which a mother worries about whether or not to evacuate her children to a safer location you might use World War II posters such as the two on the left for inspiration.

After finding a piece of World War II music, use it to create a scene in which the mother says goodbye to her children.

COMPONENT 2 DEVISING DRAMA

Genre/style

Many groups find that their work is more interesting and focused if they choose a genre or performance style for their piece. This will help you to create a piece with a more consistent tone and should aid the audience in understanding the type of theatre they are seeing. Some groups combine two genres or styles in order to create variety. Below are some genres you might consider.

Comedy

Theatre that makes the audience laugh is one way of keeping an audience interested and involved. Some common features of comedy include:

misunderstandings

physical humour (such as disguises that go wrong or accidents that cause embarrassment)

comic timing (the use of pace and pause to make the audience laugh)

exaggeration

However, do not be misled into thinking that comedy is easy. It is common to mistake something that is a bit silly or a private joke as being something that will have a wide appeal to an audience. Comedy can be used to explore serious issues and many successful devised pieces combine humour with a serious message. For example, you might make a serious political point by comically exaggerating the arguments on both sides or by creating larger-than-life characters.

Tragedy

Tragic pieces deal with large issues that have a sad outcome.
Some common features of tragedy include:

a sympathetic or worthy protagonist who experiences a downfall

warnings that things may go wrong

conflict

serious tone

A tragic subject has to be important – it would be difficult to create a tragic piece based on something trivial such as losing a shoe. You need to make sure you can sustain the tone so that it leads to a moving conclusion.

Melodrama

Melodrama is a type of theatre with exciting situations and exaggerated characters. Features of melodrama include:

characters whose role and personality are clear from their first entrance

an exaggerated acting style

a hero and a villain

dangerous situations

good usually triumphs over evil

Victorian melodramas featured 'stock' or stereotypical characters and often involved the hero saving the heroine from the villain. Modern melodramas can be altered to fit the story you wish to tell and may have a more comic tone.

Commedia dell'arte

Commedia dell'arte is a type of theatre that was particularly popular in the 16th–18th centuries, but has influenced many other types of drama. It was performed by a travelling group of actors in distinctive costumes. Features of commedia dell'arte include:

- **stock characters**, such as comic servants, old men, young lovers and boasting soldiers
- use of physical gestures and physical comedy
- tragedy
- tasks
- improvisation.

Once the style and rules of commedia dell'arte are learned, they can be applied to a number of situations. Often, much comedy can result from the master/servant relationship or the misunderstandings of the 'old men' characters.

> **KEY TERM:**
> Stock characters: easily recognised, stereotypical characters.

▲ A commedia-influenced production of 'Once Five Years Pass'.

Naturalism

Naturalism is a type of theatre that creates the illusion of reality, so the audience fully believes the characters and the situations in which they find themselves. Features of naturalism include:

- believable characters
- gestures and vocal patterns that imitate those experienced in real life
- situations that are recognisable to the audience
- realistic props and settings
- situations that may involve ordinary people who unexpectedly experience a crisis.

Naturalism can be an appealing choice, as much acting that we know from films and television is highly naturalistic. However, onstage you must make sure that this choice will give you the opportunity to demonstrate your physical and vocal skills. Remember that naturalism does not mean simply repeating real life; it is just as crafted, edited and shaped as any other dramatic form.

Epic theatre

Epic theatre is a type of theatre associated with the German writer and director, Bertolt Brecht. He rejected naturalism and instead used techniques to draw the audience's attention to the fact that they are watching a play. Features of epic theatre include:

- captions or projections with slogans or scene headings
- political goals
- comedy, sometimes even when dealing with apparently serious matters
- exaggerated characters
- 'breaking the fourth wall' by speaking directly to the audience
- use of song and music.

Brecht believed that theatre should inspire the audience to action, so he created techniques to keep them alert and interested. He wrote about political or social injustice using narration, songs and physical comedy.

Documentary theatre

Documentary theatre is drama that consists entirely or in part of factual materials, such as the words of interviews, newspaper articles or government reports. As much as possible the material is not altered but is presented **verbatim** – that is, the actual words are used. Some documentary theatre uses 'verbatim' sections contrasting with fictional situations. Features of documentary theatre include:

▶ careful and accurate research

▶ social or political themes

▶ recreation of an actual time or event

▶ naturalistic acting.

Some documentary theatre makers interview people after an important event and then carefully edit the material into a piece of drama. For example, Gillian Slovo interviewed protesters, community members and police after the 2011 London Riots. Other documentary theatre makers have edited trial transcripts to create a piece of theatre.

Physical theatre

Physical theatre is a type of non-naturalistic drama that emphasises movement such as mime, dance, clowning and mask-work in order to tell its story. Features include:

▶ stylised movement

▶ use of music and dance

▶ strong use of stage pictures and images

▶ less emphasis on dialogue.

Physical theatre can be used on its own or it may be joined with another genre of theatre. For example, you may wish to have a stylised slow motion movement section to show a difficult journey or a rapid, chaotic movement scene in order to show a character's mental state. A piece could combine a verbatim report being spoken while others mime what is in the report.

Theatre-in-Education

Theatre-in-Education (also called TIE) is a show with an education focus designed for school audiences or other groups to teach them about a certain issue. TIE productions usually have the following elements:

▶ a small-cast

▶ low-budget

▶ inventiveness, such as using multi-role or creative use of props

▶ audience interaction

▶ issue explored from many viewpoints

▶ factual information

▶ a strong, clear message

▶ simple set and props that can easily be moved to different venues.

The audience of a TIE piece needs to be one of your key starting points. Are you aiming to educate a young audience about the dangers of social media or the importance of healthy eating? A play aimed at seven-year-olds would need to be very different from one aimed at 16-year-olds. You should have a learning objective, such as, at the end of this show, the audience will now understand what the dangers of unhealthy eating are; or how to recognise healthy eating habits; or easy ways to prepare a well-balanced meal, etc.

KEY TERM:

Verbatim: using exactly the same words as were used originally.

▲ *Physical theatre and clever use of props can create impressive effects, as in this production of 'Jonah, a Musical Detour'.*

▲ *Splendid Productions' performance of 'Antigone'*

 TIP

Working in a particular style can help the audience and those assessing your work to understand your intentions.

 TIP

You could devise a piece included by theatre makers such as Brecht or Kneehigh.

REFLECTION

Which performance styles did you think added the most to the piece? Which do you think will fit in best with your devised piece?

TIP

The word 'refined' means that the Production log should note the progress and changes you have made during the devising and rehearsal process. Think about how you respond to setbacks and overcome obstacles. Did you make any changes after receiving feedback?

KEY TERM:

Objective: what the character wants.

REFLECTION

Discuss if the objectives and conflict are clear in the example on the right. What could be improved?

> **TASK 4**

Create a simple scene, such as your journey to school, and then perform it in different styles. For example:

- ▶ Documentary theatre: recreate the exact words that were spoken to you.
- ▶ Physical theatre: create a bus and mime the actions of the people on it.
- ▶ Epic theatre: write captions for each stage of your journey and speak directly to the audience.
- ▶ Naturalism: recreate the gestures and words spoken when waiting for the bus.
- ▶ Melodrama: create an exaggerated hero and villain for your journey and exaggerate the extreme danger you were in.

And so forth.

Development and collaboration

Working with others and developing ideas are part of the pleasure of drama, but these can also be difficult. Make sure that, throughout the process, you are all contributing and meeting your responsibilities. For your Devising log you need to explain:

- ▶ How you developed and refined your ideas and those of the others with whom you worked.
- ▶ How you developed the piece in rehearsals.
- ▶ How you developed and refined your own theatrical skills (performance or design) during the devising process.
- ▶ How you responded to feedback.
- ▶ How you used your refined theatrical skills in the final piece.

Rehearsal techniques

Devising is an active process and involves a great deal of 'trial and error' while you test ideas and see what works for you. Below are some rehearsal techniques to help you to develop your ideas.

Objectives

Create a short scene in which two characters have different **objectives**. Before the scene begins, clearly state what your objectives are. For example:

> **CHARACTER 1 (Employee):** I want a pay rise.
>
> **CHARACTER 2 (Boss):** I want to leave work early to go to a football game.

As you improvise the scene, think about how many different actions (the things you actually do) you can make to achieve your goal. For example, the employee might block the boss from leaving the room or show him a folder of all the work he has done. The boss might pretend to agree so he can leave or rush by the employee trying to ignore him.

First line/last line

As a group, agree the first line last line of a scene. Improvise a scene in which the characters take actions to get logically from the first line to the last. For example, the first line could be:

I'm fine, really, don't worry about me.

The last line could be:

I don't think you are ready to go back to school.

Between these you could devise a scene in which someone who is upset pretends they are fine, but then breaks down and can't carry through with their plan.

Another variation on this technique is to agree opening and closing positions for a scene. This might be two still images, such as a first image of one character on the floor, arms outraised to the other character whose back is turned. The second image might be the first character walking towards the door while the second character sits huddled in a chair. The challenge is to discover how the characters journeyed from the first image to the second.

Using performance conventions

Depending on the style of your piece, you may want to introduce various conventions. As you develop your piece you wish to try the following:

▶ Still images: these might be based on images you have researched or ones that you develop, which will help you to tell your story. You might use still images to start or end a scene or to emphasise a particular moment.

▶ Movement sequences: you could use synchronised movement, slow motion, mime, dance or other physical theatre. For example, you could recreate a protest using a silent slow motion sequence showing different people in a crowd or you could show how the internet works by having actors represent the journey a message makes through virtual space.

▶ **Choral speaking**: you could have a group of actors commenting together on a scene or you could share out lines in a speech among a number of people. You could highlight one word by having everyone saying that single word together.

▶ Breaking the fourth wall: you could use **narration** or opportunities to speak directly to the audience by introducing or interrupting the scene to comment on it.

▶ Split screen or cross-cutting: this is when you either have two scenes happening at the same time or you cut between the two scenes.

As you develop your piece, keep thinking about the meaning of it and what effect you want to have on the audience. You might think about using one of these conventions to help you get your meaning across. For example, you might want to highlight the turning point in a character's life, so you could use narration, slow motion or a still image to pinpoint that moment.

KEY TERMS:

Choral speaking: a group of people speaking together or sharing a speech.

Narration: providing the audience with background information or commentary on the action of the play.

 TIP

Avoid putting conventions in that do not help to advance your piece. Sometimes students will put in long dance or song sequences that do not help to tell their story. Part of the process is editing out anything that is irrelevant to your piece.

TASK 5

Choose a moment from your piece and rehearse it using at least two of the conventions above. Discuss which conventions work and if you could use them at other parts in your piece.

Contributing to development and collaboration as a designer

In most conventional theatre productions (and in Component 3), designers take their initial design inspiration from an existing text. However, designing for devised pieces has special challenges, especially in your ability to demonstrate your contributions to the development of the piece and to meet the practical demands of completing your work in time for the first performance. In script-based productions, if you read a script and see that you need to create a life-like, baby puppet or a sound design to depict a storm, you can plan in advance how much time and what materials you will need to complete the design.

However, with a devised piece, there will most likely be a longer period before you know what will be required. One way of avoiding a last-minute panic is to take an active role in the development of the piece. Here are some suggestions:

▶ Use design as part of the devising experience. For example, bring in music or sound effects to inspire rehearsals or aid movement sequences. Offer photos/artworks to prompt devising.

▶ Be an active participant in rehearsals and suggest how your design ideas could help the storytelling. For example, if there is a lengthy exposition section, which is slowing down the piece, could you offer to replace it with a shadow puppet show to convey the back story? Could you, as a sound designer, suggest using amplification or a distorting effect to make a moment more climactic or frightening?

▶ Take an active interest in the genre/performance style of the piece as this will affect your design choices.

▶ Establish any major design needs as early as possible. Even if the piece has not been fully devised, the group can decide on central concepts early on that you can begin developing while the script is being finalised. For example, a recent devised play had a major set change at the end, which had been agreed early in the devising process, so that everyone knew that was what the piece was leading to and the designer could begin the construction.

▶ Offer to lead rehearsals to develop a specific element of the production such as set changes, positioning onstage, use of props or puppetry.

▶ Provide rehearsal props/costumes/puppets/music, so that the actors are able to rehearse effectively.

▶ Involve the rest of the group in aspects of your design. For example, you could arrange a session with the whole group to record sound effects or a group trip to a charity shop to source costumes or props.

▶ Stay flexible, remember that ideas can change completely, especially in the early stages of devising.

TIP

Take an active interest in the whole piece. Don't think of yourself as less important than the performers. Your point of view about how the piece can be developed and shaped is as important as anyone else's.

TIP

Refer to Component 3 for more ideas on the types of design choices you can make, the materials you will need and the health and safety requirements.

Collaboration

I'm a collaborator and not precious, there are normally as many people outside watching with opinions as there are onstage. It is a collaborative process in Splendid. There are techniques that I know will just work beautifully, particularly if they're centred around what we would like an audience to do. There are some things that just don't quite work for that specific piece, so I'll hold onto them for another performance.

Kerry Frampton, director/performer/ designer, Splendid Productions

THEATRE MAKER ADVICE

Creative people often have strong opinions and this can lead to conflict. However, in drama it is important to find a way of resolving these potential conflicts. In the professional theatre, it is usually the director who settles these issues, but in group work, where everyone has an equal stake in the outcome, it can be a bit more difficult.

As a designer, you must work with the performers to ensure that your design is supporting the entire piece and the performers have an obligation to ensure that your creativity and input are seen and effective. It is no good designing a beautiful hat, if the actor refuses to wear it because they feel it hides their face or might fall off.

The designer and performer need to work together and arrive at a solution. Could the hat be refitted or altered so it fits more securely or is tilted off the face? Could the hat be worn for part of the scene and then taken off?

TASK 6

Look at the following design/performer collaboration problems and suggest how they could be resolved:

▶ You are the costume designer. You know the piece is set in the 1960s, but otherwise haven't learned enough about the characters to begin working on a costume design or sourcing items. You are worried that you won't have time to arrange the costumes if you don't get some guidance soon.

▶ You are a puppet designer. You are confident about making a puppet but aren't comfortable being onstage operating it. No one else in the group has volunteered to operate it.

▶ You are a set designer. You are excited about doing a set design, but the group has said they want a complicated and expensive set that you don't feel you could do.

▶ You are a lighting designer. Your idea is for the whole piece to be very dimly lit, but the costume designer says that means their costume/ make-up design cannot be properly seen.

▶ You are a sound designer. You want music playing underneath several scenes, but the actors say they fear their dialogue won't be heard.

 TIP

The best pieces are when all the elements work together. Don't think of yourself as in competition with the rest of the group. The goal is for everyone to succeed!

How to rehearse

**Kerry Fampton,
performer/designer/
director, Splendid
Productions**

This one is one of my favourite Splendid moments in a rehearsal room, it was the 'Seven Stages of Man'. There were three of us and a sheet. We wanted the Everyman character (played by me) to be manipulated and dressed using this sheet to represent each stage:

Birth – through a slit in the sheet a BIG baby is born.

1 Infancy – sheet becomes nappy.

2 Child –becomes a cape.

3 Lover – sheet becomes a bed cover.

4 Worker – the sheet becomes a counter, or production line.

5 Wisdom – the sheet becomes a robe like a Greek scholar.

6 Old Age – the sheet is now a gigantic beard.

7 Dependency – it becomes a nappy again and we start at the beginning.

There is no set way to rehearse, and professional theatre companies vary in how they approach rehearsals. Below are some approaches that you might find helpful:

▶ Start with a short warm-up such as a quick game or physical exercise to get focused.

▶ Agree an aim for a rehearsal such as:
  ▶ 'creating the beginning'
  ▶ 'staging the journey scene'
  ▶ 'trying out the props'
  ▶ 'working with music in the protest scene'.

▶ If possible, take it in turns to stand outside the scene and make constructive comments. Students acting as designers can helpfully comment on the work of the performers and vice versa.

▶ Spend a few minutes at the end of the rehearsal discussing how the rehearsal went.

▶ Assign tasks for people to do as homework such as:
  ▶ 'research fashion for this period'
  ▶ 'find a piece of music for the opening'
  ▶ 'learn lines for the opening'.

▶ Have one or more people in the group act as a **scribe** to write down or pull together any bits of script that emerge from the work.

▶ Agree what you will rehearse in the next session.

KEY TERM:

Scribe: someone who writes documents.

Avoiding common rehearsal problems

Common rehearsal errors:

▶ Rehearsing one section of the piece at the expense of the other scenes. Some groups end up with a perfect opening scene – and nothing else.

▶ Spreading the work unevenly – make sure that everyone is important to the success of the piece.

▶ Spending too long talking rather than getting up and doing. Often you can only tell if an idea will work by trying it.

▶ Having too many scenes with characters sitting down talking. Some groups avoid this by restricting the number of chairs in their piece and choosing active scenes where the characters have to be doing something.

▶ Having pieces that are under-researched. If you have set something in the 1920s it will be very confusing if you have people using mobile phones or talking about television.

▶ Getting discouraged and constantly changing ideas. It is normal to have some rehearsals that are less successful than others. However, if you were enthusiastic about an idea, don't give up the first time you hit an obstacle.

If you get stuck, try one of the following:

▶ Check to see if there is clear conflict in the scene. Apply the 'objective' rehearsal technique discussed earlier.

▶ See if there is a convention, such as using mime or music, that will make the scene more exciting.

▶ Write a bit of dialogue or a monologue that could kick-start the scene.

▶ Make sure you have agreed what the message and purpose of your piece is.

▲ 'The Wonderful World of Dissocia' by Anthony Neilson, costumes designed by Alice Smith in collaboration with Jasmine Swan.

 TIP

Make notes in your notebook as you go through the process of rehearsals to help you in completing your Devising log.

1 When preparing to play a character, my advice would be: Keep your eyes open! A lot of inspiration can be drawn from observing other people, for example in the supermarket, in cafes or on public transport. I was once playing a character who was never seen without a cigar. On the way to rehearsal one day I was sitting behind an old man who was wearing a cloth cap pushed right back on his head with a cigarette stuffed behind his ear. It occurred to me that I could use the same combination for my character, and from that time onwards in rehearsal I was never without a cap and a cigar jammed behind my ear. It helped me a lot.

2 The more ways you can rehearse a scene the better. it's easy to go stale when you rehearse the scene with the lines as written. One technique I have found useful is to replace the actual words with gibberish. For example the line How are you? could become Bee da su? This helps with uncovering the underlying rhythms of the text, which is often as important as to what is actually being said.

3 In rehearsal, there is no such thing as wrong. If you persevere when things aren't going well, often interesting developments can arise, which allow you to take the scene in a different direction.

Alex Harland, performer

THEATRE MAKER ADVICE

▶ The 'objective' rehearsal technique can be found on page 202.

TIP

You can use a sheet like this to make notes that will help you write your Devising log. Look at what needs to be shown in your Devising log and then note on your sheet when you have done this. For example: initial response; research, aims and intentions; responding to feedback, developing and refining ideas; etc.

Designers' and performers' rehearsal note-taking sheet

Some designers and performers find it helpful to use a grid like the one below to keep track of their progress (it is understood that elements of this will change and develop as rehearsals progress; also, the time you have to rehearse will vary from centre to centre). This will help you to complete your Devising log.

Title of piece: '2008'

Style of piece: epic/physical theatre

Date of first performance: 1 November

Role: set designer

> **KEY TERM:**
>
> Chairography: choreographed movements involving chairs.

WEEK OF REHEARSALS	WHAT HAVE I LEARNED?	WHAT DO I NEED TO DO?	WHEN DOES IT NEED TO BE COMPLETED?
WEEK 1	STIMULUS: news report about the financial crash of 2008. INITIAL RESPONSE: People carrying boxes, lives changed, office environment. OUR IDEAS: the piece is going to be set in an office building in 2008. Showing the effect of the economic crash.	RESEARCH: design for 2008, offices/office furniture. Research other plays with office sets (online). CONTRIBUTION: Bring in photos of office as stimulus for a rehearsal. Source some rehearsal furniture.	Week 2
WEEK 2	AIMS AND INTENTIONS: The style of the piece is going to be epic. (COMMUNICATE MEANING) Create sympathy for those who cannot cope with the change. Are we too focused on money/material things? Direct address. Use captions/projections? Boxes used as a recurring motif?	Make notes of scenes so far and discuss with performers possible captions. (COLLABORATION) Research what economic graphs look like for possible design idea. Sketch possible design for wall (keep copy for Devising log) (DESIGN SKILLS, CREATING AND DEVELOPING IDEAS)	Week 3
WEEK 3	Make prop lists (doughnuts, telephones, pens, paper). (PRECISE DETAILS) Feedback on design for back wall. Discuss how it could be used by performers. (COLLABORATION)	Arrange materials (flat/paint) for back wall. Schedule time in art room for painting. Arrange volunteers to help. (DESIGN SKIILLS)	Painting to be completed by Week 5, other tasks by Week 4
WEEK 4	Discuss set changes with group. How can these be accomplished? Can sound designer provide music to accompany these? (COLLABORATION) Source chairs on casters. (PRECISE DETAIL)	Make a plan for set changes. Arrange for one rehearsal with group to organise these. Bring in remaining props. Prepare for feedback session.	Next rehearsal Next week (coordinate with sound designer) Next rehearsal
WEEK 5	Change the lettering and size of captions – currently they can't be read easily. (RESPONDING TO FEEDBACK/PRECISE DETAIL) Set changes too slow!	Finish back wall set (take photos for Devising log). Rehearse set changes again (simplify!). Re-do caption slides. (RESPONDING TO FEEDBACK) Create prop list.	Next rehearsal Next week Next rehearsal Next week
WEEK 6	Set is fully painted – but needs to dry. Located chairs that can be rolled on – and go up and down (possibly incorporate in movement/chairography?).	Get set up. Locate new tray and set of mugs. Rehearse actors for tearing down graph scene. Ask for volunteers to help with technical rehearsal.	Tomorrow Next rehearsal Next rehearsal Technical rehearsal

Download a printable version from Samples & Downloads at www.illuminatepublishing.com.

Giving and responding to feedback

As you rehearse you will need to help each other to improve your performance or design. Giving and receiving feedback is an art, as you have to be constructive and helpful, while also being truthful. You also have to be open to hearing comments that may disappoint you. One good technique is to give feedback with the following structure:

One thing you liked.   One thing you didn't understand.

One thing that could be further developed/you'd like to see more.

So, for example, your feedback might be:

- I liked the tension in the opening scene because it made me wonder what was going to happen next.
- I didn't understand why the parents were fighting.
- I would like to see the characters when they are out of the home setting.

Or your comments might be more technical:

- I liked your use of an accent in the first scene.
- From the way you positioned yourself onstage, I couldn't tell how you felt about the other character.
- I would like to see you use your excellent comedy skills more, for example in the restaurant scene.

Or the feedback on a design might be:

- I liked the period music used at the beginning of the show, which helped me to picture when it was happening.
- I didn't know if there was meant to be sound effect in the second scene or if that was a mistake.
- I would like to have heard more effects that established the location — something that made clear what a busy, hectic place it was.

Once you receive feedback, you need to consider how to address any issues that arise. Of course, the person giving feedback could be wrong, but be open to the possibility that they are trying to help you. You might schedule extra rehearsals to address any problems or discuss with the rest of your group any common areas of concern.

Another way to give feedback is to use Buddy Assessor forms.

What this means is that groups get together and each person gets a Buddy Assessor from another group. At certain stages during the rehearsal process, the Buddy Assessors will watch and comment on each other's work. After receiving your Buddy Assessor's comments, you can target how you will develop and improve your work. Evidence of this process can then be recorded in Section 2 of your Devising log to show how you developed and refined your piece and theatrical skills during the rehearsals.

Buddy Assessor form – devised piece

Name of performer/designer:

Name of assessor:

What did the performer/designer do well? Please give clear examples.	
What would you like to see developed more? Explain in as much detail as possible.	
Performers: what vocal skills did the performer demonstrate? What physical skills did the performer demonstrate? **Designers: did the designer demonstrate a range of skills (think about design ideas; use of technical equipment; creativity)?** **Provide examples.**	
Performers: did the performer create one (or more) roles convincingly? **Designer: did the designer add to key moments of the piece?** **Provide examples.**	
Did the performer/designer contribute to the piece as a whole (for example, by clearly knowing cues/lines; working positively with others)? **Provide examples.**	
What did you think was the message or theme of the piece? **Explain.**	
Any comments on the piece as a whole?	

TIP

Once you have been assessed, write up your notes for your Devising log and set targets for areas needing development and improvement.

Download a printable version from Samples & Downloads at www.illuminatepublishing.com.

Structuring your piece

Kerry Fampton, performer/designer/ director, Splendid Productions

Peter Brook [a respected director] has a lovely phrase 'Hold on tightly, let go lightly.' If it doesn't serve the piece, if it doesn't do what we need it to do for an audience, then it can't stay in. Our work is lean, the aim is always clarity and truth.

In Splendid we always know WHAT we are showing/telling an audience, WHY they need to be shown or told that and finally HOW. The HOW is what theatrical technique will tell that section in the clearest way: song, naturalism, direct address, chorus, narration. The HOW is normally what we work through in the rehearsal room.

THEATRE MAKER ADVICE

Once you have arrived at the basis of your piece, you will want to consider its structure. Some basic structures are:

▶ **Linear**: this is when a piece goes in **chronological** order. For example, it might show, in order, the events of one day or one week or one year.

▶ **Non-linear**: this is when events are not in chronological order but may jump around in time. For example, there could be a scene set in the present day, then one set a century ago and then another in the future.

Other structural devices you might consider:

▶ **Narration**: having one or more characters speaking to the audience.

▶ **Bookending**: having the first and last scenes connected in some way.

▶ **Flashbacks**: providing scenes from the past that give extra meaning to the main story.

▶ **Sub-plot**: a secondary story that runs alongside the main story, so, for example, the main story may be political, but there is a romantic sub-plot.

A typical structure of a play is:

▶ **Exposition**: when you introduce the setting and main characters and what they want.

▶ **Complication**: where the obstacles to the characters' objectives are developed.

▶ **Climax**: the point of greatest tension and conflict.

▶ **Resolution**: when the plot comes to its conclusion.

An example of students using this structure would be:

▶ **Exposition**: four different characters are shown on a summer day rushing for a bus. Each has an important appointment that day.

▶ **Complication**: each character has obstacles that make them anxious and fearful they will have problems on that day. There is a flashback for each character showing why today is so important to them.

▶ **Climax**: there is a dramatic accident on the bus. A slow motion sequence shows the accident.

▶ **Resolution**: some survive and some do not. Survivors reflect on their feelings.

▲ *Spendid Productions' production of 'The Trial', telling the audience what to do.*

KEY TERMS:

Chronological: Showing events in the order in which they occurred.

Sub-plot: a secondary or less important plot in a story.

Charting the structure of your piece

It is likely that you will find you want to alter the structure of your piece. One way of refining the structure is to get a large sheet of paper and chart an axis on it like this:

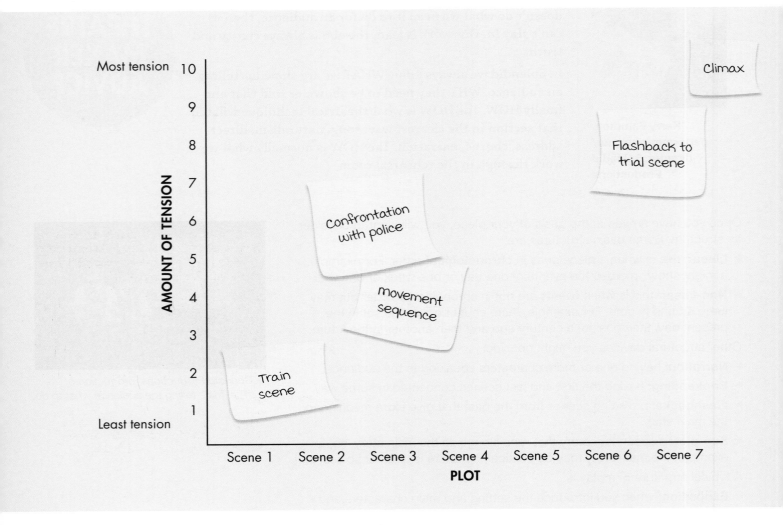

Write down each of your scenes on sticky notes and place them on the grid. As you work, you may discover that the scene you thought would be your climax doesn't work or that you want to introduce a different opening or ending scene. Keep adjusting the structure until you feel it works and there are no unnecessary scenes.

The devised performance

For the devised performance, you will be contributing either as a performer or a designer. The assessed performance may be a duologue – a performance by just two people – or a group performance of three to six performers. If there are designers in the group they can choose between the following options:

▶ lighting

▶ sound

▶ set

▶ costume

▶ puppets.

However, there can only be one designer for each specialist area. So you may have a lighting and set designer in the group, but you cannot have two set designers.

The length of the devised piece depends on the number of performers in the piece.

The designers' work must be seen in the live performance. This means, for example, that if you are a lighting design student then your lighting must be seen as part of the devised piece. Design students are assessed on their design, not on their practical ability to operate the equipment associated with the design. However, design students are encouraged to improve and develop their theatrical skills as much as possible and to realise their designs in a practical way as much as they are able to within any limitations they may discover.

Theatrical skills – performance

Performers must develop and perform one character or, if it suits the style of the play, more than one role.

You will be marked on the following:

▶ Level of use of theatrical skill.

▶ Range of theatrical skills demonstrated.

▶ Contribution to the effectiveness of the piece.

▶ Inventiveness of your work.

▶ Success in realising individual artistic intention.

For a performer, theatrical skills you will aim to show should include:

▶ vocal skills

▶ physical skills

▶ characterisation

▶ interaction and communication with audience and other performers.

Your 'artistic intention' will be judged based on your Statement of Dramatic Intentions, which you provide before your performance. Be as accurate as you can.

TIP

You will complete a 'Statement of Dramatic Intentions', where you specify what you, as a designer or performer, want to show and what you want the audience to understand from the performance.

TIP

Keep checking the timing of your piece. In the final weeks you should keep a close eye on its length in order to decide if you need to edit or add material.

TIP

It is important that your Statement of Dramatic Intentions is accurate.

How to demonstrate vocal skills

At the very least, you must ensure that your speech is clear and easily heard by the audience. But other aspects of vocal ability you might experiment with are:

▶ **Tone:**
   ▶ Are you able to adjust the tone of your voice to express the situations your character is in?

▶ **Pace and pause:**
   ▶ Can you vary the pace of your speech as appropriate for the situation?
   ▶ Can you use techniques such as pausing to heighten tension, suggest hesitation or create comic timing?

▶ **Variation in voice:**
   ▶ If you are playing more than one role, can you differentiate between characters by using vocal skills, such as accent, pitch or volume?
   ▶ If you have a character who behaves differently in certain situations can you show that by a change in voice?

Common vocal problems

It is no accident that drama schools spend years working on improving their students' vocal skills, such as breath control, diction and pitch, as these are so important for a performance. Here are some common problems for young actors:

Monotone:
   ▶ Speaking everything on the same note.
   ▶ **Effect:** dull.

Volume:
   ▶ Speaking too softly to be heard.
   ▶ **Effect:** confusing and frustrating.

Diction:
   ▶ Speaking indistinctly and running words together.
   ▶ **Effect:** confusing and irritating.

Pitch:
   ▶ Speaking either on too high or too low notes to be fully expressive.
   ▶ **Effect:** unpleasant, irritating or dull sound.

Lack of emotion:
   ▶ The tone of voice not matching the excitement of the dramatic situation.
   ▶ **Effect:** doesn't convey character or situation

TIP

Before rehearsals and performances do a short vocal warm-up, including exercises to free your vocalisation and tongue twisters to improve diction (see page 230).

TASK 7

Choose a section of the devised piece and experiment with different ways of delivering the lines. Check the list of common errors and make sure you are avoiding those.

▶ Go to pages 230–231 in Component 3 for more advice about vocal work.

How to demonstrate physical skills

You may devise a piece that demands advanced physical skills such as mime or synchronised movement. However, even a naturalistic piece offers you the ability to show physical skills. You will be assessed on how well your physical skills add to your characterisation and the piece as a whole. Some ways in which you can show physical skills include:

use of gesture   **use of stage space**

body language and stance   **variation in movement**

Common physical skills difficulties for student actors:

▶ Tight, self-conscious movement.

▶ Areas of tension inappropriate for the character or situation, such as raised shoulders or clenched hands.

▶ Repetitive movements.

▶ Wandering onstage or other movement without purpose.

▶ Inappropriate movement for character, such as too young for an older character or too hesitant or informal for a powerful, high-status character.

TASK 8

Choose a scene from your piece and take out all the dialogue. See if you can convey the meaning and emotions of the scene without any words at all.

 **REFLECTION**

What movements help you to establish your character and what they want? Can you vary your physical choices to give the scene more impact?

▲ 'Dental Society Midwinter Meeting', feeling the cold.

Theatrical skills: design

THEATRE MAKER ADVICE

Kerry Frampton, director/performer/designer, Splendid Productions

KEY TERM:

Archetypal: a typical example of someone or something; associated with an original or mythic quality of someone or something, i.e. 'he was the archetypal businessman' or 'it was the archetypal battle between good and evil'.

I normally design our work – again because my strongest ideas about character and story and atmosphere come from images or colours – every choice we make for the production then feeds into the design.

Fifty-five percent of communication is visual, the Greek root of the word theatre is 'to see' so we must think carefully about the information we are placing before the eyes of the spectator.

In a practical way there is no room for surplus set, as we are taking down and putting up our set twice a day in a selection of spaces. It must also be able to fit into the boot of a car.

With 'The Odyssey' – we needed a clear, linear, visual way to plot the 20-year journey from War to Home for Odysseus. So a blue washing line (the colour of the sea) was rigged across the back and each stop was a way of exploring another **archetypal** quality demonstrated by the hero, each archetype had an Emoji like picture at the top [see photo below] so that you could clearly understand which stop had happened.

Again, because the story was so complicated and moved around, we needed something simple that would allow an audience to feel safe. To see the progression of the piece as well as Odysseus. He was going home, we were too.

Splendid Productions' 'The Odyssey' ▶

TIP

Your 'artistic intention' will be judged based on your Statement of Dramatic Intentions, which you will provide before your performance. You will be asked to write briefly what you aim to show in the performance and what you want the audience to take away from the performance. Be as accurate as you can.

You will be marked on the following:

▶ Level of theatrical skill.

▶ Range of theatrical skills demonstrated.

▶ Contribution to the effectiveness of the piece.

▶ Inventiveness of your work.

▶ Success in realising individual artistic intention.

Design specialism and requirements

Specialism chosen:
Lighting designer

Requirement: Must create **one** lighting design. The design must show a range of lighting effects/states and cues/transitions designed to meet the demands of the devised piece being performed.

Specialism chosen:
Sound designer

Requirement: Must create **one** sound design. The design must show a range of sound effects and cues/transitions designed to meet the demands of the devised piece being performed.

Specialism chosen:
Set designer

Requirement: Must create **one** set design. The design must be for one setting, showing dressings and props designed to meet the demands of the devised piece being performed.

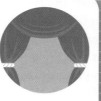

Specialism chosen:
Costume designer

Requirement: Must create **one** costume design for one performer. The design must show clothing and accessories (and hair and make-up if applicable) designed to meet the demands of the devised piece being performed.

Specialism chosen:
Puppet designer

Requirement: Must create **one** puppet design. The design must show a complete puppet designed to meet the demands of the devised piece being performed.

Your designs will be assessed in the live performance so must be visible in it.

How to show a range of theatrical skills

You may wonder how, if you are creating a single design, you can show a range of skills. Here are some suggestions:

▶ **Costume design:** you might think about using different fabrics or stitches to show a range of skills. You could choose accessories or create a make-up design to show more skills. You may choose a design that shows that you have thought about fit/shape. You might create a costume that is suitable for a quick change or can be modified for different scenes.

▶ **Lighting design:** you might demonstrate that you know how to use colours, different lanterns or special effects. Your cue sheet should be detailed and accurate. The timings should be clear, for example indicating if it is a sudden blackout or a slow fade.

▶ **Puppet design:** you could create a puppet that shows advanced skills in terms of its design and how it can be manipulated by the puppeteer. It might have a range of movements or show a well-chosen, imaginative use of materials.

▶ **Set design:** in addition to the main set design, you could provide stage furniture or other set 'dressing' to show more theatrical skills. For example, if the piece is set in a particular period, you might source or create items, such as a particular prop for the set to reinforce that.

▶ **Sound design:** you should create a detailed cue sheet showing your understanding of the needs of the devised piece. You might create original sound effects or research a variety of music to create your sound design.

▶ For more information about design specialisms look at pages 236–255 in Component 3.

Analysis and evaluation

Kerry Frampton, director/performer/designer, Splendid Productions

THEATRE MAKER ADVICE

Often we find that the simpler the idea, the better it is. Our simplest ideas are the ones that our audiences think are the most clever.

Simple and obvious are my two tips for devising. In fact here is my main preach for young devisers:

1 If your topic/stimulus/starting point is COMPLEX your way of telling the story must be SIMPLE.

2 If your topic/stimulus/starting point is SIMPLE the way of communicating your piece can be COMPLEX.

Taking something complex and then communicating it in a complex way just makes the audience hate you. Communicating an idea clearly is important. If you don't know what you are doing and why then an audience won't either. It just becomes an annoying mystery that makes the spectator feel like they don't 'get it'.

TIP

When writing your Devising log, don't be afraid to use the word 'I'. However, don't take credit for work you didn't do or work that didn't occur.

KEY TERM:

Stage business: the small movements an actor might do onstage, such as opening a book, brushing hair or straightening cushions. These movements may add to the naturalism of a scene or provide insight into the characters.

In the context of this section:

▶ To 'analyse' is to identify and investigate.

▶ To 'evaluate' is to assess the merit of the different approaches used and formulate judgements.

Section 3 of your Devising log provides you the opportunity to show your skills at analysing and evaluating your devised work. You need to include:

▶ how far you developed your theatrical skills

▶ the benefits you brought to the pair/group and the way in which you helped to shape the final piece

▶ the overall impact you personally had on the devising, rehearsals and performance.

You could also, if appropriate, consider the areas of the devising that didn't go as well as you had hoped or could have been further developed.

In order to write concisely about how well you succeeded, you need to be very clear about what you hoped to achieve.

Here is an example of a performer analysing and evaluating their work:

I knew that my role was a comic one, so I worked hard with Sam to get the timing of the office scene correct. ❶ There was a tricky piece of physical comedy where I spilled a drink on him, which didn't work at first. It seemed unbelievable and sloppy. ❷ However, I suggested that Sam should do some stage business with the folders so he seemed to be caught more by surprise and the spilt drink caused more damage. ❸ I was pleased with that scene in the final performance. Judging by the audience's laughter, it worked very well. ❹

Analysis (❶)

Evaluation (❷)

Analysis (❸)

Evaluation (❹)

Here is an example of a costume designer analysing and evaluating their work:

Evaluation

Analysis

Evaluation

Analysis

Evaluation

As our piece was set in the 1950s, I spent a long time making sure that I got every period detail as correct as possible. I found a vintage clothing shop and purchased a small handbag for Ruth that was perfect for the period ① and looked great with her dress. ② However, I was frustrated that despite studying magazines for the period, I never got her hairstyle exactly right. ③ With a larger budget, we might have thought about using a wig or perhaps I needed more training in how to get a **beehive** look. ④ However, the overall look was clearly of the period, and there were excellent details like the colour of her nail polish. ⑤

TASK 9

Choose an aspect of your contribution to the final piece and write a paragraph explaining:

▶ what you did

▶ what was successful about it

▶ what could have been improved.

KEY TERM:

Beehive: a hairstyle popular in the 1950s and 1960s for which hair was back-combed into a high cone shape.

Audience questionnaire

Name of piece:

1 When and where did you think this play was set?

2 What moments did you particularly like and why?

3 What did you think could have been improved and why?

4 Please provide some comments on the performances.

5 Please provide some comments on the design (set, costume, lighting, sound and puppet, as appropriate).

6 What do you think the message of the piece was?

7 On a scale of 1 to 10 with 1 being the worst and 10 the best, what score would you give this?

 TIP

To improve their analysis and evaluation section, some groups find it helpful to have the audience complete a questionnaire. You should write the questionnaire specifically to suit your devised piece.

For example, if you set it in a particular time period, did they understand that? If your piece had a message, did they know what it was? If you created a comedy, did they think it was funny? If you had audience interaction, did they engage with that?

Checking your Devising log

Your Devising log must be your own work. Even though you have devised as part of a group, you must put together your Devising log on your own. Your work may be presented in written form or a combination of recorded evidence and written, or entirely recorded.

As you are preparing your Devising log, keep checking it against the following checklist:

 TIP

Often students discover that one section of their log is weaker than others. Go back to that section and look at it critically. Seek out anything important that you might have missed. Some students make basic errors such as forgetting to discuss the stimulus or what they hoped to achieve with the piece.

CHALLENGE

In order to succeed at a high level, you need to provide precise details and an impressive amount of creativity. Check your work to make sure your creative journey is clear and that you have backed it up with specific details.

 TIP

The Devising log may be written, an audio/visual/audiovisual recording or a combination of the two. If you are unsure which method of creating your Devising log would be best for you, discuss this with your teacher. Don't assume that speaking in a recording is necessarily easier than writing, as it will require the same preparation and organisation. No matter which method you choose, you should make sure that your work does not exceed the maximum length/timing. Your work may be accompanied by:

- ▶ photographs and/or
- ▶ sketches/drawings and/or
- ▶ cue sheets.

- ☐ Have I written or recorded three sections with the appropriate headings?
- ☐ Are the sections roughly the same length?
- ☐ Have I stayed within the final word count/length?
- ☐ Have I provided evidence of research?
- ☐ Have I stated my dramatic aims and intentions?
- ☐ Have I shown how I developed and refined ideas?
- ☐ Have I explained how I helped the group?
- ☐ Have I shown how I responded to feedback?
- ☐ Have I demonstrated that I have developed my theatrical skills?
- ☐ Have I explained how I positively shaped the final piece?
- ☐ Have I used correct theatrical terminology to explain my thoughts?
- ☐ Have I given specific examples to back-up my points?
- ☐ Have I analysed and evaluated my work?

WHAT HAVE I LEARNED?

DEVISING DRAMA

CHOICE OF STIMULI

- A photograph, painting or sculpture
- A poem, news article or short story
- A song or piece of instrumental music
- A recent or current event
- A theme, such as 'Time' or 'War'
- A myth or fairy tale
- A cultural event, e.g. festival or ceremony

CHOICE OF GENRE

- Comedy
- Tragedy
- Physical theatre
- Melodrama
- Commedia dell'arte
- Documentary theatre
- Epic theatre
- TIE
- Naturalism

CHOICE OF SPECIALISM

- Performer
- Set
- Lighting
- Designer
- Sound
- Puppet
- Costume

HOW TO DEVISE

- Generate ideas
- Respond to feedback
- Research
- Rehearse
- Polish and refine
- Design

DEVISING LOG

- Section 1: Response to stimulus
- Section 2: Development and collaboration
- Section 3: Analysis and evaluation
- The devised performance

CHECK YOUR LEARNING

If you are uncertain of the meaning of any of the terms above, go back and revise.

Why not use the downloadable version of this summary as a basis for your own checklist of what you have learned from Samples & Downloads at www.illuminatepublishing.com.

This component is a practical component in which students are assessed on their ability to apply theatrical skills to realise artistic intentions in live performance.

For this component students must complete two assessment tasks:

▶ Study and present a key extract (monologue, duologue or group performance).

▶ Study and present a second key extract (monologue, duologue or group performance) from the same play.

Each student must choose to be assessed as a:

▶ performer or
▶ lighting designer or
▶ sound designer or
▶ set designer or
▶ costume designer or
▶ puppet designer.

You must choose the same specialism for both extracts.

ASSESSMENT FOCUS

Assessment objective: AO2: Apply theatrical skills to realise artistic intentions in live performance.

CHALLENGE

If performing, choose a role that will give you sufficient opportunities. There are many ways in which you could show an excellent range of skills by attempting roles with at least some of these qualities: emotional depth; physical precision; an interesting context; vocal variation. If you are playing two different characters in the extracts, make sure you have differentiated between them. If you are playing the same character, there may be the opportunity to show how that character has grown or changed from the earlier extract.

TIP

Keep track of the length of your piece.

Getting started

You must decide on your specialism and the play text you will be studying and presenting. **The play you choose cannot be one you studied for Component 1 and cannot have the same playwright, genre description, performance style or time period as your Component 1 play.** This is in order to give you a varied experience of drama. It will allow you to learn about different plays and styles.

You may prepare monologues, work with one other performer on a duologue or you may perform in group pieces with up to five other students. If you choose to design, you will be designing for the extracts being performed by others.

How you will be assessed

Whether you are a designer or a performer, you will be assessed on the following contribution to the performance in both extracts:

▶ Range of skills demonstrated.
▶ Skills deployed precisely and in an effective way.
▶ Personal interpretation that is appropriate to the play as a whole.
▶ Personal interpretation that is sensitive to context.
▶ Artistic intentions are achieved.
▶ The length of your piece is dictated by the number in your group.
▶ If you are doing a monologue your performance of each monologue should be between two and five minutes.
▶ If you are doing a duologue, the extracts should be between three and ten minutes.
▶ If you are doing a group performance, each extract should be between four and 20 minutes.

▲ School play

Performers

If you choose to be a performer, you must perform and interpret one role or character per extract – or more than one role if, for example, it is a multi-role. You may perform the same character in both extracts or perform different characters in each extract. For example, a performer in two extracts from 'Romeo and Juliet' could play Juliet in both extracts or Juliet in the first extract and another character such as Juliet's Nurse or even Romeo in the second extract. You may play a character of any age, gender or background.

How to approach a script

Whatever script you decide to perform, you will need to study it carefully in order to make decisions about how the characters can be interpreted. Below are examples from three different genres of scripts showing initial questions that an actor might ask and suggestions of rehearsal techniques to explore the scenes further, which could be used with a wide variety of scripts.

A naturalistic script

This scene is the opening of a play about teenagers and their fumbling journey towards adulthood. In it, Amy is getting ready to pierce the ear of her friend, Tom.

'Citizenship' by Mark Ravenhill (2006)

One

Amy, Tom

AMY: You got the Nurofen? ❶

TOM: Yeah.

AMY: Take four.

TOM: It says two.

AMY: Yeah, but if you're gonna really numb yourself you gotta do four.

TOM: I dunno. ❷

AMY: Do you want it to hurt?

TOM: No.

AMY: Then take four. Here. ❸

[AMY *passes* TOM *vodka. He uses it to wash down four Nurofen.*] ❹

AMY: Now put the ice cube on your ear.

[TOM *does this.*] ❺

AMY: Now you gotta hold it there till you can't feel nothing.

TOM: Thanks for helping. ❻

AMY: It's gonna look good.

TOM: Yeah?

---

❶ Where is this scene happening?

❷ From this opening, what do you think the relationship is between Tom and Amy?

❸ These lines are very short. What might that suggest about Amy at this point?

❹ What might Tom's facial expression be when he drinks vodka?

❺ How can the actor portray what it feels like to have a cold ice cube on his ear?

❻ Why do you think Tom says this line?

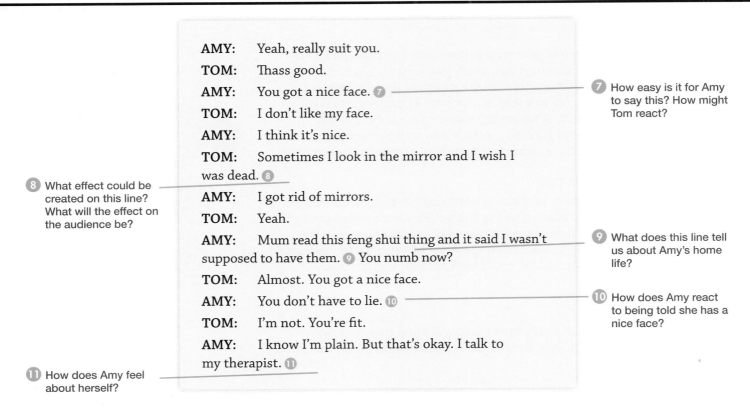

AMY: Yeah, really suit you.

TOM: Thass good.

AMY: You got a nice face. ⑦ ———————————————— ⑦ How easy is it for Amy to say this? How might Tom react?

TOM: I don't like my face.

AMY: I think it's nice.

TOM: Sometimes I look in the mirror and I wish I was dead. ⑧

⑧ What effect could be created on this line? What will the effect on the audience be?

AMY: I got rid of mirrors.

TOM: Yeah.

AMY: Mum read this feng shui thing and it said I wasn't supposed to have them. ⑨ You numb now? ——— ⑨ What does this line tell us about Amy's home life?

TOM: Almost. You got a nice face.

AMY: You don't have to lie. ⑩ ———————————————— ⑩ How does Amy react to being told she has a nice face?

TOM: I'm not. You're fit.

AMY: I know I'm plain. But that's okay. I talk to my therapist. ⑪

⑪ How does Amy feel about herself?

 TIP

There is no one right answer to these questions, but how you personally decide to answer them is the basis for your interpretation of the characters.

 TIP

In naturalistic acting, the audience will want to see how believable you can make the characters and their reactions to situations.

Try the following rehearsal exercises using the above excerpt.

Sense memory

One common rehearsal technique is to recall physical conditions and relive them. In this scene, Tom swallows Nurofen, takes a swig of vodka and puts an ice cube on his ear. All of these need to be realistically recreated by the actor. Focusing on those three actions:

▶ Recall a time when you found it hard to swallow a pill – how did it taste and feel?

▶ Recall a time when you tasted something that was surprisingly strong, sour or unpleasant – how did you feel?

▶ Recall a time when you were suddenly very cold – how did that feel?

Working individually, go through the motions of swallowing a pill, taking a gulp of an unpleasant or surprising drink and putting something very cold on your ear (some people find it helpful to do this with their eyes closed). What sensations could you remember? What physical reactions did you have? Then apply those remembered sensations to the relevant parts of the scene.

Actions

From this scene there are hints about Tom and Amy's relationship. One way to explore this is by playing different actions. That means to agree what the character wants to achieve in the scene. For example, Amy's action for the scene might be 'to get close to Tom' or 'to help Tom' or 'to show Tom how much I like him'. With your partner:

▶ Decide if your character wants the same thing throughout the scene or if it changes at some point.

▶ Choose a verb to describe what your character wants, such as 'to reassure', 'to command', 'to console' or 'to approach', for each section of the scene.

▶ Play the scene and explore how your choice of action words might affect your performance. If you chose 'to get close to', does your character find excuses to be near or touch the other character? If you chose 'to help', does your character speak in a calm and reassuring way to the other?

A stylised script

A stylised script can make different demands on the actor, as you may be creating exaggerated characters or use techniques such as physical theatre or choral speaking.

The play '**The Trial**' (1970) by Steven Berkoff, adapted from a novel by Franz Kafka (published in 1925), is about a bank clerk, Josef K, who is arrested without knowing of what crime he has been accused. Berkoff uses many stylised conventions such as a narrator, chorus, soundscapes and physical theatre.

TIP

There is no one way to play these roles. There are many aspects of personal interpretation for you to consider. For example, you may choose to use a particular accent or a certain gesture that you believe is appropriate.

TIP

As you can have no more than six performers in your group, you will need to use multi-role if you choose this script as there are many characters.

The City [Act One, Scene Two of 'The Trial']

Sound of ticking clocks made by the CHORUS. *'Josef K' sung.* ❶

NARRATOR: It was eight o'clock. The city came to life. ❷

[*Cacophony of city life.*] ❸

CHORUS 1: Someone must have been lying about Josef K.

CHORUS 2: For without having done anything wrong …

CHORUS 3: He was arrested one fine morning.

CHORUS 4: His landlady who always brought the breakfast at eight o'clock …

CHORUS 5: Failed to appear. ❹

K: That had never happened before. ❺

CHORUS 1: K waiting a little longer.

CHORUS 2: People opposite seemed to be staring at him with distinct curiosity.

CHORUS 3: Then feeling put out and hungry, he rang the bell.

[CHORUS *as bell reaches threatening crescendo.* ❻ TWO GUARDS *enter in bowler hats.*] ❼

GUARD 1: You rang?

K: I rang for the maid.

GUARD 1: What's your name?

K: Josef K.

GUARD 2: He's the one.

GUARD 1: Wouldn't you know anyway.

GUARD 2: Pale as fear.

GUARD 1: Are you frightened, K?

K: What have I done … Why! ❽

---

❸ How can the Chorus use vocal and physical skills to create city life?

❹ How will the Chorus move during this sequence? Will they stand in one place or move around the stage? Will they move as individuals or as a group?

Splendid Productions' 'Josef K'. ▼

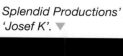

❶ How can the Chorus create the sound of the ticking clocks? Should they perform a movement sequence for this section?

❷ Is the Narrator one of the Chorus or a separate figure? Should he step out of the group and address the audience directly?

❺ How will Josef K stand out from the other characters? Is he less exaggerated and more realistic? Does he have particular mannerisms to make him seem unassuming and 'ordinary'?

❻ How can the Chorus use their vocal skills to create the sound of the bell ringing?

❼ How can two members of the Chorus transform into the two Guards? Will they change their body language and way of walking?

❽ How can the performer playing Josef K make his fear and confusion clear by using vocal and physical skills?

KEY TERM:

Ward: someone, usually a young person, who has a guardian or other legal authority responsible for them.

Rehearsal techniques

Choral movement

Follow the hand: have one person in your group be the leader. The rest of the group faces the leader. The leader raises their hand, palm towards the group, and the group must follow it, while staying in the same position in the group. So, if the leader's hand moves to the right, the group leans to the right. If the hand goes low the group squats down. If the hand trembles, then the whole group quivers in time with it.

Apply this technique to the clock sequence. The leader should conduct the group to move in time with the 'tick tock' sounds. They can experiment with changing levels or tempo.

A double act

Have the performers playing two guards experiment with pair work by trying the following:

▶ Create movements in the scene where you mirror each other.

▶ Create movements where you seem to be opposites. For example, one of you takes little steps and the other very large ones; one of you moves very quickly and the other very slowly.

▶ Create movements that show you are such a team that you are always in contact with each other. No matter how much you move some part of you is in contact with the other: a foot, an elbow, a hand, a knee, a forehead, etc.

A period script

Using scripts from different periods, such as Greek, Elizabethan or Victorian, offers you the opportunity to demonstrate particular acting skills. Your interpretation of the character and scene must be appropriate for the play's context. In the Victorian comedy, '**The Importance of Being Earnest**' (1895) by Oscar Wilde, two men, Jack and Algernon, pretend to be named Earnest in order to win the affections of Gwendolen and Cecily respectively. In this scene, Gwendolen, who lives in London, has travelled to the country house of Jack. She has met his **ward**, Cecily. At first the two women seem to like each other, but upon discovering that they are both engaged to Earnest (although in reality two different men pretending to be named Earnest) they now loathe each other. However, due to the manner in which they have been brought up, they believe they must maintain the pretence of being polite. Cecily's servant, Merriman, has just served them both tea in the garden.

1 Gwendolen is insulting Cecily who lives in the country. How could this line be delivered without making the insult too obvious, yet ensuring it has the required effect on Cecily? How could Cecily react?

3 An 'aside' is when an actor speaks directly to the audience. How should the actor make clear that they are speaking the character's thoughts? How might her tone of voice be different in the aside than it is when she speaks to Cecily?

7 How will Merriman behave at this point? Will he keep a straight face or react to what Cecily has done? Will he pause or pretend nothing has happened?

9 Does Cecily 'rise' in the same way as Gwendolen? Should Gwendolen and Cecily's movements ever mirror each other?

11 Cecily is dismissing Gwendolen, in effect, telling her to 'go away'. How could this line be delivered while still maintaining the conventions of Victorian good manners?

'The Importance of Being Earnest'

1 **GWENDOLEN:** Personally I cannot understand how anybody manages to exist in the country, if anybody who is anybody does. The country always bores me to death.

CECILY: Ah! This is what the newspapers call agricultural depression, is it not? I believe the aristocracy are suffering very much from it just at present. It is almost an epidemic amongst them, I have just been told. **2** May I offer you some tea, Miss Fairfax?

GWENDOLEN [*with elaborate politeness*]: Thank you [*Aside.*] **3** Detestable girl! But I require tea!

CECILY [*sweetly*]: Sugar?

GWENDOLEN [*superciliously*]: No, thank you. Sugar is not fashionable any more. [CECILY *looks angrily at her, takes up the tongs and puts four lumps of sugar into the cup.*] **4**

CECILY [*severely*]: Cake or bread and butter?

GWENDOLEN [*in a bored manner*]: Bread and butter, please. Cake is rarely seen at the best houses nowadays. **5**

CECILY [*cuts a very large slice of cake and puts it on the tray*]: Hand that to Miss Fairfax. **6**

[MERRIMAN *does so,* **7** *and goes out with footman.* GWENDOLEN *drinks the tea and makes a grimace. Puts down cup at once, reaches out her hand to the bread and butter, looks at it, and finds it is cake. Rises in indignation.*] **8**

GWENDOLEN: You have filled my tea with lumps of sugar, and though I asked most distinctly for bread and butter, you have given me cake. I am known for the gentleness of my disposition, and the extraordinary sweetness of my nature, but I warn you, Miss Cardew, you may go too far.

CECILY [*rising*]: **9** To save my poor, innocent, trusting boy from the **machinations** of any other girl there are no lengths to which I would not go.

GWENDOLEN: From the moment I saw you I distrusted you. I felt that you were false and deceitful. I am never deceived in such matters. My first impressions of people are invariably right. **10**

CECILY: It seems to me, Miss Fairfax, that I am trespassing on your valuable time. No doubt you have many other calls of a similar character to make in the neighbourhood. **11**

2 Cecily is very young and has apparently misunderstood what agricultural depression is (when farmers are suffering economically) and instead suggests that Gwendolen is depressed because she is in the country. How would Gwendolen react to this?

4 How will the actor playing Cecily handle the props to make clear they are intentionally giving Gwendolen too much sugar?

5 What are Gwendolen's motivations for saying this line?

6 How can this moment be made comic?

8 How can Gwendolen show her mounting anger?

10 Although both Cecily and Gwendolen are in conflict and angry with each other, this is also a source of comedy as they have gone so quickly from an apparently polite conversation to anger. How could this be played to show how completely their opinions of each other have changed?

> **KEY TERM:**
>
> **Machinations:** plots, conspiracies or schemes.

Rehearsal exercises

Rehearsal costumes and props: to help recreate the movement appropriate for a piece set in Victorian England, use ankle-length rehearsal skirts so that you can experience how that will alter your movement. For example, Victorian women such as Gwendolen and Cecily would be unlikely to cross their legs or slouch in their chairs.

Also use prop cups, saucers and cutlery so that you can practise handling them with ease. Consider what other props might be used such as Cecily's books or Gwendolen's parasol.

'The Importance of Being Earnest' ▶

Comedy of manners

One of the sources of humour in the scene is that while outwardly the two women are being very polite to each other, inwardly they are both furious. As a rehearsal technique improvise a scene in which two characters are being incredibly polite to each other. From all external signs, anyone watching them would think that they liked each other. However, despite their smiles, they are saying horrible things to each other.

Now apply any discoveries you have made about how manners can cover real feelings and play the scene as politely as possible.

REFLECTION

How can the comedy of the scene be emphasised through the characters' elaborate use of good manners?

Approaching monologues

If you choose to perform a monologue, you will be assessed on the same basis as you would performing a duologue or a group piece, including showing a range of skills and an understanding of the context. In addition, you will have some specific choices to make. Decide the following:

▶ Is your monologue being addressed to the audience or to one or more characters?

▶ If your monologue is addressed to one other character, where should you 'place' that character (where you imagine they are sitting or standing) so when you are speaking to them your eye line is consistent and your facial expressions clearly seen. If addressed to several characters, how will you make that clear?

▶ Where is your monologue located? How will your character use the space?

▶ If your monologue is directed to the audience, what is your attitude to the audience? Are you explaining things to them? Confiding in them? Entertaining them?

▶ How does your monologue fit into the play as a whole?

TIP

Avoid spending too much of your performance with your back to your audience or in profile. In order to demonstrate a range of skills, seek out any opportunities to use appropriate facial expressions, gestures and movement.

Below is an example of a naturalistic monologue.

① Asagai is speaking to Beneatha in her family's living room. At the start of the scene where should he be positioned? Where will he be looking when referring to Beneatha? What furniture or other props might be in the room, which he might use?

② What are his motivations for speaking to Beneatha like this?

③ For a monologue, this line would be cut.

④ His tone changes after this pause. Why?

⑤ Throughout the speech he speaks about contrasts, such as 'swiftly and slowly' or 'dramatic' and then 'quiet'. How could vocal skills emphasise these contrasts?

⑥ What might his facial expression be like when he dreams about being a great man?

⑦ This is a shocking idea. Would he say this in a casual, matter of fact voice or play it for dramatic effect?

⑧ For a monologue this line would be cut.

⑨ How does he change the mood on this line?

'A Raisin in the Sun' (1959) by Lorraine Hansberry [Act 3]

Set in Chicago, this play deals with an African-American family's financial struggles during a time of emerging awareness of civil rights and the fight against segregation. In this monologue from Act 3, Joseph Asagai, a bright, personable, ambitious Nigerian student, is challenging the attitudes of Beneatha (who he calls Alaiyo), including what he considers her very American attitude towards money and her African heritage. He begins by questioning her family's expectation to receive insurance money when her father died. Before this speech, Beneatha despairs because her brother, Walter, has squandered the money that would have gone towards her education.

ASAGAI: ① Then isn't there something wrong in a house – in a world – where all dreams, good or bad, must depend on the death of a man? I never thought to see you like this, Alaiyo. You! ② Your brother made a mistake and you are grateful to him so that now you can give up the ailing human race on account it! You talk about what good is struggle, what good is anything! Where are we all going and why are we bothering!

BENEATHA: AND YOU CANNOT ANSWER IT! ③

ASAGAI [*shouting over her*]: I LIVE THE ANSWER! [*Pause.*] ④ In my village at home it is the exceptional man who can even read a newspaper … or who ever sees a book at all. I will go home and much of what I will have to say will seem strange to the people of my village. But I will teach and work and things will happen, slowly and swiftly. At times it will seem that nothing changes at all … and then again the sudden dramatic events which make history leap into the future. And then quiet again. ⑤ Retrogression even. Guns, murder, revolution. And I even will have moments when I wonder if the quiet was not better than all that death and hatred. But I will look about my village at the illiteracy and disease and ignorance and I will not wonder long. And perhaps … perhaps I will be a great man ⑥ … I mean perhaps I will hold on to the substance of truth and find my way always with the right course … and perhaps for it I will be butchered in my bed some night by the servants of empire … ⑦

BENEATHA: *The martyr!* ⑧

ASAGAI [*He smiles*]: … or perhaps I shall live to be a very old man, respected and esteemed in my new nation … ⑨ And perhaps I shall hold office and this is what I'm trying to tell you, Alaiyo: Perhaps the things I believe now for my country will be wrong and outmoded, and I will not understand and do terrible things to have things my way or merely to keep my power. Don't you see that there will be young men and women – not British soldiers then, but my own black countrymen – to step out of the shadows some evening and slit my then useless throat? ⑩ Don't you see that they have always been there … that they always will be. And that such a thing as my own death will be an advance? They who might kill me even … actually replenish all that I was. ⑪

⑩ How could tension be built up through this section?

⑪ What might his final physical position be at the end of this speech?

KEY TERM:

Retrogression: going backwards, to an earlier time or state.

TIP

You do not have to use a specific accent for any monologue. If you can do an accent well that could demonstrate a theatrical skill, but it is better not to do an accent than do it badly. In a case like '**A Raisin in the Sun**', it would be advisable to make clear on your Statement of Dramatic Intentions whether or not you were aiming to show his character through your choice of accent.

TIP

It is your responsibility to time your monologue/duologue/group piece and make sure that each is the correct length. Depending on how quickly you speak or how much movement you put in the performance, performers doing exactly the same material may find that the performance length can differ widely. If a piece is too long then you must make some edits and if it is too short, you should either include a wider selection from the script or make sure that you aren't rushing your performance.

KEY TERMS:

Resonance: the quality, strength and depth of sound.

Diaphragm: the large muscle that stretches across the bottom of the rib-cage.

Rehearsal techniques

Subtext:

A. There are a number of mood shifts in this speech. Go through it and break it into smaller bits each time you think Asagai's motivations change. For example, for the first few lines his motivations might be 'to shame Beneatha' or 'to scold Beneatha'. Later sections might be 'to impress her', 'to shock her', 'to show her a different way of life' and so forth. Then experiment with playing the scene with those intentions.

B. After this speech, Asagai asks Beneatha to go to Nigeria with him. Experiment with ways of performing this scene with the subtext of making Beneatha love him and want to be with him.

Characterisation:

Asagai comes from a different background than the other characters in the play. This influences his accent, manners and attitudes. Experiment with specific choices, such as a Nigerian accent (accents can be researched online), a very strong, upright posture and powerful gestures.

Vocal warm-ups

Whatever piece you choose you will be expected to display your vocal skills. One way to improve your vocal ability is to undertake vocal warm-ups. These help to free up your voice, increase your vocal range and **resonance**, and improve your diction.

1 **Breathing:** making sure that your neck and shoulders are relaxed, place your hands on your **diaphragm**. Breathe in slowly for ten counts and then out for ten counts. Make sure that your shoulders and chest are not rising up and down when you breathe. The action should come from your diaphragm.

2 **Vowels:** slowly breathe in and then breathe out making the vowel sounds (A, E, I, O, U), with an 'm' sound in front: Mah, Mee, Mie, Moh, Moo. The 'M' sound should help you to bring your voice forwards and the vowels should sound open and free.

3 **Diction:** over-enunciate tongue twisters such as:

THE **LIPS**, THE **TEETH**, THE **TIP OF THE TONGUE**

NEW YORK **UNIQUE**, **UNIQUE** NEW YORK

ROUND THE **RAGGED ROCKS** THE **RAGGED RASCALS RAN**

I find sighing for a minute or two at the beginning of the warm-up very useful as it's a gentle way to ease into a vocal warm-up. As well as this, making a noise like a siren on an 'ng' is very good to warm up the range of the voice. Finally, making an 'ooo' sound on a really low note whilst in a squatted position is good for focusing the sound lower in the body so I am grounded and more resonant.

Baker Mukasa, actor

THEATRE MAKER ADVICE

Physical warm-ups

Physical warm-ups are useful to relax areas of tension and increase flexibility and energy. Try the following:

1 **Gentle head rolls:** standing, drop your head to your chest and then gently roll it up to one side and then back to the other so that you are making half-circles from side-to-side.

2 **Shoulder rolls:** gently roll both shoulders backwards several times and then forwards several times. Then straighten one arm and swing that in wide circles, checking that your shoulder is relaxed while you are rotating your arm. Then repeat on the other side.

3 **Loosen up:** lay on the floor and, starting with your feet and working upwards, tense and then relax each part of your body. End with scrunching up your face and then relaxing it.

4 **Shake out:** standing up, shake out each arm and leg eight times, counting aloud as you go. Then repeat for a count of four. Then for a count of two. Lastly, a count of one. Then shake your whole body out.

5 **Mirror:** facing your partner, take it in turns to mirror each other's actions and then switch leaders. See if you can become so in tune with each other that eventually you can continue without knowing who is the leader. This exercise is good for focus and teamwork.

 TIP

As with any physical exercise, know your limits and be particularly careful with any work involving your neck and spine. When rising from the ground, don't spring up, but roll to one side, bend your knees and stand up one foot at a time.

◀ *Actors perform a range of physical and vocal warm-ups before rehearsals and performances, like this cast.*

THEATRE MAKER ADVICE

Baker Mukasa, actor

Rolling down the spine is a great way to begin a physical warm-up, as it increases the mobility of the spine and makes you feel more connected to your body. The more mobile and connected you are to your spine the more you will be able to not only physicalise other characters convincingly but also avoid injuries that may occur due to the physical demands of a play.

Swings are great full body warm-ups. Raise arms above head and then drop upper body towards the floor letting legs bend and arms brush the floor as they swing back and then up again bring you back to standing. It warms up and releases tension in your shoulders, warms up your legs and gets you heart rate up.

Doing high knees is a great warm-up to get the heart rate up and give you the energy you need in order to go onstage.

Characterisation

Your performance must show your understanding of the characters, the play and its context. In order to show this understanding, make sure you understand what has happened before your excerpt begins and what will follow it. What is the world of the play (date, location, etc.) and how does your character fit into this world?

THEATRE MAKER ADVICE

Baker Mukasa, actor

I look at first understanding the basic story, what are the key themes and ideas expressed and where does the action of the play take place. From there, I then focus specifically on my character by listing what my character says about others, what my character says about himself, what other characters say about my character and what does my character do in every scene. This will act as the foundation of ongoing character work and help me understand how he is perceived and his relationships with everyone around him.

In '**A Raisin in the Sun**' the fact that Asagai comes from a different society and disapproves of the values of the American characters is important to the play. Performers can show this through their use of accent, tone, body language and gestures.

The very different rules of Victorian society influence the vocal and movement choices of the performers in '**The Importance of Being Earnest**'.

Although '**Citizenship**' is a more modern English text, character choices, such as a choice of accent and use of teenage body language, will allow you to show characterisation.

'**The Trial**' is set in a nightmarish world in which your character might be a victim or a tormentor, which will guide your choices, for example if you are a tormentor you might be obviously dominant in your movements or you might hide your intentions.

Baker Mukasa, actor

When I was playing Harry Dalton, a stable owner in '**Equus**', I was struggling to find the weight he would have commanded. As he was a stable owner, used to commanding and taking care of horses, he needed to be grounded. To try and lock into this I did an animal study of a horse to inform how I characterised him, as they are very heavy and have a commanding presence. I used how heavily they breathed and their stance to inform how I played Dalton. Using the horse as a reference really helped me to key into Dalton's character and play him truthfully.

THEATRE MAKER ADVICE

TASK 11

Think of an animal that might share some of the characteristics of your character. Are they are proud as a peacock or as timid as a mouse? Can you find ways of adding these characteristics to your character?

Rehearsal techniques for developing and polishing your performance

Below are common performance problems and suggested rehearsal techniques to help.

PROBLEM	POSSIBLE REHEARSAL TECHNIQUE
Lack of tension	Focus on reactions. Use numbered cards to increase the reactions, with the higher the number the more intense/extreme the reaction. How is a '5' reaction different from a '10'? Which is appropriate for this play?
Rushed	Focus on pause and pace: try using pauses to increase tension or allow for reactions. Do a subtext exercise, such as thought-tracking, making sure you know what the character is thinking on every line.
Slow/dull	Do a double-time run: perform all the lines and actions but in double-time. Did this help you to discover any wasted moments/slow transitions? Increase the stakes: give the characters a deadline/time limit. If they don't convince the other character of X by Y amount of time it will be the end of the world, for example.
Lack of commitment/ not believable	Create the world of the character: use props or costumes that will help you to put yourself fully into the character's shoes.

Dealing with performance stress

Nerves and stage fright are common for even the most experienced of actors. It would be a very unusual actor who hasn't felt that tightening of muscles, the dry mouth and shaking hands that go with the stress of performing. Learning to manage nerves is part of an actor's job. Below are some techniques to help you:

▶ Know your role inside out so that you could do it in your sleep or standing on your head if you had to.

▶ If you are still struggling with lines shortly before the performance even the slightest distraction can throw you off.

▶ Another example from a Theatre Maker on characterisation can be seen in the 'A Midsummer Night's Dream' section (page 150), where Peter Forbes describes his approach to the character of 'Bottom'.

- ▶ Imagine what your character is doing right before they enter. Have they run in from the rain or argued with a parent? Whatever they have done, bring a bit of that world onstage with you. For example, if appropriate for your character and their situation, you might enter shaking out your umbrella or jog on out of breath. Focusing on actions will help prevent self-consciousness.

- ▶ If you are performing with others, really listen and react to them onstage. Create a bubble of concentration that excludes distractions.

- ▶ When performing, imagine that someone supportive is in the audience and keep that image in your mind.

THEATRE MAKER ADVICE

Baker Mukasa, actor

I deal with the stress by doing things which immerse me in the story of the play I am in and the character's journey. If I am focusing on that then I won't focus on the things that tend to stress me out, e.g. what will people think, will I remember everything? One thing that helps me do this is I find music that echoes the atmosphere of my first scene, so if it's a confrontational scene I will listen to something aggressive and energetic. By shifting the focus away from the anxiety I am feeling and just focusing on the story it helps me to feel less stressed.

What if something goes wrong?

In theatre, sometimes things go wrong. A prop might be dropped, a line forgotten, a door won't open or a costume rips. These accidents do not have to be a disaster if dealt with well.

The best course of action is prevention. Make sure that you have tried out all your props and costumes before your first performance. Double-check that costumes fit and are not pulling at the seams or causing you to trip. Some props, which are not handled by the actors, may be secured to the set so that they don't accidentally fall over. None of the technical elements of the production should come as a surprise during the performance and any glitches should be ironed out beforehand.

If something still goes wrong, if possible, stay in character. For example, if someone in your group forgets a line, it is far better to stay in character and help them to find their place by either **ad-libbing** a line that will help them to remember where they are or to carry on to your next line rather than dropping out of character and telling them what their line is.

If a prop is dropped, you will need to make a quick calculation whether you need to pick it up or if it should be left. If you do pick it up, do so in character.

KEY TERM:

Ad-libbing: saying lines that aren't in the script.

Whatever happens, don't judge or give up on your performance if there are mistakes. Recovering from a mistake and carrying on with confidence is always the best course of action.

Health and safety

As you plan your performance, make sure you consider any possible health and safety considerations. Some common risks and actions are listed below (but you may discover many others).

RISK	ACTIONS
Slipping onstage	Make sure stage is dry. If, in the course of a scene, liquid is spilt, avoid that area of the stage and then ensure the floor is dried before the next scene. If the stage itself is slippery, consider if the surface needs to be altered. If using a rug as part of the set, ensure it is stuck down and won't cause actors to trip. Ensure that chairs and other set furniture are not set too close to the edge of the stage, where they might tip off.
Injuries during stage fights/physical actions	Any stage fights need to be carefully choreographed. Using techniques such as slow motion can create a more effective and safer fight. **Never** use actual weapons or sharp objects onstage. There should be no actual contact on slaps or punches. Focus instead on acting the reactions.

TASK 12

Go over the demands of your script and list any possible health and safety issues and decide what the solutions should be.

Avoiding errors checklist

Checking your work and avoiding common errors:

✓ Do you know all your lines?

✓ Do you know all your movements?

✓ Do you understand the play from which your excerpts come?

✓ Do you project and vary your voice?

✓ Do you stay in character even when you are not speaking?

✓ Do you listen and react to others?

✓ Are you confident about what comes next (rather than looking to others for direction)?

✓ Do you maintain your focus and energy throughout your performance?

✓ Do you establish your character by the way you speak and move?

✓ Do you help to create the world of the play (its location, period, style and themes) through your use of the performance space?

✓ Do you achieve your artistic intentions for the role (for example, if you have stated it is a comic role, have you refined the comedy to amuse the audience or if your character is heroic, have you managed to create a character with whom the audience has a sympathetic response)?

Design

As a designer you will be working collaboratively with performers to help convey the meaning of the extracts that are being performed. Throughout the process, you must work together making sure that the end product allows everyone to show their theatrical skills and demonstrate a sensitive insight into the extracts.

Lighting designer

If you choose lighting design for your specialism, you must create one lighting design per extract. Your designs should show a range of lighting **effects/states** and **cues/transitions** designed to meet the demands of the extracts being performed. Your design must be appropriate to the play as a whole and its context.

Sample stages of work

Below is a sample of the order in which you might approach the various demands of lighting design.

1 Read the play and make notes on the excerpts of various opportunities for lighting.
2 Explore the lighting capabilities of the performance space, such as available lights/lanterns, size of space and location of audience.
3 Draw a plan of the stage configuration and make notes on what areas need to be lit (angles, direction, etc.).
4 Experiment with various colour and intensity options.
5 Consider any special effects you may wish to create.
6 Hang, set and focus any lights as appropriate.
7 Create an initial lighting cue sheet.
8 Work with performers and, if appropriate, other designers to ensure that lighting is effective. For example, can the actors be seen, is the correct mood created, is the set appropriately lit?
9 Run a technical rehearsal to ensure that all lighting timings are correct.
10 Finalise lighting cue sheet.

Approaching a script

> **KEY TERMS:**
>
> **Effects:** special lighting such as strobes or using lighting to recreate headlights, lightning, fires or other unusual lighting.
>
> **States:** the settings and positioning of lighting to create certain lighting conditions, such as a bright afternoon or a moonlit scene.
>
> **Cues:** instructions indicating when a change in lighting should occur.
>
> **Transitions:** moving from one lighting state to another, such as a fade to darkness or a sudden blackout.

TIP

Be sure that your lighting is appropriate for the chosen stage configuration. For example, for an in the round configuration, make sure you avoid lights shining into the eyes of the audience.

THEATRE MAKER ADVICE

Gavin Maze, lighting designer and technician

When I've designed shows, my first step is to read through the script and highlight any mention of location, weather, atmosphere, etc. Some play texts/authors are very specific and will give direct instructions about sunlight, for example coming through windows. I actually prefer the more vague instructions as it lets me put my own stamp on it.

The play '**Macbeth**' by William Shakespeare begins in a battlefield where three witches discuss Macbeth who has successfully defeated the enemy.

Below are sample lighting designer annotations on one version of the play, which begins with the following stage direction:

1 Dark, grey lights, soft (fresnel), not sharp lines, to create grim battlefield. Possible use of gobos to create eerie patterns.

> **1** *The battlefield: thunder and lightning.* **2**
> *Enter three witches.* **3**

2 Use of strobe or other flashing lights to create lightning effects.

3 Three distinct pools of light (downlighting, profile spots) one for each witch, green filter to make them look otherworldly or else possibly have each witch enter with a handheld light?

Later in the script the witches describe the weather:

5 Blackout or fade for their exit? Possible cross-fade?

> **ALL:** Fair is foul and foul is fair
> Hover through the fog and filthy air. **4**
> *Exeunt.* **5**

4 Should this be from the beginning of the scene? Green side lighting to highlight effect of fog (can we use dry ice or other smoke machine effect)?

> ### KEY TERM:
> **Cross-fade:** fading lights out on one area of the stage while simultaneously bringing them up on another area.

TASK 13

Go through the excerpts you are working on and make notes for any possible lighting effects. You might consider how you create the time of day, location and season. You might want to use lights to pick out particular characters or to add to the atmosphere of a scene.

Lighting equipment

Depending on where your performance will be held, you may have a fully operational professional lighting set-up with computerised controls or you may be working with a basic lighting rig with a manually controlled dimmer board. The lighting equipment that you may have access could include:

▶ **Floodlight**: typically a light without a lens so it cannot be focused, but it throws out a large amount of light. They can be used to light a backscreen or to provide a 'wash' (an undefined light) over a large area.

▶ **Profile spots**: provides more sharp-edged spots of light. They have a lens and are easy to focus. They usually come with a 'gate' which can hold gobos to create special effects.

▶ **Strobe light**: a device which produces flashes of lights. The number and timing of the flashes can be controlled. These are often used to create effects such as lightning or reporters' flash bulbs or to break up movement so that the audience only sees it in flashes. Health and safety warnings must be issued when these are used as some people have negative reactions to flashing lights.

▶ **Follow spots**: these are usually manually operated lights which are used to highlight performers and follow their movements onstage. Most have changeable colour filters which can tint the light.

▶ **Colour filters**: also sometimes called 'gels', are sheets of plastic used to alter the colour of stage lighting. These are made in hundreds of different colours and can be combined to achieve just the right colour.

▶ **Gobo**: metal cut-outs which are used to project patterns, such as leaves, stars, swirls or waves.

THEATRE MAKER ADVICE

Gavin Maze, lighting designer and technician

Whilst at university one of the spaces we used had a massive pillar in the middle of the performing space. On a production of 'Into the Woods' we did in that space, we turned it into a tree and used a few different gobos to create some cool shadows and the illusion of leaves and branches. Don't let a building quirk get in your way – think of a way you can bring it in, the director will probably thank you!

TIP

Early in your design you may begin thinking about the colours and brightness you will use.

Specific effects can be achieved with handheld lights, as used in 'The Old Man and the Old Moon'. ▶

Making choices as a lighting designer

Even for the simplest lighting there are a number of choices you will make including:

▶ Where will the lights be positioned?

▶ What colours will be used?

▶ What will be the direction or angle of the light?

▶ What will be the intensity of the light?

An instruction of 'light comes in from the window' can be interpreted in many different ways:

TIP

In addition to standard stage lighting, you may use other sources of light such as torches, fairy lights or a 'disco ball' if these will create the effects you desire.

Gavin Maze, lighting designer and technician

For light through a window, generally a fresnel would be good, but this can be achieved with a profile too. You'd need to think about time and location. If the play was set abroad somewhere traditionally hot, the sun might be a bit brighter and 'whiter', whereas say it was an autumnal sunset you'd try and pick a lovely orangey/amber. Generally, the light would be rigged in a way behind the window but it all depends on angles and accessibility. Barn doors would be used here to direct the light in the way you'd want it if you had a fresnel, if you were using a profile lantern you'd use the shutters.

THEATRE MAKER ADVICE

Excerpt from a sample lighting cue sheet

CUE NUMBER	PAGE NUMBER	CUE	NOTES
1	2	Preset	FOH lights up. Single spotlight onstage
2	2	Opening Act 1 Afternoon	Room brightly lit
3	4	Darkens to dusk	Over the scene the room darkens to dusk
4	5	Gunshot	Sound cue: blackout
5	5	Sally stands centre stage	Visual: actor arrives centre stage. Spotlight up
6	7	Car approaching	Sound cue (car): headlights flash through windows of room

Note: FOH = front of house

Gavin Maze, lighting designer and technician

Look for any ideas that could enhance a scene; for example, is someone entering a room and turning on various light switches, what type of cue will that be (a visual cue or a called cue depending on if you've got someone [like a stage manager] calling the cues to you). Try and attend as many rehearsals of the show as you can as you'll pick up on something new each time.

THEATRE MAKER ADVICE

Health and safety

There are many aspects of health and safety which you should consider. Below are just a few:

RISK	SOLUTION
Burns	Wait a few minutes after switching off before removing colour filters and gobos or touching a lamp. The lamps get extremely hot and can cause injury.
Electric shock	Any work involving electricity should be done with approved equipment known to be safe. Make sure that power is off when hanging or adjusting lights.
Falls	If working on a ladder to place or adjust a lantern, make sure that someone is with you, ensuring that you are safe. Do not put lighting in any location where it could easily fall. All brackets, etc. must be checked by a professional.
Tripping over wiring or cables	Ensure that all wiring, which could cause performers or audience members to trip, has been taped down. None should be placed in locations, such as entrances, where tripping would be most likely.

Sound designer

If you choose sound design for your specialism, you must create one sound design per extract. This means that you will create two different sound plots, demonstrating a range of skills, one for each extract. Your design must show a range of sound effects and cues/transitions designed to meet the demands of the extract being performed.

Your sound design may be recorded or performed live and may include sound effects and music. Your design must be appropriate to the play as a whole and its context.

How to approach a script

THEATRE MAKER ADVICE

Max Perryment, sound designer

After reading the script, I'll talk to the director about specific themes and characters of the play, the overall directorial vision and what are the important things that an audience will need to understand. I'll then go through the script and mark every moment, however vague, where sound could be used. I'll usually mark moments that will create a sense of time and place and also opportunities where sound can be used to create certain mood or atmosphere.

Naturalistic or abstract sound design

The play '**Kindertransport**' (1993), by Diane Samuels, offers opportunities for both naturalistic and abstract sound design choices. In the play, Eva, a young German girl, travels to England by train. Throughout the play a frightening character from a storybook, *The Ratcatcher*, appears, symbolising her fears. There are sounds necessary to establish location or events and others that show how the characters are feeling or to establish an atmosphere.

Here is an excerpt from page 17 with example designer notes:

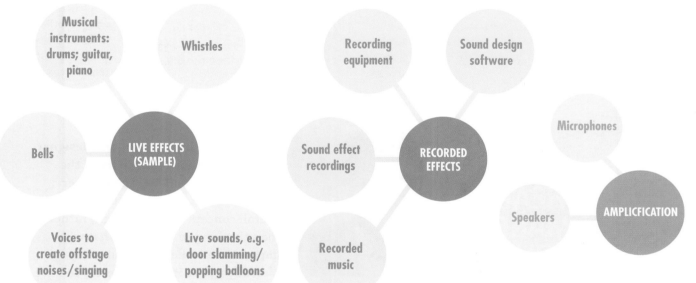

1 Abstract: ominous theme to accompany every appearance of Ratcatcher.

4 Naturalistic: train whistle – probably recorded but could it be live?

1 **RATCATCHER:** I will take the heart of your happiness away.

[*The* RATCATCHER *plays his music.* **2**

The sounds of the railway station become louder and louder. **3**

Another train whistle.] **4**

EVA: Mutti! Vati! Hello! Hello! See. I did get into the carriage. I said I would. See. I'm not crying … **5**

2 Abstract: a haunting tune. Perhaps played live on a recorder or flute?

3 Naturalistic: recorded sounds to establish train station: crowd noises, bustling.

5 Abstract: under this speech soft orchestral theme, increases in volume as speech continues.

Sound equipment

The sound equipment you will need depends on your design for the excerpts. Some typical equipment might include:

- Musical instruments: drums; guitar, piano
- Whistles
- Bells
- **LIVE EFFECTS (SAMPLE)**
- Voices to create offstage noises/singing
- Live sounds, e.g. door slamming/ popping balloons

- Recording equipment
- Sound design software
- Sound effect recordings
- **RECORDED EFFECTS**
- Recorded music

- Microphones
- Speakers
- **AMPLICFICATION**

Use of microphones and musical instruments may form part of your sound design, as in 'The Old Man and the Old Moon.' ▼

Possible opportunities to use music or sound

Beginning of or during scenes (establish locations)

Before play begins

During scene changes/transitions

The curtain call

SOUND OPPORTUNITIES

MUSIC OPPORTUNITIES

A theme when certain characters appear

Create atmosphere during scenes (shrill noises, ominous thuds)

Note key plot events (gunshots, doorbell, phone ringing)

Part of the performance (e.g. in a musical)

Underneath dialogue/action to underscore mood or create an effect (tension, comedy)

THEATRE MAKER ADVICE

Max Perryment, sound designer

TIP

There are a number of sound effects/sound mixing products available online. Technology is advancing all the time and many of the resources are free or inexpensive.

KEY TERM:

Subliminally: so that it barely registers; the audience is affected without consciously being aware of what is affecting them.

TIP

You may use sound equipment to create special effects such as a 'reverb', which is an echoing effect. This can create an ominous mood or could suggest a location, such as a large empty building.

Whatever the budget, a sound designer is responsible for telling part of the story. Even if you have one speaker and an iPhone, focus on story and the overall concept of your design, rather than thinking in terms of what will impress the audience. Decide very carefully where it may be better to have no sound at all or perhaps where sound could be used subliminally underneath scenes. Think about where you want to be naturalistic or abstract in the sound world you create. Whatever your approach your decisions will change the way the audience experiences the play.

A vital piece of software to get to know is QLab, which you can download for free. It is an industry-standard and it enables you to be very creative with sound very easily.

Creating original sound effects

You may choose to use pre-recorded sound effects or you may record your own. Using easy to find materials you can create the sound of rain, wind or a noisy crowd.

Max Perryment, sound designer

On using sound design to create atmosphere, location and character:

I think a sound designer aims to do exactly these things throughout the entire duration of the play. As an example, I recorded several solo French horn drone-like noises for the play 'Creditors'. The French horn at its quietest was reminiscent of a boat foghorn, and since the play was set near a harbour it worked as a little reminder, although quite abstractly, of the location. Additionally, there's a character called Gustav, who slowly and cruelly manipulates the other two characters. The sound that began as a distant horn became more dissonant and menacing, conveying his growing power and control over the other characters.

THEATRE MAKER ADVICE

Sample working order

1 Read script and note sound/music ideas.

2 Discuss ideas with performers and, if appropriate, other designers.

3 Decide which sounds, if any, will be recorded and which live.

4 Record or source recorded sound effects/music or locate materials for live sound effects/music.

5 Create cue sheets noting volume and duration of sound.

6 Arrange any technical requirements such as microphones, speakers or amps.

7 Decide if there are any live cues and rehearse them.

8 Rehearse cues making any necessary adjustments.

9 Have a technical rehearsal making sure all cues are accurate and all health and safety considerations have been followed (such as taped-down wires).

TIP

In addition to the volume you might consider the direction of the sound. By placing your speakers in certain positions, you may create the effect that the audience is surrounded by sound or that a sound is coming from a certain place.

KEY TERMS:

Visual: a cue that the technician must judge by watching the action onstage.

Snap: quickly on or off.

Sample sound cue sheet

CUE NUMBER	PAGE NUMBER	CUE	NOTES	DURATION
0.5	11	**Preshow music**	Preshow music. Quiet	20 mins
1	11	**Preshow music stops**	Loud ringing	Slow fade
2	21	**Alarm clock**	Visual cue when Sally switches on tablet	**Visual.** Until Sally hits alarm clock
3	24	**'You don't know love'**	Visual cue. Headlights through window	Throughout scene
4	51	**Car approaching**	Reverb increases throughout	10 secs
5	58	**Dripping water**	Crunching gravel	End cue: SALLY: No, it wasn't like that
6	76	**People approaching**	Line cue: SALLY: Stand back everyone	10 secs
7	87	**Firework bang**		**Snap**
8	87	**Firework bang x3**		Snap

Health and safety

There are many aspects of health and safety that you should consider:

RISK	SOLUTION
Tripping over wires	Ensure that any sound equipment wires are carefully taped down. Notify all performers and backstage staff of their location.
Electric shock	Any work involving electricity should be done with approved, safe equipment.
	Before adjusting speakers, amps and other equipment make sure that they are turned off.

Set designer

If you choose set design for your specialism, you must create one set design per extract. This means that you will either create two different sets to suit the two extracts or you will adapt a single set to suit each extract. The design must show dressing and props designed to meet the demands of the extract being performed.

Below are suggestions on how to approach the process of set design.

THEATRE MAKER ADVICE

Tim Shortall, set and costume designer

Q. How do you research your ideas?

A. It would depend entirely what is required.
A contemporary UK setting, for example, may be something I am already familiar with, or, if not, may be set somewhere I can visit, for first-hand experience – beats any amount of online and other research, as you get an immediate personal response to that environment, involving touch, smell, etc., as well as merely the visual.

If it's a 'period piece' I will mostly do research online, and through museums, books, documentary film.

Below are typical stages for a set design:

1 Carefully read the script. Note the practical requirements of it and first impressions of possible settings and style.

2 Discuss with the rest of the group the possible setting requirements and the atmosphere and style of the piece.

3 Research: this could include: art books; the internet; visits to museums; trips to locations; taking photographs; etc.

4 Put together initial 'mood boards' – collections of inspirations and ideas, usually mounted on a large board. They might include: sample colours; architectural details; samples of furniture; textures and patterns; inspiration from other theatre designs; etc.

5 Make first sketches and discuss with rest of the group.

6 Measure the stage area and make a **ground plan.**

7 Optional: create a card model of the set. Use this to experiment with colours, textures and placement of set furniture.

8 Make a ground plan and then work with the performance group to make sure the set will work with their requirements. For example, are the entrances and exits in the right place? Is there enough room for any physical actions?

KEY TERM:

Ground plan: a bird's-eye view of the set showing the scale of the stage and set and where key elements of the design will be located, as shown in the illustration opposite.

9 Begin creation and assembling of actual set. This may involve a number of tasks from locating pieces of furniture, painting scenery, making drapery or a backdrop, adapting existing pieces of set and so forth.

10 Check your work for health and safety issues.

11 Have a technical rehearsal to make sure that the set operates correctly and that any scene changes can be done safely and efficiently. Make any necessary adjustments.

TASK 14

Create your own ground plan for the text you are creating a set design for.

Mark the following on it:

▶ Where the audience will be.

▶ Where the entrances/exits will be.

▶ Where any large pieces of scenery will be (flats/backdrops/ large high-backed pieces of furniture).

Then check your work:

▶ Do any pieces of scenery block entrances/exits?

▶ Will the scenery fit on the stage and leave enough room for acting?

▶ Will the audience have clear sightlines of the action?

▶ Can any technology you may wish to use, such as projections, work successfully?

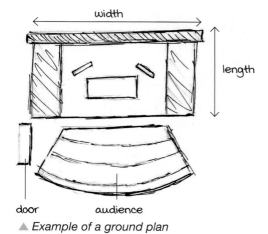

Example of a ground plan

Tim Shortall, set and costume designer

THEATRE MAKER ADVICE

Q. Can you explain how important colour and texture are in a design?

A. The power of colour to affect mood is very well known, of course. And texture can transform and give life to an otherwise dull surface, and, by providing contrast, it will give layers of interest, To give an extreme example: say I'm designing a play set in a grand Victorian house. I've researched the period, and I've tried to recreate every little detail to give as accurate a portrait as I can of the lives these people would have led at the time. There are heavily patterned wallpapers, lots of detailed mouldings, thick drapes at the tall windows, dark colours, brown woodwork and paneling, etc. But when it's finished, I think it lacks 'life' – it doesn't get to the 'heart' of the play, for me. It's too naturalistic. Without changing the structure in any way, I decide to paint the entire thing blood-red. Walls, cornicing, floor, ceiling. All in layered shades of deep, dark reds. I make the paint look as though it's peeling off the surfaces. The floor I paint in a high-gloss red, but cracked all over like a shattered mirror, reflecting the decaying surfaces in kaleidoscopic detail … The dramatic alteration in colour and texture has changed the visual impact of the entire play. So colour and texture are both powerful tools.

▲ *Sample set designs by Tim Shortall, for 'Sweet Charity', under the Manhattan Bridge (left) and 'Pitcairn' (right).*

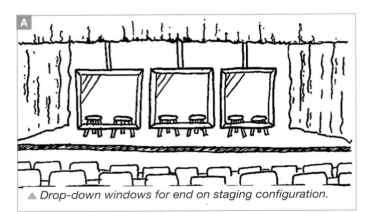

▲ *Drop-down windows for end on staging configuration.*

▲ *Painted mountain backdrop for thrust staging configuration.*

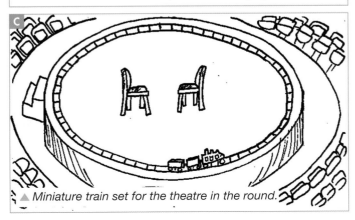

▲ *Miniature train set for the theatre in the round.*

Sample work

On the left are the first sketches of a student who is designing the set for a performance where scenes take place on a train. At this point, the group has not decided what theatre configuration or style of performance it will have so the designer is just experimenting with ideas.

All of these ideas would probably have practical challenges in a school setting, but sketches like these are a good way of beginning to develop your ideas. Some questions you might ask yourself about your initial designs include:

▶ Is this a set that could be created within the time and budget available?

▶ Do I have (or can I obtain) the necessary skills and equipment to create this set?

▶ Is this set appropriate to the mood and style of the performance piece?

▶ Will the sightlines be good for the audience?

▶ Will the set be safe for the performers and audience?

TASK 15

a   Based on the extracts with which you are working, quickly draw several sketches showing different ways you could approach the set design. At this stage, don't worry about how practical the designs are, just use this as a way of getting ideas down on paper.

b   Note any ideas that you particularly like.

c   Discuss with your group the practicalities of the space in which you are working, your budget, your skills and amount of time you have. Based on these discussions, note any ideas that you think could be further developed.

TIP

Many designers consider the descriptions of a set in a play as suggestions rather than requirements that cannot be altered. Often designers read the description for clues and hints as to what the playwright believes the atmosphere or the set should be and it is up to the designer to interpret these hints.

Working with a script

It is the role of the designer to interpret the requirements of the play. Some playwrights offer no description of what the set should be like, while others will give detailed descriptions. However, no matter how detailed the description is, the designer interprets this in order to create the desired effects.

Minimalistic or abstract sets

In '**The Trial**', the playwright Steven Berkoff describes the set requirements as follows, with sample designer notes provided in the margin:

① We have a cast of five, so will only use five chairs and five screens. What style of chair? All the same colour or different?

④ Screens can be painted differently – one side black, the other representing different images

> The stage is bare. Ten screens and ten chairs and a rope are the set. **①** The screens are the structure of the city – lawcourts, houses and endless corridors. **②** They are a maze and a trap – they are mirrors and paintings **③** – they are external and internal worlds. **④** The cast are the environment of K. The rope is his route as well as his death. **⑤**

② How big should the screens be? Should they all be the same size? Is it easier to create the impression of a city, with different or the same heights?

③ Screens need to move, so lightweight or possibly on wheels for quick changes

⑤ Where should rope be onstage? Should it be used in different scenes and then hung as a noose later? Check health and safety considerations

 TIP

While this designer plans to use the idea of chairs, screen and rope in Berkoff's suggestions, another designer might ignore this advice. For example, if the staging configuration is in the round or traverse, the designer might think that the screens would block too much of the set, so would choose something else for their set. Another designer might want to incorporate technology such as projections or videos.

▲ *Use of projections in the set of 'Once Five Years Pass'.*

Period settings

Below is an example of the description of a Victorian set from Oscar Wilde's **'The Importance of Being Earnest'** (beginning of Act 2) with sample designer notes.

2 Cut steps, not needed

3 Use pots with artificial rose trees?

5 Need at least two matching chairs. Wicker table and chairs or wrought iron? Do we need tree? Possibly make a wooden two-dimensional cut-out one?

7 Watering can needed. Where best to position roses? Stage left?

Garden at the Manor House. **1** A flight of grey stone steps leads up to the house. **2** The garden, an old-fashioned one, full of roses. **3** Time of year, July. **4** Basket chairs, and a table covered with books, are set under a large yew-tree. **5**

Miss Prism discovered seated at the table. **6** Cecily is at the back, watering flowers. **7**

1 Flats used upstage to show back of house or doorway into house?

4 Use pastels, yellows and pinks, to highlight season

6 Position table downstage, slightly stage right

THEATRE MAKER ADVICE

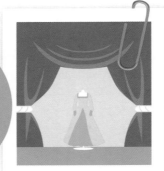

Tim Shortall, set and costume designer

For designers working on very small budgets, the fact that you have almost no money to play with means you are forced to think differently, and to spend very selectively and wisely – what is most important, what can you simply not do without.

 TIP

You need to show your interpretation of the play and your artistic intentions. Your set needs to be more than purely functional. Even if you are doing a minimalistic set, you need to demonstrate your skills through the choice of materials and style of design.

TASK 16

a Using the excerpts you are working on, make a list of the minimum requirements of the script. Be precise. If it requires chairs, how many? If it says 'a table' is the table used or is it just for decoration or scene setting – in which case do you need it?

b What dressings (additions to the set) and props (things that are handled by the actors) are required by the script?

c Can you think of one additional item of dressings or props that would add meaning or impact to the script? For example, the set of **'The Trial'** might have a large clock hanging above it to show how time is running out for Josef K. Or the set of **'The Importance of Being Earnest'** might have a tea trolley that could be wheeled on (which could be used for comic business for Merriman) or a curved arbor covered in vines and flowers (to highlight the beauty of the garden and provide an entrance and exit point).

Health and safety

There are many aspects of health and safety that you should consider. Below are just a few:

RISK	SOLUTION
Injuries when moving set	Avoid making set pieces that are too heavy.
	Ensure that you have a sufficient number of people for any set changes and rehearse these so that they go smoothly for the performance.
	When possible, use 'hand trucks' or other wheeled devices.
Broken glass	Avoid, when possible, using glass in your designs. If necessary (for example, a wine glass), ensure that it is handled and stored carefully.
	Should any glass break onstage, it must be carefully swept up to avoid injuries.
	If it is a requirement of a script that a glass or bottle is broken, then specially purchased 'breakaway' glass made from a plastic resin or 'sugar glass' should be used.
Injuries due to falls	Should any of the set involve constructing steps, platforms, ladders, etc., ensure that they are reinforced and suitable for weight-bearing.
	The stage floor should not be slippery.
Set falling down	Any flats that are used in the set need to be properly bracketed and weighed down to ensure that they don't fall over.
Sharp edges	Avoid having any sharp edges on the set as these could be dangerous should actors fall or bump into them.

Costume design

If you choose costume design as your specialism you must create one costume for one performer per extract. This means that you will either design two different costumes, one for each extract, or adapt a single costume for each extract. The design must show clothing and accessories, and hair and make-up if appropriate, which meets the demands of the extract being performed.

 TIP

It is important to know that collaboration with the actors is vital. There is no point in designing a costume that contradicts the performer's ideas about the character, restricts their ability to move or does not fit appropriately.

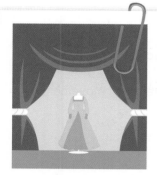

Tim Shortall, set and costume designer

Costume designs will be ongoing during this lead-up to the start of rehearsals. If it is a 'period' piece, it is likely I will have done a considerable amount of work prior to this, especially if the costumes are to be made, as this will involve a great deal of design, fabric and trim sourcing, and the timescale to start the makers will be very tight.

On a modern show, I much prefer to wait to do the costumes until I can talk in detail with each actor, to see what their view of their character is, and what they think they should wear. There is no point trying to give an actor a modern-day outfit without at least knowing in what direction they are heading with their characterisation! They need to feel absolutely comfortable and 'right' with the choice of clothes I have given them.

KEY TERM:

Trim: in sewing, this refers to any extra decoration such as ribbons, thread, lace, tassels, braid and cord.

Possible stages for your costume design:

1 Carefully read the script. Note its practical requirements and your first ideas of possible costumes.

2 Discuss with the performers the possible costumes and choose which costumes you will design.

3 Research: this could include art books, the internet, visits to museums, magazines, taking photographs, etc.

4 Put together initial mood boards. These might include: sample colours; swatches of fabric; photographs from books or magazines; examples of textures and patterns; inspiration from other costume designs, sample silhouettes; make-up and hairstyle examples; etc.

5 Take measurements of performer(s).

6 Create initial sketches.

7 If appropriate, make pattern for costume.

8 Source and obtain necessary materials such as fabrics and trim.

9 Begin making actual costume.

10 Arrange costume fittings and make any necessary adjustments.

11 Source any necessary accessories.

12 If appropriate, experiment with hair and make-up design.

13 At dress rehearsal make sure that the costume fits correctly and creates necessary effect. Make any necessary adjustments.

14 Check all details of costume, accessories, hair and make-up before first performance.

 TIP

At any rehearsals or performances when the costume is being used, have a small sewing kit to hand, including thread, needle, safety pins, scissors, etc., in order to make last-minute repairs.

TASK 17

Focusing on the excerpts you are working with, draw a few quick initial sketches of possible costumes. Once you have completed them, check your ideas against the following checklist:

✓ Are these costumes that could be created within the time and budget available?

✓ Do I have (or can I obtain) the necessary skills and equipment to create these costumes?

✓ Are these costumes appropriate for the character and style of the performance piece?

✓ Will the costume work practically onstage in terms of movement and comfort of performer?

Working with a script

It is the role of the designer to interpret the requirements of the play. Some playwrights offer no description of what the costumes should be like, while others will give detailed descriptions. Sometimes requirements of the costume are mentioned in the dialogue. For example, Eddie Carbone in '**A View from the Bridge**' complains about his niece, Catherine, wearing high heels, so for that moment to make sense, she must wear high heels. However, no matter how detailed the descriptions and dialogue are, the designer interprets these in order to create the desired effects.

The best costumes will reveal aspects of the character, and the style and meaning of the play.

Naturalistic period costumes

'**Kindertransport**' has scenes set both in the 1930s and in recent times.

The play begins with Eva, a nine-year-old German girl, and her German-Jewish mother, Helga, as they prepare for Eva to travel to England. Below are sample designer notes on the descriptions of the characters in the script:

> EVA, dressed in clothes of the late thirties, ① is sitting on the floor, reading. The book is a large, hard-backed children's story book entitled *Der Rattenfanger*.
>
> HELGA, holding a coat, ② button, needle and thread, is nearby. She is well turned-out in clothes of the late thirties. ③

① What sort of dress would a nine-year-old girl wear in the 1930s? Fabric? Length? Colours?

② Eva's coat, she will put this on later

③ What does 'well-turned out' mean for the 1930s? Fur? Jewellery? Skirt suit? Make-up?

Later in the script (page 16) Eva is further described:

⑤ What should label be made from? Cardboard? String or chain or pin to attach? Handwritten number or printed?

> EVA *puts on her coat and hat* ④ *and label with her number on it –* 3362. ⑤

④ What type of hat? Hairstyle? Plaits? Loose?

TASK 18

From the script of the excerpts that you are working on, choose either a description of a character or any information you can gather about a character such as occupation, age, location, time period, etc. Then, basing your ideas on the types of questions listed above, write any questions or observations you have about possible costumes for the character.

Fantasy or stylised costumes

The 1985, Peter Hall's adaptation of George Orwell's novel *Animal Farm* presents many challenges for the costume designer, as it depicts animals who speak and, in many ways, behave like humans. In his adaptor's note about the original production, Peter Hall writes:

▲ '*Animal Farm*'

> The actors wore black, except for brightly coloured elements – their animal masks, tails and feet. Until the end of the play, they went on all fours, using crutches of varying heights on their hands. The 'human' characters also wore masks. This was one solution to the production of the play. There are many others.

TASK 19

You have been asked to design a costume for one of the following animals in '**Animal Farm**':

▶ Old Major, a large old pig

▶ Boxer, a huge cart horse

▶ Moses, a tame raven.

However, in your design you choose not to use masks or crutches as you fear these will impede the actors' ability to speak or move freely. Sketch at least two other solutions to creating an animal costume.

Hair and make-up

In addition to costumes, styling of hair and make-up can greatly increase the visual impact a character makes. It's hard to imagine a 1950s costume looking truly effective, if it is not accompanied by an appropriate period hairstyle.

Some considerations:

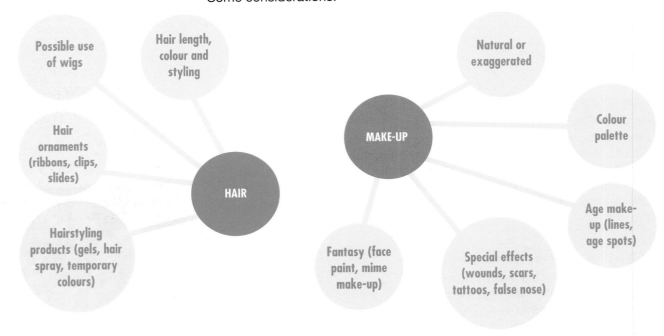

TIP

In order to demonstrate a range of skills you may wish to design hair and make-up as well as costumes.

Health and safety

There are many aspects of health and safety that you should consider. Below are just a few:

RISK	SOLUTION
Tripping	Check that length of costume does not pose a trip hazard. Ensure that actor has enough time working in costume to be comfortable moving in it.
Impeded vision	Ensure that any masks or head coverings have eye holes large enough for unimpeded vision. Check that the fastenings (elastic, etc.) are secure so that they do not slip.
Sharp objects	Scissors should be used with care and put securely away when not being used. No loose pins should remain in costumes (safety pins can be used, if securely closed).

Puppet designer

If you choose puppet design as your specialism you must create one puppet per extract. This means that you will either design two different puppets, one for each extract, or adapt a single puppet for each extract. The design must show a complete puppet, designed to meet the demands of the extract being performed.

Types of puppets

One of your first choices will be what type of puppet you wish to make. Below are just some examples:

Shadow puppets

Shadow puppets are two-dimensional puppets that are operated between a light and screen. They can be jointed to create movement.

The photo on the right shows the use of shadow puppets in Pigpen Theatre Company's storytelling theatre production of '**The Old Man and the Old Moon**'.

A hand puppet

A cloth puppet worn over a hand, traditionally the puppeteer's thumb serves as the jaw of the puppet's face.

Marionette

A puppet, usually made from wood controlled by wires or strings.

Hand and rod puppets

Where the puppeteer uses one hand to control the mouth and rods to control the arms of the puppet.

Backpack puppets

Large puppets attached to the puppeteer by a backpack-like device.

Below is an example of Nikki Gunson's puppet designs for '**Sinbad the Sailor**' at Stratford East Theatre, including a hand and rod monkey puppet and two large backpack puppets.

▲ *Shadow puppets in PigPen Theatre Company's production of 'The Old Man and the Old Moon'.*

◀ *Nikki Gunson's puppet designs for 'Sinbad the Sailor' at the Stratford East Theatre. Director Kerry Michael; Designer Hattie Barsby; Photographer Sharron Wallace; Puppet Designer Nikki Gunson; Lighting Designer David Plater*

THEATRE MAKER ADVICE

There are few things I look at when deciding what sort of puppet to make:

Where is the puppet to be performed? – Theatre, street or bus?

What is the puppet? – Human, animal, mythical or talking chair?

Size? 8 or 8,000 cm?

The part they play?

Their character, what they need to be able to do, animation required? – Simple flapping Snow Geese or all-singing and dancing parrot?

Nikki Gunson, puppet designer

How it needs to be operated and by how many people? – A giant octopus operated by nine people or one person? Three blind mice operated by one person or three people?

Q. What are the basic stages of the design process for you?

A 1   Receive brief/script for – or on the odd occasion decide what – character is to be created.

   2   Collect images and ideas, from all sorts of places: brainstorming, books, internet, photos, sketched thoughts and ideas.

   3   Working drawings – when I start my working drawings, I work on squared paper and sketch to scale.

   4   First draft – starts as a rough sketch, using brief and research images to get an idea of look/style, possible materials, where to put joints, estimate cost of and time taken to build.

   5   Rub out and work on until sketch is readable enough to have puppet design okayed.

   6   Second draft – Drawing is larger, and while sketching I am working out, how and where to animate and what materials could be used, drawing certain things like joints and how they work to the side or on a separate piece of paper.

   7   I build up my drawing in the same way I build puppets, constructing it in my mind – Skelly [Skeleton]/joints, Muscles Skin: materials, techniques and style used, varies depending on the needs of each puppet.

Materials

Puppets may be created with a wide variety of materials. For example, if creating a puppet with a three-dimensional head, materials you could consider using include:

foam rubber   **polystyrene**   wood

papier mâché (paste and paper)

plaster filler and muslin (a type of thin cotton fabric)

Additionally, you will want to think about whether or not your puppet is costumed, which will lead you to thinking about different fabrics. You may want to give it its own costume, and limbs that either hang limply or can be operated separately with a rod.

Working with a script

In Tim Supple's adaptation of '**Grimm Tales**' (1994), one of the tales is 'The Golden Goose'. In the original production a puppet was used to create the goose.

The goose is described in the dialogue as follows:

> Dummling went straight over to the tree and cut it down, and when it fell there was a goose sitting in the roots with feathers of pure gold. He lifted her out, tucked her firmly under this arm, and set off for an inn where he intended to stay the night.
>
> Later in the play the landlord's daughters become fascinated with the goose and want to steal its feathers. Each of the three daughters becomes stuck to the goose and, as the story progresses more and more people become stuck to the goose as Dummling carries it to show the king.

TASK 20

From this description, copy and complete the following mindmap by adding more legs to it to incorporate your ideas:

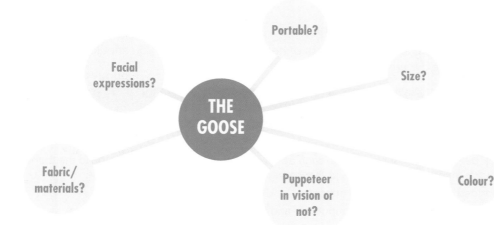

Nikki Gunson, puppet designer

Q. Any advice for making effective puppets?

A. Depends on venue and puppet: for large spaces – go larger than life; striking, bold and simple; don't get bogged down with too much detail that won't be noticed: Bright is always good, you can't beat a bit of glitter.

Exaggerate – head, face, eyes and hands, bring attention to the parts of the puppet you use interact/communicate with.

Finish – paints; satin is my finish of choice, matt tends to flatten and dull, gloss is good for the wet look, gloss varnish on eyes, reflects light, makes them look moist and brings them to life.

THEATRE MAKER ADVICE

Puppeteers

If you or someone else is operating the puppet you must decide if the puppeteer will be in vision or not. It may be that the script will dictate this. For example, in the example on the previous page, the actor playing Dummling would usually operate the goose puppet, as the script requires him to carry it from place to place. You may choose to have an onstage character working the puppet; an onstage puppeteer who isn't a character in the piece operate the puppet; or the puppet may be operated off-stage by an unseen puppeteer, for example by wires or strings.

THEATRE MAKER ADVICE

Nikki Gunson, puppet designer

With the puppets I make and operate, the puppeteer is usually in sight, I tend to wear black, shadow-like clothes, not wanting to distract from the puppet (unless a costume is part of the puppet) – sometimes I wear a veiled hat.

To me the magic of being a puppeteer is, even if you are in plain sight, you become invisible. It happens whether operating a large backpack puppet or a small rod puppet – I have a photo of me clearly visible operating a 10ft backpack and people ask 'Where are you?'

Health and safety

There are many aspects of health and safety that you should consider. Below are just a couple:

RISK	SOLUTION
Danger to audience	If there is any audience interaction (particularly with young or vulnerable people) make sure that you use soft, non-toxic materials.
Danger to puppeteer	With backpack puppets, use light materials, such as willow, rather than metal rods to build the frame, so there is not too much weight on the puppeteer's back. Use secure padded straps to attach the puppet. Ensure puppet doesn't obscure view of puppeteer and that they can clearly see any hazards.

 TIP

Write your Statement of Dramatic Intentions with care. You will need to express what you, as a performer or designer, want to show and what you want the audience to understand from the performance. This is an opportunity to show what you are attempting in terms of characterisation, context, atmosphere and meaning.

Texts in practice: checking your work and avoiding common errors

☐ Have you allowed enough time for your work to be completed?

☐ Have you taken into account the equipment and skills available to you to complete your design/performance?

☐ Have you considered any health and safety implications?

☐ Have you displayed a range of skills? (For example, if you have only created a single costume of a black leotard or a set that consists of one chair, it will be difficult to demonstrate a range of skills.)

☐ Have you used your skills precisely and in a highly effective way? (For example, are the sound cues accurate and at the appropriate volume? Does the costume fit? If there is group movement are you on time and precise?)

☐ Is your interpretation appropriate for the play as a whole? (For example, if the play is a non-naturalistic play in which frightening things happen, does your music help show that or have you just inserted popular songs you like?)

☐ Is your interpretation sensitive to the context of the piece? (For example, if it is set in a certain period do your costumes and music reflect that? If the scene takes place on a moonlit field, does your lighting help to convey that?)

☐ Are you artistic intentions entirely achieved? (Have you completed what you said you would or is the work incomplete or entirely different? For example, if you said you would create a beautiful backpack dragon puppet, have you instead made a glove puppet?)

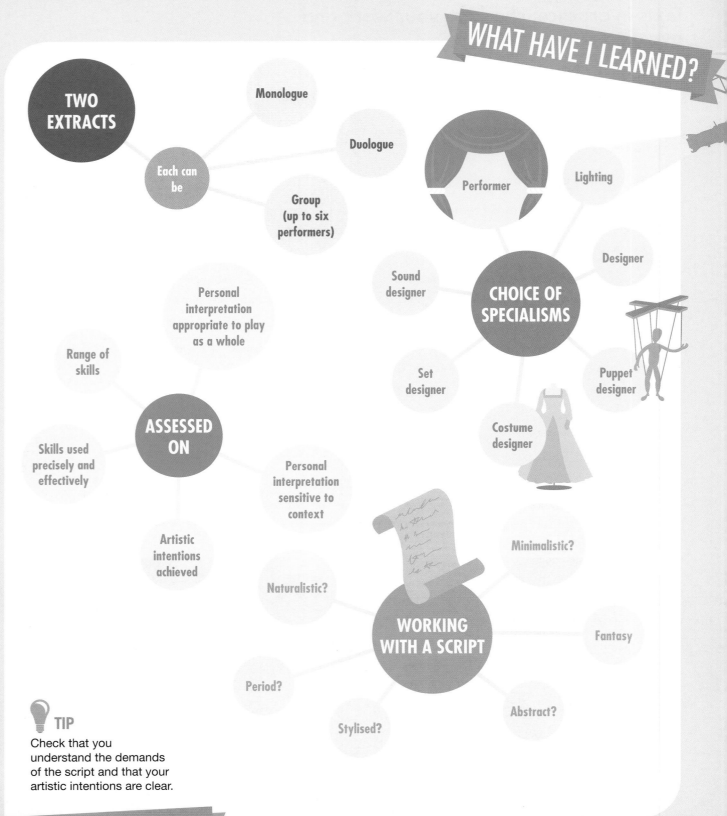

TWO EXTRACTS

Monologue

Each can be

Duologue

Group (up to six performers)

Performer

Lighting

Designer

Sound designer

CHOICE OF SPECIALISMS

Personal interpretation appropriate to play as a whole

Range of skills

Set designer

Puppet designer

Costume designer

ASSESSED ON

Skills used precisely and effectively

Personal interpretation sensitive to context

Minimalistic?

Artistic intentions achieved

Naturalistic?

Fantasy

WORKING WITH A SCRIPT

Period?

Abstract?

Stylised?

 TIP

Check that you understand the demands of the script and that your artistic intentions are clear.

CHECK YOUR LEARNING If you are uncertain of the meaning of any of the terms above, go back and revise.

Why not use the downloadable version of this summary as a basis for your own checklist of what you have learned from Samples & Downloads at www.illuminatepublishing.com.

GLOSSARY OF KEY TERMS

Abstract: not realistic or life-like, but instead using colours, shapes, textures, sounds and other means to achieve an effect.

Accent: a way of pronouncing words that is associated with a particular country, region or social class. This includes foreign accents, such as an American or German accent.

Ad-libbing: saying lines that aren't in the script.

Amplification: how sound is made louder.

Analyse: to examine something, perhaps by looking at the different elements of it, and to explain it.

Apron: the area of the stage nearest the audience, which projects in front of the curtain.

Archetypal: a typical example of someone or something; associated with an original or mythic quality of someone or something, i.e. 'he was the archetypal businessman' or 'it was the archetypal battle between of good and evil'.

Asides: when a character breaks out of a scene to speak briefly to the audience.

Audience interaction: involving the audience in the play, for example, by bringing them onstage, going into the audience to speak with them or passing them props to hold.

Backdrop: a large painted cloth hung as part of the scenery.

Beehive: a hairstyle popular in the 1950s and 1960s for which hair was back-combed into a high cone shape.

Blackout: in lighting, suddenly switching all the lights off.

Blocking: the movements of the actor. These are often written down by the stage manager to ensure that they can be repeated. For example, '*Jo enters and moves DSL* (downstage left)'.

Bower: an enclosed, shady place under branches of trees.

Box office: those who sell tickets.

Box set: a set with three complete walls, often used in naturalistic set designs, for example to create a believable room.

Breaking the fourth wall: breaking the imaginary wall between the actors and performers by speaking directly to the audience.

Chairography: choreographed movements involving chairs.

Character: a person or other being (such as talking animal) in a play, novel or film.

Characterisation: how the qualities of a character are shown, typically through description, dialogue and actions.

Choral speaking: a group of people speaking together or sharing a speech.

Chronological: showing events in the order in which they occurred.

Clapboards: wooden boards used to cover the outside of buildings.

Concept: a unifying idea about the production, such as when it is set or how it will be interpreted and performed.

Conflict: when two or more characters' desires are in opposition (external conflict) or when a character experiences opposing emotions (internal conflict).

Context: the circumstances of the setting of a play, such as the location, period of time or conventions.

Costumes: what the characters wear onstage.

Covering: learning the words and movements for a part that you do not usually perform.

Cross-cutting: alternating between two different scenes.

Cross-fade: fading lights out on one area of the stage while simultaneously bringing them up on another area.

Cues: instructions indicating when a change in lighting should occur.

Describe: to write what you saw, heard or experienced.

Designer: person responsible for an aspect of the production, such as lighting, costumes, set, sound or puppets.

Devising: a way of creating drama that begins not with writers or a script but is based on the collaborative efforts of a group of people.

Diaphragm: the large muscle that stretches across the bottom of the rib-cage.

Diction: how clearly and precisely words are spoken.

Direct address: speaking directly to the audience.

Director: the person responsible for the overall production of a play including the performances and overseeing the designers.

Dirndl: a dress or skirt, often seen in traditional Austrian or Bavarian outfits, which is gathered at the waist and falls to about knee-length.

Drapes: curtains or other hanging fabric.

Dynamic: energetic, forceful.

Dystopian: referring to an imagined world where society is presented in a highly negative light. Writers often create dystopian worlds in order to warn people about present dangers.

Effects: special lighting such as strobes or using lighting to recreate headlights, lightning, fires or other unusual lighting.

End on staging: a staging configuration in which the audience sits along one end of the stage, directly facing it.

Ensemble: an approach to acting involving everyone working together, rather than singling out 'star' performers. It can also refer to a group of actors who play many roles in a play or a chorus. In the case of Kneehigh, there are a number of collaborators, including the musicians and designers.

Enunciate: to pronounce or articulate words.

Episodic: a series of loosely connected scenes.

Evaluate: to judge or form an opinion of something, such as explaining what effect was created and how successful it was.

Fade: in lighting, gradually getting lighter or darker.

Fade: in sound, gradually getting quieter or louder.

Filters: also sometimes called 'gels', sheets of plastic used to alter the colour of stage lighting.

Flapper: a girl in the 1920s associated with daring behaviour, wearing short skirts and dancing to jazz music.

Flat: a piece of scenery mounted on a frame.

Fly: raising and lowering scenery or other items onto the stage using a system of ropes and pulleys.

Fly space: area above the stage where scenery may be stored and lowered to the stage.

Footlights: lights placed at the front of the stage at the level of the actor's feet, with their light directed upwards.

Fourth wall: an imaginary wall between the audience and the actors giving the impression that the actors are unaware they are being observed.

Front of house: ushers and others who deal with the audience.

Fresnel: a common stage lantern which provides a soft-edged beam of light. It can be used to cover a large area of the stage creating a 'wash' of light'. They often have 'barn doors', which are metal flaps at the side to provide some control of the spillage of light. They are usually fitted with a colour slot in which colour filters can be inserted.

Furnishings: furniture on the set, such as chairs, cushions, tables.

Gel: coloured tranparencies used to create different-coloured lighting.

Genre: a category or type of music, art or literature.

Gobos: metal cut-outs that are used to project patterns, such as leaves, stars, swirls or waves.

Ground plan: this is a bird's-eye view of the set showing the scale of the stage and set and where key elements of the design will be located.

Harris Tweed: a high-quality, handwoven, woollen cloth.

Hot seat: one performer sits in a chair and, in character, answers questions.

House lights: lighting that makes the audience visible.

Improvise: to act without a script.

Interpret: to make choices about a play. There may be many possible interpretations.

Interval: a break in a performance for both the performers and the audience. This often occurs between the first and second acts of plays. Some plays have more than one interval and some run without an interval.

Lanterns: the equipment used to produce light onstage, such as floods, fresnels or profiles.

LED lights: light-emitting diodes (LEDs) are light sources that have a high light output but use relatively little power.

Lighting rig: the structure that holds the lighting equipment in the theatre.

Machinations: plots, conspiracies or schemes.

Melodrama: a piece of drama with exaggerated characters and exciting events.

Minimalistic: simple; using few elements; stripped back.

Motif: a repeated image or idea.

Motivations: what a character wants or needs in a scene. For example, 'I need to escape' or 'I want you to admire me'. These are sometimes called 'objectives'.

Multimedia: using film or other media in a live theatre production.

Narration: providing the audience with background information or commentary on the action of the play.

Naturalistic: life-like, realistic, believable.

Non-naturalistic: stylised, not realistic.

Objective: what the character wants.

Parody: an exaggerated imitation for comic effect.

Performance conventions: techniques used in a particular type of performance, such as soliloquies in Shakespeare or direct address in an epic play.

Physical theatre: theatre that emphasises physical movement, such as mime.

Playwright: responsible for the writing of the script of the play. This includes the dialogue and stage directions.

Projection: projecting a film or still image to form a theatrical backdrop.

Promenade: to promenade means 'to walk' and promenade theatre is when the audience stands or follows the actors through the performance.

Prompt book: a master copy of the script, annotated with blocking and technical cues.

Props: small items that actors can carry onstage.

Proscenium arch: a stage configuration particularly popular for larger theatres or opera houses. The proscenium refers to the frame around the stage which emphasises that the whole audience is seeing the same stage picture.

Prosthetics: make-up that uses moulds and sculptural techniques to create special effects, such as scars or a false nose.

Proximity: the distance between people or objects; how near or far.

Received pronunciation: how clearly and precisely words are spoken.

Register: the vocal range of the voice (upper, middle or lower registers); the variety of tones of voice.

Repressing: holding back or restraining.

Resonance: the quality, strength and depth of sound.

Retrogression: going backwards, often to an earlier time or state.

Reverb: an echoing effect.

Revolve: a large turntable device that can be turned to reveal a different setting.

Rig: what the lights are positioned on (a lighting rig) or 'to rig the lights' is to set them in position.

Scribe: someone who writes documents.

Sets: items put onstage such as furniture or backdrops to create the world of the play; sometimes called scenery. There may also be props, which are objects used onstage.

Set dressings: items on the set not actually used as props, but that create detail and interest in it, such as vases or framed paintings on a wall.

Sightline: the view of the audience.

Silhouette: the outline or shape created by a costume on a figure.

Site specific: a performance in a location, such as a warehouse or a park, which is not a conventional theatre. The space has often been adapted to suit the production.

Snap: quickly on or off.

Soliloquy: a speech when a character is alone onstage.

Soundscape: drama technique where performers use their voices (and sometimes other items) to create sounds to enhance the mood or theme of a piece of drama.

Spotlight: a lamp projecting a narrow intense beam of light directly onto a performer or area of the stage.

Stage business: the small movements an actor might do onstage, such as opening a book, brushing hair or straightening cushions. These movements may add to the naturalism of a scene or provide insight into the characters.

Stage manager: responsible for the backstage elements of the production, such as calling cues and checking props.

States: the settings and positioning of lighting to create certain lighting conditions, such as a bright afternoon or a moonlit scene.

Staging configuration: the type of stage and audience arrangement.

Still image: a frozen image showing the facial expressions and physical positions, including posture and gesture, of one or more characters.

Stimulus: a resource in drama used to start a creative process by providing context, inspiration or focus.

Stock characters: easily recognised, stereotypical characters.

Stock gestures: stereotypical gestures to signal certain emotions, such as shaking a fist to show anger.

Strobe: a stroboscopic lamp that produces flashes of light.

Style: the way in which something is written or performed, such as the use of realistic dialogue or choreographed movement.

Stylised: non-realistic, done in a particular manner, perhaps emphasising one element.

Sub-plot: a secondary or less important plot in a story.

Subtext: the unspoken meaning, feelings and thoughts 'beneath' the lines, which may be shown in the characters' body language, tone of voice and facial expressions, for example, although not explicitly stated in the text.

Subliminally: so that it barely registers; the audience is affected without consciously being aware of what is affecting them.

Supernature: usually means something which is beyond the rules of nature. This may refer to the extraordinary ability of the animals in the play to exhibit many human or extraordinary characteristics, such as the ability to speak.

Symbolic: using something that represents something else. Examples of symbolic design might be characters dressed in white to symbolise their purity or a set resembling a boxing ring to symbolise the conflict between the characters.

Technical rehearsal: a rehearsal which is used to make sure that all technical elements such as lighting, sound and set changes are operating correctly.

Tension: a sense of anticipation or anxiety.

Theatre in the round: a stage configuration when the audience is seated around all sides of the stage.

Titillated: excited, thrilled.

Thought-track: speaking aloud the thoughts of the character.

Thrust: a type of stage configuration in which the stage protrudes into the auditorium with the audience on three sides.

Tragedy: a play involving the downfall of its lead character leading to an unhappy ending.

Transitions: moving from one lighting state to another, such as a fade to darkness or a sudden blackout.

Trapdoor: a door in the floor of a stage allowing objects or performers to be dropped, lifted or lowered.

Traverse: a stage configuration is when the acting takes place on a long central area with the audience seated on either side facing each other.

Trim: in sewing, this refers to any extra decoration such as ribbons, thread, lace, tassels, braid and cord.

Truck: a platform on wheels upon which scenery can be mounted and moved.

Verbatim: using exactly the same words as were used originally.

Visual: a cue that the technician must judge by watching the action onstage.

Ward: someone, usually a young person, who has a guardian or other legal authority responsible for them.

Wing spaces: areas to the side of the stage. This is the area where actors, unseen by the audience, wait to enter and where props and set pieces may be stored.

Yodelling: a type of singing which involves rapidly alternating between low and high pitches.

INDEX